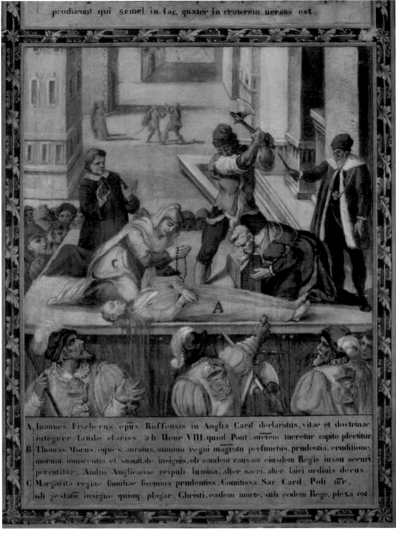

producunt qui semel in lac, quater in cruorem uersus est.

A, Ioannes Fischerus, epus Roffensis in Anglia Card declaratus, vitae et doctrinae
integerr. Laude clariss. a b Henr VIII.quod Pont. auctem tueretur capite plectitur.
B Thomas Morus, eques auratus, summo regni magratu perfunctus, prudentia, eruditione,
morum innocentia et suauitate insignis, ob eandem causam eiusdem Regis iussu securi
percutitur. Ambo Anglicanae reipub. lumina, alter sacri, alter laici ordinis decus.
C Margarita regiae familiae foemina prudentiss. Comitissa Sar. Card. Poli ur.
ob gestasū insigne quinq plagar, Christi, eadem morte, sub eodem Rege, plexa est.

A schematized depiction of the executions of John Fisher, Thomas More, and
Margaret Pole, from the church of the Venerable English College in Rome. It
replicates a scene from the lost 1583 fresco-cycle by Nicolo Circognani, tracing the
history of England through the deaths of her Catholic martyrs, ancient and modern.
Engravings of Circognani's frescoes circulated widely in Catholic Europe, to fuel
Counter-Reformation militancy.

Saints, Sacrilege and Sedition

Saints, Sacrilege and Sedition

Religion and Conflict in the Tudor Reformations

Eamon Duffy

BLOOMSBURY
LONDON · NEW DELHI · NEW YORK · SYDNEY

First published in Great Britain 2012
Paperback edition, 2014

© Eamon Duffy, 2012

The moral right of the author has been asserted

Bloomsbury Publishing Plc
50 Bedford Square
London WC1B 3DP
www.bloomsbury.com

Bloomsbury Publishing, London, New Delhi, New York and Sydney

A CIP record for this book is available from the British Library

ISBN: PB: 9781472909176

10 9 8 7 6 5 4 3 2 1

Typeset by Fakenham Prepress Solutions, Fakenham, Norfolk NR21 8NN
Printed and bound in Great Britain by CPI Group (UK) Ltd, Croydon CR0 4YY

Contents

Part IV Catholic voices 211

List of Plates and Figures

Colour Plates.

Frontispiece: The Executions of More, Fisher, and Margaret Pole, Venerable English College, Rome.

Black and white figures.

Part I

Reformation unravelled

Introduction

Let us begin with two contrasting summaries of the course and causes of the English Reformation, both provided by an American historian of Tudor England, Professor Norman Jones.

> Once upon a time the people of England were happy medieval Catholics, visiting their holy wells, attending frequent masses and deeply respectful of Purgatory and afraid of hell. Then lustful King Henry forced them to abandon their religion. England was never merry again.

Or, alternatively,

> Once upon a time the people of England were oppressed by corrupt churchmen. They yearned for the liberty of the Gospel. Then, Good King Harry gave them the Protestant nation for which they longed.[1]

Nobody, I take it, would nowadays admit to holding either of these positions in their crude and chemical purity. Nevertheless, these two contrasting caricatures undoubtedly represent recognizable approaches to the Tudor past. The second version is an exaggeration of the traditional account of the Reformation, criticized in the second chapter of this book. The first is a parody of the account of the Tudor Reformation often nowadays dubbed 'revisionist'. That 'revisionist' view of the English Reformation is sometimes identified with *The Stripping of the Altars*,[2] a book I myself published in 1992, but it takes its name from a collection of essays edited by Dr Christopher Haigh five years earlier, under the title *The English Reformation Revised*.[3]

The Stripping of the Altars was a self-consciously polemical book.[4] It had long been an axiom of historical writing about the establishment of Protestantism in England that the success of the Reformation had been a more or less inevitable consequence of the dysfunction and unpopularity of late medieval Catholicism. By the early sixteenth century, it was claimed, ordinary people had lost confidence in church institutions. They resented the oppressive power of the clergy, and so greeted with relief and enthusiasm the doctrinal critique of the entire sclerotic medieval religious system launched in 1517 by the German monk Martin Luther. The translation of the bible into English in the 1520s and 1530s revealed that many of the most fundamental teachings of the medieval church, from the authority of the pope and the presence of Christ in the bread and wine of the Eucharist, to the intercession of the saints or the fiery punishment of erring souls in purgatory after death, had little or no basis in scripture. Under the leadership of the crown, therefore, the whole elaborate construction of medieval Catholicism came crashing down, and a liberated population enthusiastically embraced a simpler, cleaner and more English form of Christianity.[5]

The Stripping of the Altars questioned this account of things in two different ways. The first part of the book analysed in detail the workings of late medieval Christianity at parish level, in order to demonstrate the strong imaginative hold that the beliefs and practices of late medieval Christianity continued to exert right up to the point at which they were outlawed and dismantled by the Tudor state. Some reviewers and readers of the book imagined that what was being claimed was that everyone in the Middle Ages in England was a devout Catholic, but I maintained no such thing. The book acknowledges, though it does not concern itself in detail with, the existence of religious dissidents (notably the Lollards) and the religiously indifferent. My concern, rather, was to demonstrate that late medieval Catholicism in England was a functional symbolic and religious system, whose range and complexity met the often divergent and socially divided religious needs of late medieval English society. A novel feature of this part of the book was the sustained use of the material culture of medieval Christianity – the architecture and furnishings of parish churches and shrines, surviving religious imagery in glass and paint, in wood and stone, and printed (and often illustrated) devotional books. This material culture, more often than not the product of lay investment, had been largely neglected by previous Reformation historians, but it provided, I suggested, abundant and concrete evidence of the vitality and extent of lay commitment to Catholic beliefs and practices, a commitment at odds with the conventional narrative of lay disenchantment.

The second part of the book provided an overarching account of the reformation process in England over the course of three generations, and drew attention both to the widespread dismay with which religious change was often greeted, and to the laborious and often fraught processes of enforcement to which successive protestant regimes were obliged to resort. The argument of this part of the book was not, as was sometimes assumed, that there was *no* popular support for the Reformation, but I did argue that many people, and probably the majority, did not in fact welcome it, or did so reluctantly and, as the rapid restoration of Catholic practice in the reign of Mary was to demonstrate, provisionally. The Protestantizing of England, therefore, was never a landslide, but a task achieved with labour and difficulty, and its outcome was not secure till the second half of the reign of Elizabeth.

The Stripping of the Altars offered the fullest exploration in English to date of the workings of late medieval Christianity, and was also unusual in ignoring the conventional period divide between medieval and early modern British history, since it devoted as much attention to the fifteenth as to the sixteenth centuries. But its general line of argument was by no means new. In the fifteen or so years before its publication, several other Tudor historians, notably Professor J. J. Scarisbrick and Dr Christopher Haigh, had led the way with broadly similar accounts of the sixteenth-century English Reformation.[6] A number of medieval historians had also offered more positive perspectives on the workings of English religion on the eve of the Tudor religious changes.[7] But widespread media interest in *The Stripping of the Altars*, and the publication the following year of Christopher Haigh's *English Reformations*,[8] contributed to a sense that a distinctive 'school' of Reformation history had emerged, and proponents of this more quizzical view of the Reformation were bunched together as 'revisionists', and even, and in Haigh's case quite erroneously, as 'Catholic revisionists'.[9]

In fact, in any hard and fast sense, the 'revisionist' model of the Reformation was itself largely a critical construct, for the differences between so-called 'revisionists' were at least as significant as their agreements. It is, for example, a fundamental contention of *The Stripping of the Altars* that the Reformation represented a deep and traumatic cultural hiatus with the medieval past, a notion that has since been taken up in different ways by art and architectural historians like Andrew Graham Dixon and Sir Roy Strong, and by literary critics like Stephen Greenblatt.[10] By contrast, it is a fundamental contention of Christopher Haigh's masterly and mischievous *English Reformations*, that when the dust had settled on all the Crown-imposed religious upheavals, nothing very much had in fact happened. Nor were the contributors to *The English Reformation Revised* in any sense a movement, for they shared no single agenda. In so far as their essays had something in common, it was a sense that the reformation process in England had been precisely that, a *process* and a labour, difficult and long drawn-out, whose outcome had been by no means a foregone conclusion. They shared also, perhaps, a more positive assessment both of the activities of the proponents of Tudor Catholicism like bishops John Longland or Edmund Bonner and, more generally, of the 'traditional religion' (a term coined in *The Stripping of the Altars* and now widely adopted) which the reformers assailed.

But it is worth noting that the perception that the Reformation had not been achieved on a tidal wave of popular enthusiasm, but instead had to be worked for, by force, persuasion and slow institutional transformation, certainly did not originate with card-carrying 'revisionists' of any stamp. The year before Haigh's collection appeared, the leading historian of English Puritanism, Professor Patrick Collinson, had given the Anstey lectures at Kent, which he subsequently published as *The Birthpangs of Protestant England*.[11] The published version opened with the ringing declaration that 'if I were to be asked when Protestant England was born I would answer … after the accession of Elizabeth 1, some considerable time after'.[12] Collinson dedicated the book to Professor Geoffrey Dickens. Unsurprisingly, Dickens, who had ended his celebrated (and celebratory) history of *The English Reformation*[13] soon after the accession of Queen Elizabeth in 1559, was not greatly delighted by Collinson's gesture, and perhaps did not quite know what to make of the dedication which credited him with having both 'led and pointed the way', since Professor Collinson assumed that the story of the birth of English Protestantism began more or less at the point where Professor Dicken's history of the Reformation left off. And, speaking autobiographically, the book which contributed most to my own realization of the contested character of the Tudor reformations had been no 'revisionist' work, but the late professor Sir Geoffrey Elton's masterpiece, *Policy and Police*, published as long ago as 1972, when revisionism was barely a twinkle in Christopher Haigh's infant eye.[14] Elton, who was not in fact greatly interested in religion, never questioned Dicken's conviction that by the end of Edward's reign England was more or less ineradicably Protestant. Nevertheless, his use of Thomas Cromwell's 1530s postbag to chart both widespread popular resistance to, and criticism of, the Henrician Reformation, and the Henrician regime's resort to the systematic use of both force and persuasion to forward it, undermined some of Dicken's foundational assumptions, and set the agenda for much subsequent work.

So a good deal of what is now described as 'revisionism' has nothing to do with a conscious revisionary agenda, but is simply the routine work of historians doing what historians always do or are supposed to do: trying to get a clearer picture of what happened in the past. The more positive re-evaluation of late medieval religion which has made so crucial a contribution to much recent thinking about the Reformation, for example, (and to which chapters three to six of this book aim to contribute a little more), was pioneered by medievalists only marginally concerned with the background to the Reformation, and working independently of each other.[15] Among historians more directly concerned with the sixteenth century, several are indeed Roman Catholics – Jack Scarisbrick, myself, and more recently Richard Rex and Peter Marshall[16] – and that has contributed to a perception that 'revisionism' represents the unfortunate revival of confessional history, the grinding of papistical axes. Remarkably, no-one appears to have thought it worth comment or concern that before these recent debates most British Reformation historians were in fact practising or at least cultural Protestants – Dickens himself, my own supervisor Gordon Rupp, Claire Cross, Andrew Pettegree, Diarmaid MacCulloch, and many more.

I should myself attribute the growing presence of Catholics among British historians of late medieval and early modern religion at least in part to the

accident of the passing of the 1944 Butler Education Act, which led to a
post-war flood of Catholics into higher education, and the professionalization
of the formerly largely plebeian Catholic community. There are thus simply
more Catholics writing history in the academy than there used to be. But
there is also a notable Catholic presence among historians of late medieval
and early modern religion, and not merely English religion, but that of Europe
more widely. Their influence, moreover, has been disproportionate to their
actual numbers, if one considers the names of John Bossy,[17] Peter Burke,[18] and
the late Bob Scribner,[19] and, I would add, the social anthropologists Victor
Turner[20] and Mary Douglas,[21] whose writings have influenced much recent
historical thinking about early-modern religion.

This British Roman Catholic interest in late medieval and early modern
religion may be in part a product, I suspect, of sub-cultural formation, and
the heightened religious preoccupations of a minority religious group. But
since several of those I have mentioned have by their own account been firmly
'lapsed', and their Catholicism therefore a matter of cultural formation rather
than ideological commitment, I suspect also that their apparently 'revisionist'
take on the religious past stems not from gladiatorial denominational concerns,
so much as from the fact that to anyone formed in a Catholic religious ethos,
the religion of the late Middle Ages simply *looks* more coherent, less odd
or repellent, than might be the case for those formed in a different (i.e. a
Protestant) religious tradition. In that sense, 'Catholic revisionism', in so far
as it exists at all, may represent the absence of a Protestant historiographical
agenda, at least as much as the presence of a Catholic one. These are delicate
and fraught issues, in which intellectual integrity can often appear to be at
odds with more visceral allegiances: I have offered my own perspectives on
them in the first two chapters of this book.

Yet whatever the reasons, there is no denying that even in our secular
age, the ghosts of old religious passions continue to haunt perceptions of the
Tudor past. This was borne in on me a few years ago by the publication in
the *Sunday Times* of a vehement review of Sir Roy Strong's *Little History of
the English Country Church* by the well-known journalist, Simon Jenkins.[22]
In discussing the Reformation and its aftermath, Sir Roy had adopted the
general interpretative stance of *The Stripping of the Altars*. This stance Mr

Jenkins directly repudiated, and he delivered himself of the judgement that 'most Britons had, by the late-15th century, come to regard the Roman church as an alien, corrupt and reactionary agent of intellectual oppression, awash in magic and superstition. They could not wait to see the back of it.… The dynamic of the Reformation was that Catholicism claimed a power over the British state that Britons would not accept.' Britons, in a word, never ever shall be slaves. The historical realities behind such claims are considered in chapter nine of this book, but historical realities hardly enter into such utterances, which are declarations of a stance, not deductions from evidence. Though himself no longer a Christian believer, Mr Jenkins is the son of a Welsh non-conformist minister, and old habits of mind evidently die hard: these are robustly Protestant sentiments. But they are woefully lacking both in objective historical foundation, and in historical precision. As I argue later in this book, there is no evidence for widespread hostility to the papacy on the eve of the English Reformation. Hostility to the papacy was not the cause of the Reformation, it was one of its consequences.[23] And there was of course no 'British' state, nor any 'Britons', in 1500. The very concept of Britain, and the actual political union of the archipelago, maintained when necessary by force of English arms as well as by the power of persuasion, lay far in the future. All the same, Mr Jenkins' resort to the rhetoric of an instinctively Protestant Britannia over against the shoddy superstition and tyranny of the pope of Rome, proclaims its pedigree clearly enough. Behind his review stood generations of pulpit and populist declamation, from the service of thanksgiving for deliverance from Gunpowder treason which was part of the Book of Common prayer till 1859, with its prayers against 'Popish Tyranny and arbitrary Power', to the raucous Hanoverian anti-Catholicism of Hogarth's prints, celebrating the Roast Beef of Old England, satirising funny foreigners and lecherous monks, equating Protestantism with prosperity, and popery with oppression and wooden shoes.[24]

The alleged opposition between Englishness and Catholicism is in fact an invention of the age of Henry VIII, and a notion, as I argue in chapter nine, that before 1534 was confined to the lunatic fringe. Where, by contrast, might one locate the heart of England and Englishness? No doubt there are as many answers to that question as there are readers of these words, but one could certainly make a case for the sanctuary of Westminster Abbey, the sacred space which shelters both the coronation chair and the tomb of Edward the Confessor. King Henry III built the abbey as a national shrine round the burial-place of its monarchs. But to clothe this innermost core of Englishness, he chose Roman vestments. He sent to Rome for its most famous decorative masons, the Cosmati brothers. With porphyry and jade and purbeck marble, these Italian workmen remodeled the shrine and its surroundings to resemble the holy places of Papal Rome.[25] This resting-place of the first English saint ever canonized by a pope would become the mausoleum as well as the coronation church of England's kings. It would lend to the Confessor's successors both the glamour of the Roman Empire, and the immemorial religious validation of the papacy. For till 1534, Henry III's successors felt no conflict between English greatness and Roman allegiance. On the contrary, they sought papal ratification for their conquests, and the thanksgivings for the victories at Agincourt and Cressy and Flodden were Catholic celebrations. Henry VIII himself rejoiced in the title 'Defender of the Faith', bestowed by a pope for a book against the Protestant reformer Martin Luther. And when he needed to rid himself of an unwanted wife, it was the authority of that papacy to which he appealed.

What changed all that was not, as Mr Jenkins supposed, that the papacy began to make claims over the English state that no right-thinking English heart could tolerate, but that the pope failed to oblige the king. The English crown responded by asserting a new power over conscience and over the English Church, which no modern Englishman would be likely nowadays to put up with for a second. Christian kings had always believed themselves obliged to defend the Christian faith, by force if necessary. But they received that faith, like everyone else, from the Church which taught it. What was entirely new in the 1530s was that the Crown asserted an unprecedented right over against the papacy to redefine what the Christian faith was, and to coerce English subjects to repudiate the allegiance of a thousand years and accept that new faith. The monarch became the ultimate arbiter of conscience, the spiritual independence of the Church was thereby abolished and the notion of an autonomous realm of the spirit, over which no state had any say, formally and explicitly repudiated. From a Catholic perspective the doctrine of the

Royal Supremacy, far from being a form of liberation from papal tyranny, was in fact an entirely new form of human enslavement, a declaration that neither individual conscience nor the collective convictions of Christendom had any weight against the wishes of the Crown. The claim that 'the bishop of Rome hath no jurisdiction in this realm' boiled down for them to the notion that there was no appeal from the diktat of the state even in matters of innermost conscience. That was the issue for which Thomas More went to the block, and that was the fundamental issue between Catholics and the Protestant state until 1829.

For Catholics in the generations immediately following the Reformation all this was experienced as a form of internal exile: they lamented the nation's reconfiguration into what they took to be a foreign mould, the abandonment of ancient certainties in favour of dissonant and alien fashions from Zurich, Geneva and Wittenberg.

> A Gospel new she hath found out
> A bird of Calvin's brood
> Abandoning all memory
> Of Christ his holy rood.
> Unity is clean exiled,
> for preachers do agree
> As do our clocks when they strike noon,
> Now one, now two, now three;
> But all together never jump
> As when our elders all
> Of faith and doctrine did accord
> In points both great and small.[26]

The Protestant iconoclasm explored in chapters five and eleven of this book destroyed much of the architecture and most of the art of medieval England, and left behind Shakespeare's 'bare ruin'd choirs where late the sweet birds sang'. That seemed to Tudor Catholics more than a sacrilegious exercise in fanaticism. They experienced it as a deliberate cultural revolution, designed to obliterate England's memory of who and what she had been. Catholics alone, they felt, stood where they had always stood. The formidable Lady

Cecily Stonor, under mounting pressure to conform to Protestantism in
the wake of the arrest and execution of Edmund Campion in 1581, put the
matter forcefully.

> 'I was born in such a time when Holy Mass was in great reverence', she
> told her judges, 'and was brought up in the same faith. In King Edward's
> time this reverence was neglected and reproved by such as governed. In
> Queen Mary's it was restored with much applause, and now in this time it
> pleaseth the State to question them, as now they do me, who continue in
> this Catholic profession. The State would have the several changes which
> I have seen with my eyes, good and laudable. Whether it can be so I refer
> to your Lordship's consideration. I hold me still to that wherein I was born
> and bred, and find nothing taught in it but great virtue and sanctity, and so
> by the grace of God I will live and die in it'.[27]

But of course, the issues were much more complicated than antiquity,
virtue or sanctity. Catholics had long seen Christendom as an entity which
transcended mere national sovereignty. Pope and Emperor represented
authorities which, in extremes, could call princes to account before the
wider laws of Christendom. It was a notion which, by the sixteenth
century, even Catholic princes were coming to reject, and the rise of nation
states demanding absolute loyalty from their subjects seemed increasingly
incompatible with that older vision. English Catholics themselves were
divided about the theoretical extent of the state's claim on their loyalties, but
whatever they thought of the theories, practical allegiance to an increasingly
hostile regime, in the form of loyalty to its Protestant Queen, became for
all of them increasingly difficult to square with fidelity to a religion which
that regime proscribed and persecuted.[28] For vital life-lines like the English
Catholic schools and seminaries abroad, and for an end to persecution, they
were forced to look to the greatest Catholic world power, to Spain, whose
king Philip II a few years before had of course also been king of England.
And so Catholicism as treason, a grimly laughable fiction under Henry VIII,
became a reality under Elizabeth. In 1588 an English Cardinal, after a lifetime
of increasingly equivocal protestations of loyalty to the Crown, formally
blessed the Armada as an army of liberation, and called on Englishmen

everywhere to rise against their bastard queen, and restore the true faith to England.[29] That dilemma, and the ramifications of Cardinal Allen's action, would divide Catholics themselves for generations.

For its part, over the next century, Protestant England would feel itself increasingly part of a beleaguered Protestant international, shrinking back into the cold north-west corner of Europe. In the light of that fear, Catholicism would be imprinted on to the national consciousness as the ultimate enemy, the embodiment of the hostile 'other', whether at home or abroad. Catholic Englishmen loomed as a danger out of all proportion to their actual number, a fifth column allegedly eager to surrender the nation's independence into the hands of foreign tyrannies, spiritual and material. The discovery of the Gunpowder Plot gave form and substance to these fears, and they were stoked by carefully fostered memories of the fiery enforcement of Catholicism under Queen Mary, by the chronic inability of the Stuart monarchs to find themselves permanently Protestant wives and, ultimately, by the return of the House of Stuart to the religion of their Catholic great-grandmother, Mary Queen of Scots. A century and three quarters after Henry's break with Rome, the Act of Settlement would finally declare that no Catholic might rule over England, an exclusion which still pertains.

The essays which make up the chapters of this book aim to illuminate one aspect or another of the fraught and highly confessionalized history of religion in Tudor England. Chapters one and two consider how Tudor religious conflict has been deployed to shape English self-awareness, and the ways in which religious allegiances have conditioned the understanding and writing of Tudor history. Chapters three to five explore what it meant to be a Catholic Christian in early Tudor England, by examining aspects of the material culture of religion in medieval and early Tudor England – the traces of the lavish investment by late medieval and early Tudor lay people and their priests in the worship of the English parish church. Chapter three considers one of the main focuses of lay benefaction, the great screens which in the later Middle Ages divided the chancel, the preserve of the clergy, from the people's part of the church, the nave. Chapter four offers a case-study of what the documentary and architectural evidence for a single church, Salle in Norfolk, can tell us about Tudor religion and its transformations. Chapter five considers the material culture of the Tudor parish more generally, through the lens of the official records of the state-sponsored plunder of every parish church in England in 1552–3. Chapters six to nine move from medieval objects to Tudor people, and explore the character of militant Catholicism, and its relation to the crown and nation, through the careers and teaching of two of Tudor England's most remarkable clerical leaders, both of them Cardinals. John Fisher, bishop of Rochester and the most distinguished Catholic theologian in the Europe of his day, was beheaded in 1535 for his opposition to the Henrician Reformation. Reginald Pole masterminded the restoration of Catholicism under Mary Tudor, and his exalted understanding of the centrality of the papacy would decisively shape both English and European Catholic perceptions of the English Reformation for generations. Each of these two in their own day enjoyed a European celebrity which far outstripped that of any of their Protestant contemporaries and opponents, though history has reversed that order of celebrity, and it is their lesser adversaries – Cranmer, Ridley, Latimer – who are remembered as the greatest of Tudor churchmen. I hope that my focus on these neglected giants will do something to offset suggestions that opposition to the Reformation in early and mid Tudor England was the work of 'devoted mediocrities'.[30] The final two chapters of the book explore aspects of what might be called the afterlife of Tudor Catholicism, by considering the ways in which that 'old religion' was spoken about in mid Tudor England, and the language in which it was remembered in the age of William Shakespeare.

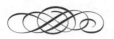

1

Reformation, Counter-Reformation and the English nation

As the Blitz began in wartime London, George Orwell sat down at his typewriter and tried to define English national identity. In the essay that resulted he argued for an ineradicable English distinctiveness: over here 'the beer is bitterer, the coins are heavier, the grass is greener, the advertisements more blatant'. English people *looked* different, with their mild knobby faces, and the rhythms of English life were utterly distinctive, from the rattle of the pin tables in the pubs of Soho to the old maids biking to communion through the mists of an autumn morning – yes, that's where John Major got it. The English were culturally different, with their aversion to art, their horror of abstract thought, their obstinate clinging to everything that is out of date and a nuisance, a spelling system that defies analysis and a system of weights and measures intelligible only to the compilers of arithmetic text-books. Real English culture was to be found not in the art gallery or the concert hall but in things which, even when they were communal, were not official: the pub, the picture postcard, the football match, the back garden. Liberty was the fundamental value. Not a grandiose, abstract liberty, fraternity, equality, no principles of 1789, but small liberties: liberty to have a home of your own, to do what you like in your spare time and above all, liberty to refuse the collective: no party rallies, no youth movements, no coloured shirts, no Jew-baiting or demonstrations, and, he hoped, no Gestapo either.[1]

Orwell disliked religion (especially Catholicism), and thought organized churches had little to do with Englishness.[2] The common people, he thought, retained a deep tinge of Christian feeling, in their extreme gentleness, their strong sense of morality, but they rejected churchly values – they were inveterate gambles and drinkers, were devoted to bawdy jokes, and used the foulest language in the world: above all, they were without definite religious belief, and had been so for centuries. The Anglican Church, he thought, had never had a real hold on them, being simply the preserve of the landed gentry, and nonconformity had influenced only minorities.

Orwell knew that, even as he wrote, all these markers of national distinctiveness were passing away for reasons that had something, but not much, to do with war, but which stemmed rather from larger and deeper forces of collectivization and globalization: the English, like all other modern people, he thought, were in the process of being numbered, labelled, conscripted, coordinated. And in the seventy years between the writing of that marvellous essay and the writing of this book, not only have most of the distinguishing features of national distinctiveness he identified atrophied or been swept away, but we have become far more aware of the deep structures which make national distinctiveness appear decorative rather than constitutive. The financial crisis which still envelops us should have taught us, if we had not already grasped, that capital, trade and information are all trans-national forces, the deep determinants of who we are or are allowed to be, against which even national governments are ultimately impotent.[3] To walk down the high street of any English town and look at the shop names, or to switch on the TV and consider the choice of programmes on offer, is to grasp that we are members of a world community – or a world consumeriate – in which national distinctiveness, even as decoration, is increasingly marginal.

The Reformation marked, for England, the end of the notion of Christendom. The foundation doctrine of the English Reformation was neither *sola scriptura* nor *sola fide*, but the Royal Supremacy: Henry VIII utterly rejected justification by faith and burned those who preached it, and he understood the authority of scripture to reside chiefly in the fact that the scriptures taught obedience to the king.[4] The Act in Restraint of Appeals had insisted that it was clear from 'divers sundry old authentic histories and chronicles' that 'this realm of England' was and always had been 'an Empire … governed by one supreme head and king having the dignity and royal estate of the imperial crown of the same'. To that one supreme head all subjects, clerical or lay, owed absolute obedience, in spiritual as well as temporal matters. England, in other words, was a closed system, complete in itself, answerable to no external law and recognizing no legitimate external authority.[5] It would be anachronistic to speak of a nation state in the sixteenth century, but here was an insistence on the legal and spiritual autonomy of the kingdom which drove a dagger deep into the heart of the medieval under-standing of the interconnectedness of all Christian realms, and their common answerability to a transcendent Christian world order represented by pope and emperor. That of course was the nub of Thomas More's rejection of the Henrician Act of Supremacy, and the basis of his claim that the legislation under which he was tried and condemned had no legal or moral standing within Christendom at large, and therefore could not be legal in England: 'this realm, being but one member and small part of the Church', could not make a particular law 'disagreeable with the general law of Christ's Universal Catholic Church'. And so, famously, he declared, 'therefore am I not bounden … to conform my conscience to the Council of one realm, against the general Council of Christendom'.[6]

That opposition between English legislation and loyalties, the council of one realm, and allegiance to the universal Catholic Church, would become one of the most consistent points in contention between Catholics and defenders of the English Reformation: acceptance of the Royal Supremacy would become the mark of the loyal Englishman, repudiation of it the badge of a traitor.

'What art thou fellow, that seem so bragging bold,'

asks King John in Bale's Reformation drama, and gets the answer:

'I am Sedycyon, that with the pope wyll hold
So long as I have a hole within my breche.'[7]

For Catholics, by contrast, the absolute claims of the crown over consciences represented by the exaltation of the monarchy above the pope seemed idolatrous, a usurpation of the authority of Christ himself. It seemed to them to find perfect symbolic expression in King Edward's reign, when crucifixes in the chancel arches of parish churches everywhere were torn down and burned, to be replaced by the royal arms. Nicholas Harpsfield declared:

> Then should you have seen instead of Christ his Crucifix, the arms of a mortal king set up on high with a dogge and a lyon, which a man might well call the abomination of desolation standing in the temple that Daniell speaketh of.[8]

Protestantism as patriotism, popery as treason. The terms of that trope were set by King Henry himself, and the opposition would be played out in English history over and over again. But to begin with, the matter was by no means so simple. For Protestantism had begun in Germany, and the early Catholic polemicists in England had emphasized that foreign pedigree: this was already a major theme in Thomas More's writings against heresy beginning with the *Dialogue Concerning Heresies* of 1529.[9] There he had called for the forcible suppression of Protestantism, evoking an apocalyptic vision of Protestantism as a terminal social disease that, unless it were halted in its tracks, would overwhelm England as it already had Germany, where the destruction was far advanced:

> theyr secte hath all redy fordone the faythe/ pulled downe the chyrches/ polluted the temples/ put out and spoyled all good relygyous folke/ joined freres and nonnes togyther in lechery ... caste downe Crystes crosse/ throwne out the blessyd sacrament/ refused all good lawes/ abhorred all good governaunce/ rebelled agaynste all rulers / ... all the lawes of the worlde/ all reason among men/ set all wretchedness a broche/ and finally turned the nature of man in to worse than a beste/ and the goodness of god in to worse than the devyll.[10]

More's polemical strategy, identifying the Reformation as an alien import, bringing German turmoil into England and undermining not merely religious orthodoxy and practice but all political and social stability, might have seemed far-fetched in Henry's reign, but gained enormously in plausibility in the light of the reign of Edward VI. The boy-king's regime backed a sweeping programme of iconoclasm. The Mass was both denounced and reviled in a government-sponsored press campaign which began in 1548, and then legally abolished in favour of increasingly stark vernacular communion services. These moves precipitated rebellion in the West Country in 1549. Archbishop Cranmer, himself secretly married to the niece of the German reformer Andreas Osiander, saw these English reforms as part of a Europe-wide process of religious purification, and he summoned to his aid in England a group of high-profile European reformers to assist and advise: from Wittenberg Luther's right hand man Melancthon, who in the event never turned up; from Strasbourg Martin Bucer and his Italian protégé, Peter Martyr Vermigli; from Emden the Pole, Jan Laski.[11] With the accession of Edward's elder step-sister Mary, Catholic preachers and pamphleteers would seize on this foreign influx as a powerful propaganda weapon against the new faith – the Protestants' 'chief captains', it was endlessly pointed out, were John Calvin, Peter Martyr, Henirich Bullinger, Musculus, 'and suche other rutterkyns'. The Marian pamphleteer Myles Hogarde, wrote:

> O devylyshe libertie, I wold to God Germany might have kept thee
> still, so England had never bene trobled with the. I would to God thou
> haddest had all our English bere to drink dronk with Hans and Jacob
> in Strassburg, upon condition London had never reteyned the. I would
> to God thou haddest remained in Switzerland a conqueror, so that thou
> haddest never made conquest in Englande. For sythe thy arrival hether,
> many poore men by thy ungracious merchandise are undone. Many a
> good English man at the first glad to entertain thee, for curtesie as a
> stranger, would now be rid of their guest, but they cannot.[12]

That insistence on the Reformation as a foreign corruption of honest English minds and morals had a lot mileage in it: well into the Stuart age Catholics could go on denouncing Edward and his advisers for importing into England the religion of Calvin, Bucer and Peter Martyr, and portraying Protestantism as an alien novelty which undid ancient order and truth. So Richard Broughton condemned Edward's 'tutors and protectors', who,

> seeking for new Evangelists in forraine countries, founde Bucer, Martir,
> and others ... who coming in to the countrye and finding the people

generally inclined to libertie easily made their entrance into change of Religion, and so in a shorte tyme … they introduced a forme of Religion never heard of in England …[13]

In all this, loyalty to the Crown played a crucial part. Henry had made obedience to the monarch the defining mark of a good English Christian, and the Royal Supremacy itself had been the lynch-pin of the English Church's unilateral declaration of independence from the papacy and the wider Catholic communion. Henry's Catholic daughter Mary rejected the Royal Supremacy, but her supporters insisted nevertheless that religious obedience to the Queen was the mark of a good Englishman. In 1554 the priest John Proctor published a pamphlet describing and denouncing Wyatt's rebellion as the work of Protestant malcontents. He appealed against them to 'his dear brethren and naturall countrymen of England', and branded the rebels themselves as un-English aliens: at the end of his book, England herself spoke, denouncing the Protestants as a 'cursed and hellishe generation', and begging them to

> consider bothe me and youre selues. You haue been the cause of my great griefes, and yet you envie me the remedie. You knowe if I perishe you can not florish, yet disdaine you to be refourmed, that I maye bee confirmed in myne auncient and blisfull state. You resiste to be subiect to good gouer-naunce, … and contrarye to your allegeaunce, contrarye to nature, wil thus vexe and trouble me.[14]

But that appeal to loyalty was of course a dangerously double-edged weapon. Within five years, Proctor's Catholic queen, Mary, had been replaced by her Protestant half sister Elizabeth, and the trumpet of royal sovereignty was being blown once more on behalf of renewed rejection of papal obedience, and with it the unity of Catholic Christendom. Clearly the Englishness of English Christianity had to be grounded in something more stable than the shifting religious demands of successive Tudor monarchs. Early Elizabethan Catholics were intensely aware of this, and the dilemma implicit in their repudiation of the Royal Supremacy became acute after 1570. The rebellion of the Northern earls of 1569 and the Papal Bull of 1570, *Regnans in Excelsis*, excommunicating and deposing Elizabeth, combined to brand Catholicism as intrinsically treasonous. From the mid 1570s a series of savage executions by half-strangling and disembowelling would inscribe that association between Catholicism and treachery into the quivering flesh of more than 200 unfortunate men and women.[15]

Meanwhile the polemicists on both sides of the Reformation divide were constructing long-term narratives of Christian England designed to exclude their opponents and validate their own religious positions as the only possibility for a patriot. Probably the most effective, because the least fanciful, of these efforts was the Louvain exile Thomas Stapelton's translation of Bede's *Ecclesiastical History of the English People*, which appeared in 1565. Stapelton's version of Bede, one of the great achievements of England's greatest age of translation, was designed to demonstrate the continuity of Catholicism as the ancient religion showed 'our dear country of England' to have been more ardently Catholic 'than any one country in all Christendom beside'. Modern Catholics, Stapelton told the Queen in the dedication of the book, believed exactly as Bede had believed, by contrast with the wavering and unstable Protestants who 'had altered the faith we were christened in, condemning our dear forefathers of almost these thousand years'. The reformers had thereby proved themselves aliens, 'no Christian inhabitants of your grace's dominions'.[16]

For Stapelton, England's Christian identity and her national identity emerged at the same moment, and Bede's story of the Christianizing of the Saxon invaders of England was the foundation story of both church and state, 'the coming in of the Christen faith into our country, the heavenly tidings brought to our land, the course, increase and multiplying thereof, the virtuous behaviour of our forefathers, the first Christen Englishmen'.[17]

But there were, of course, origin stories that located the genesis of Christian England – or perhaps more correctly Christian Britain, much further back. If there were few in the sixteenth century who believed, like Blake, that the Lamb of God himself had walked our fields, and that the countenance divine had indeed shone forth upon our clouded hills, it was widely believed that Joseph of Arimathea had preached the gospel in England and lay buried at Glastonbury, and there were some who even believed it possible that St Peter himself had founded churches in Roman Britain. These earlier origin legends were pressed into polemic service by both Catholics and Protestants.[18]

Perhaps the most interestingly protean of these origin legends, used by both sides for opposite purposes, was the story of the conversion of King Lucius. Lucius was an entirely legendary second-century King of Britain who had allegedly sent to Pope Eleutherius sometime in the last quarter of the second century to ask for baptism for himself and his entire kingdom. The pope duly despatched two missionaries to Britain, which thereby became the first Christian kingdom to embrace the Gospel. Later elaborations of the story have Lucius abandon his throne, and travel to Germany as a missionary. There he became bishop of Chur in the Swiss canton of Graubunden, where he died a martyr's death.[19]

The Lucius story is mentioned by Bede and embroidered by Geoffrey of Monmouth. Even in its simplest form, it was a godsend to Catholics seeking proof that from the very beginning British Christians had acknowledged the jurisdiction of the pope, and that indeed Christianity was a papal import into Britain. That was the aspect of the story seized on by one of the most influential English Catholic thinkers of the sixteenth century, Cardinal Reginald Pole. Pole, cousin of Henry VIII and Italian-educated humanist churchman, had broken with his ferocious cousin in 1536, when he sent him from Italy a manuscript treatise on the Unity of the Church, denouncing the Henrician schism and Henry himself in particular. Pole used the conventional New Testament passages to prove the pope's primacy in spiritual matters, but he went far beyond merely constitutional or even doctrinal theories of papal sovereignty, and sketched out instead a providentialist account of the role of the papacy in England's history. Historians have long emphasized the importance in English Protestant thought of the idea of God's special providential care for England, the notion of an elect nation. Cardinal Pole elaborated just such a providentialist theory from a Catholic perspective. From the beginning, he suggested, God had shown special favour to England, always through the popes. England had first received Christianity from Pope Eleutherius, who sent missionaries at the request of the second-century British King Lucius. The special relationship between God and England thus begun had persisted. When Britain had been overrun by Saxon paganism, the faith was restored by Pope Gregory the Great. Ever since, the English people had been ardently attached to the popes, their fathers in the faith, and the nation had prospered as a nation in proportion to this filial devotedness. But even now, when England under her apostate king had repudiated her spiritual father, God remembered his special love for England. He had raised up to himself witnesses to the unity of the church and the authority of the pope, martyrs whose blood both accused and pleaded for the nation which had fallen away from Christ and his vicar. The blood of the Henrician martyrs, above all the blood of Thomas More and John Fisher, was God's special grace to England. The privilege of martyrdom had been granted to no other country afflicted by religious division. These two men, the paragons of their age, were special legates from God to their country, their credential letters written in blood: 'They have accomplished their embassy; they have reported; they have brought back the most certain opinion of Christ'.[20]

Between 1536, when he first sketched out these ideas, and 1554, when he returned to England as Cardinal legate to reconcile the kingdom to the papacy, Pole developed this linkage between papal Christianity and English nationhood to new heights. In his momentous speech to Parliament in November 1554, Pole revisited and extended these ideas. Henry's break with Rome, Pole claimed, was a repudiation of England's special place in history, for under King Lucius England had been the first kingdom 'by the public consent of king and people to accept the faith'. Ever since, England had been cherished by the popes, and in return had given 'singular obedience ... unto their father in faith the Pope of Rome'. They had exported this obedience: it was English missionaries who had brought the Christian faith and fidelity to the Holy See to the other nations of northern Europe. But Henry's 'fleshly wille full of a carnal concupiscence' had forced his people into an utterly un-English schism, from which all the evils of the last generation had flowed. As England had first received the gospel with the universal consent of king and people under Lucius, under Henry the consent of the people in Parliament had implicated all in guilt. But God was not mocked: every nation which repudiated the papacy brought on itself terrible punishment – war and anarchy in Germany, or the enslavement of the Christian peoples of Greece and Asia, who had also abandoned papal obedience, and who now groaned under Turkish tyranny.[21]

These ideas were to remain fundamental, not merely to Marian Catholic propaganda, but to English Catholic thinking about faith and nation, for the rest of the Tudor century and beyond. William Allen's *A Defense of English Catholics* addressed to Lord Burleigh in 1584 culminates in a chapter in which he argues that separation from the papacy was 'the only cause of all the present fears and dangers that the state seemeth to stand in'. The argument will now be familiar. England had first received the faith from Rome. All princes and peoples can only be happy, their kingdoms can only be stable when they have learned 'faithfully to submit their sceptres to Christ's sweet yoke' by obedience to Christ's Vicar. The 'See of succession of the Church of Rome' is 'an impregnable rock', the cornerstone 'such as whoever falleth upon it shall be broken'. The papacy has outlived kingdoms and empires, worn out heresies and schisms: all who oppose or separate from it bring ruin on themselves:

> Into what desolation all Africa was finally brought by the schism and sect of the Donatists … how the division of the Oriental Church from the See of Peter hath been the loss of liberty and … eternal destruction … no man can be ignorant.

And what ruin the 'devilish doctrines' of the Reformation has brought on Flanders, Germany, Poland, and on England too. By contrast,

> when our kings of England had good intelligence with the pope and mutual offices of love and honour passed betwixt them … then had we a most happy and victorious country, blessed of God with all spiritual and temporal benediction.[22]

Perhaps the most remarkable expression of this Catholic providentialist reading of English history was embedded not in a text, but in a notable series of pictures painted in the church of the English College in Rome in 1583. Established in 1578 to train priests for the mission to Elizabethan England, the College had been quickly placed under Jesuit supervision. Counter-Reformation spirituality laid great emphasis on the value of martyrdom: the recent rediscovery of the Roman catacombs had promoted an idealized understanding of the early church as a martyr community. That proved a powerful model for a church whose missionaries, especially the Jesuits, found themselves frequently called to work in hostile Protestant states. In 1581 the Jesuit order commissioned a series of gruesome frescoes, depicting the sufferings of the martyrs of the early church, in San Stefano Rotundo, the retreat church of the German and Hungarian College on the Caelian hill. Designed to be meditated upon, the frescoes became one of the sights of Counter-Reformation Rome. They were of course primarily intended to inspire readiness for martyrdom among the young priests destined for missionary work in Protestant Europe. Two years later, the same artist, Nicolo Circognani, was commissioned to paint thirty-four equally daunting frescoes for the English College. But here the programme of the cycle treated not the martyrs of early Christianity in general, but specifically the martyrs of England. The whole cycle was devised by William Good, the College's Jesuit spiritual director, a West Country man who had been born in Glastonbury. It was paid for by George Gilbert, a wealthy young lay convert to Catholicism who was resident in the College. Good's scheme was based on Pole's providentialist and papalist reading of the history of Christian England, but for good measure he included St Peter's preaching in England and the mission of Joseph of Arimathea to his native Glastonbury. The essential outline and theology of the cycle, however, follows Pole, from King Lucius' baptism and martyrdom in church, through the sending of Augustine to England by Gregory the Great and the papal reconversion of the Kingdom, down to the recent Tudor martyrdoms – the cycle included the executions of alumni of the Douai and Roman colleges who were certainly known to some of the student priests who first saw the pictures – Cuthbert Mayne, Ralph Sherwin and Edmund Campion. News of the last martyrdom portrayed, that of Richard Thirkeld at York in May 1583, came to the College while Circognani was actually at work on the cycle. Within this framework derived from Pole, the cycle inserted material designed to emphasize the indissoluble links between the English Church and the wider Christian story of Europe, in the form of images of English martyr missionaries to Germany, Scandinavia and Holland. The central image of the sequence is, predictably, the martyrdom of Thomas Becket, symbol of the perennial struggle between the liberties of the church and a tyrannical monarchy. It ended with an image of the mission of a new Gregory the Great, Gregory XIII, who had founded the English College in Rome to train martyr missionaries to recover England for Catholic Christendom [*see Frontispiece*].[23]

If English Catholics used the Lucius legend to emphasize the immemorial links between papal Christendom and the national church, Protestant polemicists used it for precisely opposite purposes. One of the bogus documents generated by the Lucius legend was a letter, probably forged during the quarrels between Pope Innocent III and King John in the early thirteenth century, when England lay under interdict. The letter purported to be from Pope Eleutherius to King Lucius, telling him that he had no need of papal or imperial instruction or permission to discharge his mission as Christian monarch: he had the scriptures, which contained the whole of God's law, so 'Out of them by Gods grace, with the Councel of your realme, take ye a law, and by that lawe (through gods sufferance) rule your kingdome of Britayne. For you be Gods Vicare in your kingdome'.[24]

Even in the sixteenth century, plenty of people had the critical nous to realize that this was a highly suspect document, even if one accepted the historicity of the Eleutherius/Lucius legend in the first place. But for a monarchy seeking warrant for the Royal Supremacy it was far too valuable an exhibit to be discounted: it was almost certainly one of the principle pieces of evidence produced by Henry's theological poodles in the run-up to the break with Rome, and it was routinely pressed into service by apologists for the autonomy of the English or British Protestant Churches from John Foxe to James Usher.

I have been arguing that sixteenth-century English Catholics faced in two directions: they celebrated the affinity between Catholicism and Englishness, emphasising God's special regard and providential care for English Church and nation from their very beginnings. But they also insisted that English religious particularity in no way detracted from the fundamental connectedness of England and Catholic Christendom, and more specifically, it did nothing to detract from the paternal authority of the popes over the English Church, which, whether in the person of St Peter himself or Pope Eleutherius or Pope Gregory the Great, had called that Church into existence in the first place, and had nourished it ever since.

But Tudor Protestants were also confronted by the need to reconcile English Christian particularity with a wider understanding of Christian history. If the Royal Supremacy tended to lock the reformed English Church within national boundaries, as we have seen, the sense among the leaders of

English Protestantism that they were participants in a European religious awakening turned them outwards to the other European reformed churches. This perception was of course strongest among those Protestants who under Queen Mary had fled to Switzerland, and had found refuge there. Laurence Humphrey and Thomas Sampson told Henirich Bullinger in 1566 that the English Church should look to 'you, who are our brethren of the Reformation. We have the same confession in our churches, the same rule of doctrine and faith'.[25]

Humphrey and Sampson were men of the left, puritans angrily rejecting the rags of popery in what they saw as Elizabeth's half-reformed church. But their sense of fraternity with the churches of reformed Europe was by no means a peculiarly puritan position. Elizabethan Anglican self-perception as part of a Protestant international appears particularly clearly in a rather neglected set of sources, the Occasional Forms of Prayer issued through the agency of the bishops for use in the parishes in times of special crisis.[26] The occasions for these prayers varied greatly, from plague, dearth or earthquake to the victories of the Turks in Malta and in Eastern Europe. A recurrent theme, however, is the threat of militant counter-reformation Catholicism, from the likelihood of an invasion from Scotland led by the Duke de Guise in the early 1560s, through the rising of the Northern Earls in 1569, to the Armada and the wars of the French Catholic League against the Huguenot leader Henri of Navarre in the 1590s. From the very beginning Catholicism appears in these prayers as thoroughly un-English, synonymous with treason, cruelty, tyranny, superstition and opposition to the Gospel. In the wake of the Massacre of St Bartholomew in 1572, for example, the parishes of England were required to pray

> not only to abate their pride, and to stay the fury and cruelty of such as either of malice or ignorance do persecute them which put their trust in thee, and hate us, but also to mollify their hard hearts, to open their blinded eyes, and to lighten their ignorant minds, that they may see and understand, and truly turn to thee.[27]

Notice that this prayer makes a simple identification between the cause of the French Protestants and the Church of England: the papists here hate 'US': the Protestant cause in England and France is one cause, popery the common enemy.

As the reign progressed, the polarization between international Catholicism and international Protestantism sharpened, and with it, English Protestant solidarity with the reformed churches of Europe. One of the forms of prayer circulating in the wake of the 1580 earthquake pleaded for the overthrow of Catholicism, asking that Elizabeth should be given strength

> to strike the stroke of ruin of all their superstition, to double into the bosom of that rose-coloured whore that which she hath poured out against thy saints, that she may give the deadly wound not to one head, but to all the heads of the cruel beast.[28]

That apocalyptic note, rare in the early part of Elizabeth's reign, was prominent in the official formularies of the early 1590s, which were no less emphatic about the fundamental polarity between Catholics and Protestants. England was increasingly seen as the chief bastion and refuge of Protestantism: the Catholic League in France was seen not as a force against the Huguenots alone, but against all Protestants: 'Thou knowest O Lord, how they that fight against us have entered into a league, and combined themselves, never to desist, until they have destroyed all such as profess thy Gospel'. The 1590 English state prayers for Henri of Navarre identified the French Huguenots quite simply as belonging to the same church 'their enemies and ours are all one, and the chief cause of their Malice the same: we together with them, as true members of the same Communion ....'[29]

But the centrality of the Royal Supremacy in the English Reformation, and the religious anomalies that flowed from the Supremacy – the retention of bishops and of many Catholic elements in the Elizabethan Prayer Book, made the balance between English particularism and Protestant internationalism difficult to sustain. Jacobean and Caroline high-churchmen would increasingly reappraise the Elizabethan religious enterprise. Informed in part by the political realigning of Europe, in part by shifts in patristic theology, and in part by second thoughts about the pillaging of the Church and the reduction of clerical influence and status for which they blamed the Reformation, they would seek simultaneously to distance themselves from reformed Europe, and to re-appropriate large tracts of the repudiated English Catholic past.[30]The direction of that evolving process emerges with startling clarity in the contrasts between two well-known and interconnected poems which attempt to relate the Church of England to the Church of Rome on one hand, and to the European Protestant Reformation on the other. The first is the opening quatrain of Donne's Holy Sonnet XVIII, where Donne, in seeking the true church, implies that there are essentially two alternatives: – the Church of Rome, or international Protestantism, of which the Church of England is a part.

> Show me dear Christ, thy spouse so bright and clear.
> What! is it she which on the other shore
> Goes richly painted? or which, robb'd and tore,
> Laments and mourns in Germany and here?[31]

George Herbert knew that poem (Donne presented a copy of his Holy Sonnets to Herbert's mother, Magdalene), and a generation later, he composed what is in effect a reply, in which he establishes clear blue water between the Church of England and the foreign Protestant Churches: no question here of being one and the same Church 'robbed and tore, in Germany and here'. Herbert's poem, a celebration of the uniqueness of the Church of England, is called *The British Church*.

> I joy, dear Mother, when I view
> Thy perfect lineaments and hue
> Both sweet and bright.
>
> Beautie in thee takes up her place,
> And dates her letters from thy face,
> When she doth write.
>
> A fine aspect in fit aray,
> Neither too mean nor yet too gay,
> Shows who is best.
>
> Outlandish looks may not compare:
> For all they either painted are
> Or else undrest.

She on the hills, which wantonly
Allureth all in hope to be
By her preferr'd,

Hath kiss'd so long her painted shrines
That ev'n her face by kissing shines
For her reward.

She in the valley is so shie
Of dressing that her hair doth lie
About her eares.

While she avoids her neighbour's pride
She wholly goes on th'other side
And nothing wears.

But dearest Mother, (what those misse)
The mean, thy praise and glory is,
And long may be.

Blessed be God, whose love it was,
To double-moat thee with his grace,
And none but thee.[32]

And none but thee. In that breath-takingly arrogant phrase we cross a threshold in the evolution of Anglican particularism, pregnant with significance for the future relationship of the Church of England to all other churches. Under the influence of a high-church tradition as it developed under the influence of the Tractarians of the 19th century it would develop into a full-blown repudiation of the Lutheran and Reformed traditions. In insisting on the unique character of the English Reformation, that high-church tradition was forced to rewrite history, and to edit out the sense of Protestant solidarity which I have dwelt on here. The mental gymnastics which such a move necessitates were brought home to me twenty years ago when Professor Gillian Evans published a 600-page volume of source materials entitled *The Anglican Tradition*.[33] It had a preface by Archbishop Robert Runcie, which gave it a semi-official status, and it was in many ways an admirable and wide-ranging collection. It had two notable peculiarities, however. The first was that under the rubric 'The Anglican Tradition' it included not only a large amount of patristic material (which one might reasonably expect), but also some surprising medieval documents, which did not at once suggest themselves as specially Anglican, for example the Fourth Lateran Council's definition of Transubstantiation. Secondly, not only were a mere 60 of its more than 600 pages devoted to the Reformation, but the word 'Reformation' itself did not occur at all as a section heading. Instead, the foundational events of the Church of England were represented under the heading 'The Sixteenth-Century Emergency'. And among the extracts from Reformation writers, there was not a single passage from any of the continental divines of the Reformed tradition who had played so decisive a role in shaping the emerging Church of England: no Calvin, no Bucer, no Bullinger.

Behind these significant inclusions and absences lay a distinctive account of the English Reformation which had its roots not only in the Tractarian revival of the nineteenth century, but in older high-church historiographies which can be traced back to the seventeenth century, and to the mind-set emergent in Herbert's 'none but thee'.[34] This account emphasized continuities between the modern Church of England and the patristic and medieval past which would have horrified the founding fathers of the Church of England, and, by the same token, minimized the similarities between the Church of England and continental Protestant Churches of every hue.

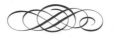

2

Reformation unravelled: facts and fictions

Whatever else the Reformation was, it represented a great hiatus in the lived experience of religion. It dug a ditch, deep and dividing, between people and their religious past, and in its rejection of purgatory and of the cult of the saints, of prayer to and for the holy dead, it reduced Christianity to the mere company of the living. Overnight, a millennium of Christian splendour – the worlds of Gregory and Bede and Anselm and Francis and Dominic and Bernard and Dante, patterns of thought and ritual and symbol that had constituted and nourished the mind and heart of Christendom for a thousand years – became alien territory, the dark ages of popery. Protestantism was built on a series of noble affirmations – the sovereignty of the grace of God in salvation, the free availability of that grace to all who seek it, the self-revelation of God in his holy Word. But in England it quickly clenched itself around a series of negatives and rejections: as it smashed the statues, whitewashed the churches and denounced the pope and the mass, Protestantism came to be constituted by its NO to Catholicism, in a way that it seems to me Counter-Reformation Catholicism, even at its most ferociously intolerant, was never defined primarily by its repudiation of the Reformation.

The result in England was a perceptible narrowing of spirit visible, above all, in the arts. In the century of Reformation, England's greatest musicians, Tallis and Byrd, were Catholics, and it had no great painters at all.[1] Only in words, the one current coin of the Protestant imagination, did English art excel. The Reformation silenced the prayers of men and women for their parents, it banished the saints, it drastically reduced the sacramental life of every Christian. The destruction of monasticism did more than take the roofs off some of the best buildings in England: it amputated one of the Church's perennial and most precious sources of Christian inspiration and renewal. The abolition of religious vows for women closed off a world of opportunity for female self-expression and self-definition: for Protestant women, the only coherent Christian vocation became marriage.

And English religion became parochial. Think of Fielding's Mr Thwackum: 'When I mention religion, I mean the Christian religion, and not only the Christian religion but the Protestant religion, and not only the Protestant religion but the Church of England.'[2] Whatever the theories of later theologians and apologists, experientially the Reformation cut the English Church off from the *Catholica*, the union of peoples of every race and tongue, from the rising of the sun to its setting, in one great sacrifice of praise. It was not *at first* alone: as I argued in chapter one,[3] the Elizabethan Church of England was, and felt itself to be, a member of the northern European family of reformed churches, united by a common Calvinism. But it rapidly came to dislike the company it was keeping, and within a century, until the Evangelical revival, the Church of England was to all intents and purposes going it alone, its Christianity an aspect of Englishness, ironically made prisoner of that tame subjection to the very rhythms and demands of the nation's life which one might argue had been one of the fatal weaknesses of the medieval *Ecclesia Anglicana*.

And so until at least the rise of evangelicalism English religious horizons did not reach beyond England and its colonies. There was to be no Protestant equivalent of Francis Xavier or Matteo Ricci or Roberto Nobili, those visionary missionaries who laboured for a Christianity which could encompass all the cultures of humanity. And early modern England would be cut off, too, from the great outpouring of the Spirit which produced the flowering of Counter-Reformation sanctity. The established church's quiet and rather dour domestic ideal of Christian holiness had little space for the heroic, and no room at all for explorers of the spirit: no English Reformation bishop is remotely to be compared to Carlo Borromeo, Torribio de Mogriveja, Nicholas de Pavillon,

Francois de Sales, just as there would be no English John of the Cross, Teresa of Avila, or Vincent de Paul.

But that, of course, was not how it seemed to Elizabethan Protestant commentators nor to their successors. They were indeed intensely conscious of alienation from European Catholicism, which is to say, from the bulk of European society, but they understood that isolation as a providential escape from the toils of antichrist, and the sign of God's special favour to England. The execution by burning of almost three hundred Protestants under Queen Mary provided proof of the diabolical cruelty of contemporary Catholicism, and of its implacable hostility to the Gospel. The deteriorating relationship between England and Spain, and the growing fear of foreign Catholic intervention in the affairs of England, culminating in 1588 in the Armada, promoted Protestant imaginings of England as a beleaguered isle, a fortress of truth and integrity in a sea of devilish aggression from Catholic powers without and a treacherous Catholic fifth column within.[4]

Much of the intellectual energy for this self imagining was provided by John Foxe. His *Actes and Monuments*, the massive chronicle of popish cruelty and conspiracy against God's elect across the ages went through four steadily expanding editions between 1563 and 1583.[5] It provided English Protestants with an apocalyptic and providentialist reading of history as a whole, and their own recent past in particular. In Foxe's writings the papacy and Catholicism were, and had been from time immemorial, the perpetual enemy. The war between the persecuted church of God and the synagogue of Satan had been waged since the world began, but had climaxed in the sixteenth century, with the rise of Luther and the open confrontation between the true and the false Churches. In that struggle Elizabethan England was a specially favoured land, snatched from damnation and darkness by the miraculous preservation of Princess Elizabeth in the desperate times of the Catholic Queen Mary, and so given the priceless gifts of peace, plenty, and Protestantism,

> in such sort as the like example of Gods aboundant mercies are not to be seene in any nation about vs ... first in hauing the true light of Gods gospel so shining among vs, so publickly receiued, so freely preached, with such libertie of conscience without daunger professed, hauing withall a Prince so vertuous, a Queene so gratious vnto vs, of our owne natiue country,

bred and borne amongst vs, so quietly gouerning vs, so long lent vnto vs, in such peace defending vs, agaynst such as would els diuoure vs: briefly what could we haue more at Gods hand, if wee woulde wish?[6]

Foxe projected this happy situation backwards into the remote past, insisting that the English had always been happy in proportion to their independence of Rome, and he comprehensively denied that the nation had ever received any benefits from the seat of the antiChrist. Foxe particularly denied Pole's claim that England owed its Christianity to the papacy, insisting that the conversion of England predated the time of Pope Eleutherius and King Lucius, and might indeed go back to the apostle Philip and Joseph of Arimathea, though in fact he was not terribly interested in the details of the origins of Christianity in this island.

Foxe's great book provided the materials on which were built all subsequent versions of the black legend of popish craft and cruelty, and in particular the notion of an age-old opposition between the spirit of popery and the spirit of England: already by the end of Elizabeth's reign ardent English patriots, like Sir Francis Drake, had absorbed Foxe's distinctive ideas, and they had helped foster a bitter animosity to all things Catholic. But it was the involvement of the house of Stuart in the affairs of England which gave existential urgency to these Protestant imaginings, and which cemented into the national psyche the conviction that Englishness and Catholicism were simply and utterly incompatible.[7] All the Stuart Kings of England married Catholic wives, and though the Gunpowder Plot absolved James I and VI from any suspicion that he might himself be a crypto-papist, that suspicion hung increasingly vehemently round his son and grandsons. And, as fears that Protestant England might soon find itself groaning under the rule of a popish king mounted, Foxe's narrative was increasingly deployed to fuel those terrors. The burnings of Mary's reign had always, of course, been prize exhibits for the association of Catholicism and cruelty, but Mary's own reputation had remained surprisingly uncontaminated: she was seen as a simple and long-suffering woman led astray by crafty clergy and sly Spaniards. The epithet 'Bloody Mary' doesn't appear in any publication until the late 1650s, and it was not until the late seventeenth and early eighteenth centuries that cheap reprints of the relevant parts of Foxe's enormous book began to circulate widely, some of them in weekly serial form.

Englishness was now identified with the spirit of Protestantism and liberty, a notion which admittedly required some drastic reinterpretation of the reign of bluff King Hal. Popery, by contrast, was identified with tyranny, slavery and arbitrary government: the reign of Bloody Mary became a stalking horse for Whig opposition to the House of Stuart, the history of mid Tudor England a form of propaganda about the inevitable rekindling of the fires of Smithfield were James II or his Catholic successors to have their wicked way, designed to help prevent any such eventuality.

So it is unsurprising that the Revolution of 1688, glorious or not depending on your point of view, should have been justified in terms which drew directly on the religious oppositions I have been discussing. A key indicator here is the success and importance of Gilbert Burnet's *History of the Reformation*, a major work which would dominate the historiography of the English Reformation for the next century and more. Burnet's first volume appeared in 1679, at the height of the Popish Plot. It originated as a reply to a new edition of an Elizabethan Catholic polemical classic, Nicholas Sander's *Origin and Growth of the Anglican Schism*. Burnet, however, wrote quite explicitly with an eye on the current political situation, to warn the nation what to expect from a Catholic monarch, a warning infused with apocalyptic menace.[8] With fear of Catholicism at frenzy pitch, the political impact of his book was electric. Burnet received a formal vote of thanks from both houses of Parliament, not a common accolade for ecclesiastical historians.

Unsurprisingly, Burnet was to be one of the principal apologists for the Revolution of 1688 and, in mounting an apologia for William's ejection of James II, he plundered the Tudor debates on religion and nationhood which I discussed in chapter one. So, preaching before the House of Commons in January 1689, he reverted to the issue of the origins of English Christianity: Popery, he declared, was, and always had been, simply tyranny and, therefore, utterly alien to the English.

> As it is a yoke, so it is foreign to us; we owe no dependence to the See that pretends to be the Mother Church: we received not the Gospel from any sent by them. The Christian religion was in this island for several ages before we had any commerce with that See, nor were we ever subject to it

any other way than as a prisoner in the power of him that took him ... And though we did run the common fate of the rest of Europe of falling under the prevailing superstition of some dark ages, yet this nation did even during the darkness, maintain its liberty the best it could.

Conscious even in medieval times of groaning under papal and clerical tyranny, at the Reformation England at last broke free from her reluctant servitude and would never now return to bondage. Hence the implacable hatred and restless scheming of the papists, against which Britons must be eternally vigilant: 'they hate us, because we dare to be freemen and Protestants'.[9] Fear and hatred of Catholicism, therefore, was the bloody thread which ran through all the upheavals and revolutions of the political history of early modern England: fear of the crypto-Catholicism of the Stuart kings and their Catholic wives, and fear of the tyranny that was assumed to go along with Catholicism.

The cod scholarship underpinning this anti-Catholic tradition was to have a long life. As late as 1819 Thomas Burgess, one of the most learned bishops on the Anglican bench, could publish a treatise proving that the Church of Rome had broken away from the Church of England in the sixteenth century, and arguing that English Christianity owed its origins not to Rome but to St Paul, and had retained its independence till the Norman yoke had temporarily eclipsed primitive Christianity, which the reformers restored:

> To the labours and preaching of the great apostle of the gentiles, St Paul, we are indebted for the first introduction of the Gospel ... the rejection of the Pope's authority in the seventh century stamps the first feature of our Protestant character.[10]

Till well into the nineteenth century, therefore, the polemical theological constructions of the sixteenth century and the bogus history of origins devised to underpin them – apostles preaching in England, Protestant Anglo-Saxons demonstrating their independence of the papacy, and all the rest – continued to shape perceptions of just what it was that had happened at the Reformation. Fear of popery sent the historians into the archives, to find documentary proof of the evils and cruelties of Catholicism. Narratives, hammered out as political ammunition in late Stuart England, survived to shape scholarly perception of the religious history of the sixteenth century well into modern times. That remained true even when, in Victorian England, English historical studies began to be put on a far more secure scholarly base. The Public Record Office was founded in 1838, gathering together for the first time the major state archives into a single location, and the process of sorting, listing, calendaring and publishing the basic materials made a thorough reappraisal of the Reformation period possible. But in fact, no such reappraisal took place. One of the first researchers into the newly accessible archives was James Anthony Froude, and his wonderfully vivid twelve-volume history of the English Reformation, from the fall of Cardinal Wolsey to the defeat of the Spanish Armada, a masterpiece which was in many ways the foundation of the modern study of Tudor England, in fact endorsed and strengthened the ancient stereoptypes.[11] Froude was a fiercely patriotic liberal Protestant, anti-clerical, suspicious of dogma, but persuaded that a robust and rationalistic Protestantism was a sort of spiritual and moral disinfectant, which had helped to liberate sixteenth-century England from the dark ages of monkish superstition and opened the way to modernity. His *History of England* in the sixteenth century, genuinely scholarly and largely based on archival research, was also an enormous tract for the times, designed to dispel the cobwebs of Catholic clericalism and dogma, and to inculcate sound rational religious values, the values which underpinned England's rise to imperial greatness.[12]

So Froude regarded the advent of Protestantism and the repudiation of papal authority in England as an immense blessing, a necessary step in the emergence of the modern world and of English values. The power of a personal monarchy, embodying the lay and secular virtues which were the essence of Englishness, above all the gargantuan figure of Henry VIII, therefore, had enabled and indeed enforced the transition from a backward-looking Catholic Middle Ages to a new age of English greatness. And if for Froude, with his fear of religious fanaticism and contempt for clerical dogmatism, the opposing forces in that struggle were not those of Christ and Antichrist, as in the traditional theological historiography, they nevertheless represented equally momentous polarities and contradictions – priestcraft, sentimentalism, pious excess, bogus supernaturalism, on one side, pitted against the secular virtues and secular decencies which were the heart of England and Englishness. You get the flavour of these oppositions in the sentence in which he characterized the opposing fleets, and opposing civilizations, as the English line themselves to repel Philip's Catholic Armada.

> The names on both sides, either by accident or purpose, corresponded to the character of the struggle: the St Matthew, the St Philip, the St James, the St John, the St Martin and the Lady of the Rosary, were coming to encounter the Victory, the Revenge, the Dreadnought, the Bear, the Lion and the Bull: dreams were ranged against realities, fiction against fact, and imaginary supernatural patronage against mere human courage, strength and determination.[13]

In the modified and partially secularized form popularized by Froude, and passed from him to twentieth-century Tudor historians like Albert Frederick Pollard, these visceral Protestant sentiments passed into the blood-stream of the nation and were canonized in school and university history syllabuses. Until very recently, and even if they never darkened the door of a church, most educated English people probably took it for granted that Protestantism was, if not necessarily *true*, then at least not, unlike Catholicism, obviously *false*. It was widely agreed that the Reformation was, among other things, a vital stage along the road to modernity, the cleansing of priestcraft, ignorance, and superstition from the English psyche, a moral and intellectual leap forward. These stereotypes were much more than the public-house rantings of redneck bigots: the Whiggishly 'progressivist' assumptions they underpinned affected even scholarly thinking and writing about the Reformation, as they had done since the sixteenth century. In 1971, ironically just on the eve of an efflorescence of supernaturalist belief and the dawning of the new Age of Aquarius, Sir Keith Thomas, a man with no acknowledged religious allegiances or interests, could begin his magisterial treatment of the relationship between religion and magic in early modern England with the confident assertion that 'Astrology, witchcraft, magical healing, divination … are now all *rightly disdained by intelligent persons*'.[14] And in similar vein almost twenty years later, the most respected modern historian of the English Reformation, Professor A.

G. Dickens, could start a new edition of the best-selling textbook which had
dominated English academic opinion about the Reformation for a generation,
with this equally blithe assertion:

> In England as elsewhere, the Protestant Reformation sought first and
> foremost to establish gospel Christianity, to maintain the authority of New
> Testament evidence over mere church traditions and human inventions.[15]

Needless to say, all this was reflected by a correspondingly assertive Catholic
historiography, represented in the early nineteenth century by the priest-
historian John Lingard, who scoured the archives of Catholic Europe as well
as the English public records for material to disprove the received Protestant
narrative.[16] Lingard combined apologetic intent with a scrupulous attention
to accuracy. Rather less scrupulously and infinitely less accurately, at the turn
of the twentieth century the slapdash monastic historian Aidan Gasquet and
the frankly propagandist popular historical writing of Chesterton and Belloc
put apologetics first. In the early twentieth century, indeed, discussion of the
late medieval Church and the Reformation was as much coloured by sectarian
polemic as ever, above all in the unequal gladiatorial struggle between Cardinal
Gasquet and Dr George Gordon Coulton. This is not the place to recount the
detail of what became an excruciating and unrelenting exercise in bear-baiting
by the terrier-like Coulton. Gasquet was a generously talented man, whose
first book, *Henry VIII and the Monasteries* (1888), contained a good deal of
fresh and worthwhile research and offered a spirited challenge to traditional
Protestant historiography of the Reformation. It caused a considerable stir,
became a best-seller, and was welcomed not only by Catholic, but by Anglo-
Catholic historians, as doing much to rescue a crucial aspect of late medieval
religion from the calumny of centuries. Gasquet was to follow it with a series
of almost equally successful books with titles like *The Old English Bible*,
The Eve of the Reformation and *Parish Life in Medieval England*, all of them
containing a good deal of valuable information, and all offering a highly
idealized picture of Catholic England from which every shadow and blemish
had been air-brushed out or explained away. His last book of real value was the
collaborative study, with Edmund Bishop, *Edward VI and the Book of Common
Prayer*, published in 1902.[17] Thereafter his work was increasingly based on

hasty and half-remembered reading, and it was riddled with gross mistakes which, however often or politely pointed out to him, he failed, and sometimes refused, to correct. As David Knowles remarked, towards the end of his life, 'Gasquet's capacity for inaccuracy amounted almost to genius': in a serious historical essay offered to one of the greatest and most meticulous historians of the day, his friend and collaborator Edmund Bishop, he could write blithely and repeatedly about Gibbon's *Rise and Fall of the Roman Empire*. As Coulton declared contemptuously, 'inaccuracy grew on him like a crust'.[18]

In the early 1950s, however, an English Catholic perspective on the Tudor Reformations, free from Gasquet's relentless apologetic urge and backed by first-rate scholarship, found formidable expression in a three-volume history of the English Reformation by Monsignor Philip Hughes.[19] Hughes' book offered a masterly overview of the long struggle between the old and new religions in England, and surpassed any other available account in its attention to Catholic as well as Protestant sources. Sixty years on, many of Hughes' judgements and intuitions seem shrewd and percipient, and his book has worn far better than any of the older histories of the subject. But Hughes's bleak view of Tudor England as a repressive state organized in the interests of the wealthy, his scepticism about the integrity of major reformers like Cranmer, his apologetic defensiveness about such neuralgic issues as the Marian burnings, his personal history as a Catholic convert and a priest, and the fact that his books carried the Imprimatur of official Roman Catholic approval, combined to ensure that his work never achieved the recognition, nor the scholarly impact, it deserved.

By and large, therefore, even the weightiest and best of these Catholic counter-narratives failed to persuade the wider public. Froude's great history, controversial when it appeared, had eventually prevailed and set the agenda for scholarly writing on the English Reformation for the next hundred years. In all essentials, the accounts of the Reformation mounted by A. F. Pollard in the first half of the twentieth century, and by Professor A. G. Dickens in the second, were variants, updatings or extensions of Froude's main emphases.

Dickens himself provides a fascinating case-study of the all-pervasiveness of the instinctively Protestant assumptions underlying this historiographic tradition. Dickens was ninety when he died in 2001, and had been ailing for some years before, so we need to remind ourselves that in his prime and, indeed, long past it, he was for forty years one of the most powerful and influential figures in English academic life – Director of the Institute of Historical Research, Chairman and General Secretary of the British National Committee of the Historical Sciences, Foreign Secretary of the British Academy, he dominated and helped shape the English historical profession. For two generations there was scarcely an appointment to a University chair in history about which he was not consulted.

Dickens deplored the fact that Reformation history had remained a sectarian battleground, and in his own writing he scrupulously strove to avoid sounding like G. G. Coulton. But he could not help being touched by Coultonian presuppositions all the same, for Dickens himself came from impeccably Protestant stock. His paternal grandfather was an old-style Tory churchwarden. His maternal grandfather was a Primitive Methodist local preacher, with whom Dickens remembered as a child walking, Sunday by Sunday, hand in hand to chapel, and he recalled a household where strict sabbatarianism, teetolism and fundamentalism were the norm. That inherited religious outlook coloured all his work as an historian. For Dickens, the advance of Protestantism was a liberation of the human spirit which carried its own inevitability. With the appearance of Tyndale's bible translations, therefore, 'the Catholic ascendancy over the English mind was inevitably doomed', for Englishmen had 'developed spiritual needs widely different from those of the mediterranean people'. Writing in the aftermath of two world wars, he was a passionate believer in England's moral superiority, a superiority to which the Reformation was integral. Considering the failure of the religious risings in the north of England in 1536, he could ask

> What serious English patriot can wish that the Pilgrimage of Grace … had succeeded? … They were swimming directly against that stream which bore our nation to far higher destinies than any it had attained in the age of neo-feudalism.

The rebels were attempting 'to roll back the march of history'.[20]

Despite meticulous courtesy and a conscious desire to be fair in all that he wrote, for him 'Catholic' would always carry a whiff of the exotic, would always in his hands be a term of at least mild disapprobation, and 'Protestant', by contrast, an accolade. This emerges with startling and comical clarity in one of his most charming books, his *Portrait* of the East Riding of Yorkshire (*charming*, by the way, is a thoroughly Dickensian word, although in his hands it usually means engagingly untrue – thus Catholic legends of the saints were 'charming'). Dickens closed this genial and unbuttoned guidebook to the East Riding with a pen-picture of the town of Beverley. Discussing the minster there, he developed a revealing comparison with Chartres Cathedral. Chartres, he thought, in its exuberant elaboration represented 'the Catholic Church, organized on every side by logic and law, yet within this compass luxuriously human, infinitely anthropomorphic', 'seething' with the figures of men and women, not merely the 'bible in stone' but 'a petrification of all Christian and pagan history'. Early English Beverley seems by contrast proto-Protestant; it suggests the crags of the mountain-top or, more properly, the bare glade in early spring, where the individual soul stands in loneliness face-to-face with its own sense of God. 'I call it half Protestant', he wrote.

> the symbol of *ecclesia anglicana* ... yet might one not rather regard the spirit which informed its builders as a survival of the Celtic strain in English Christianity? Despite the Roman philosophies and forms of adminis-tration, did not this more truly native strain continue to grow underground and then, in the thirteenth century, when English literature also broke its long silence, did it not escape from the closer forms of continental tutelage to create these grave, sweet harmonies?[21]

This is, of course, the purest tosh, and one can only hope that he had his tongue in his cheek as he wrote it, although he was prone to get carried away by the temptation to fine writing. But it is revealing tosh all the same, every word of which is worth weighing as a key to his thinking about medieval Christianity, and not least his manifest conviction that all that is best and dearest in English religion, even in the Middle Ages, must somehow have remained free of the influence of 'Roman philosophies and forms of administration', and must either look forward to the Protestantism which was to come, or backwards to an unsullied Celtic strain of Christianity, reflecting the purity of the bare crags and vales, and the lonely soul in communion with its maker.

Dickens' influential writings about Reformation and counter-Reformation set the tone of academic study of the subject in England for decades. At the centre of that work was his manifest conviction that everything that is dearest and best in English religion, even in the Middle Ages, even in a church like Beverley Minster, built to house the relics of one of the great pilgrimage sites of the English Middle Ages, the tomb of St John of Beverley, must somehow have remained free of the taint of Romanism. It is no surprise therefore to find at the heart of Dickens' account of the Reformation the conviction that the English had a natural affinity with Protestantism, that the Marian restoration of religion was 'the least English episode in our history', and that Queen Mary failed ultimately because 'of her inability to be, unlike her successor, "mere English"'.[22]

Dickens' patriotic and essentially Protestant confessional account of the Reformation was already looking shaky by 1989, the year in which he reissued what turned out to be the final edition of his best-selling textbook. In the twenty years since then that account has totally unravelled. A raft of studies of the local and national scene have offered radical reassessments of the nature and progress of the English Reformation both on the micro and macro levels. Cumulatively, they suggest that far from being corrupt, priest-ridden and ignorant, the religion of the English parish churches on the eve of the Reformation was vigorous, adaptable and popular. Correspondingly, it is also now widely accepted that the Reformation itself was at first unpopular, slow to gain a hold over the minds and hearts of the people of England, and that its success was a slow and difficult labour which, at every stage, owed a great deal to the support and initiative of the Crown.[23]

This decisive retreat of an essentially Protestant account of the English Reformation, however, has produced worries of its own about religious bias in an opposite direction, and it has not marked the disappearance of confessional influence over the interpretation of the religious upheavals of four and a half centuries ago. For, as I have already pointed out in the introduction to this book, many of the historians involved in establishing the new perspectives on the Reformation happen to be Roman Catholics. That fact has led to a widespread perception that the 'revision' of the narrative of the English Reformation does not in fact represent abandonment of confessional history, but its revival, the grinding of papistical axes, Chesterton and Belloc *redevivus*. Revisionist writing about the Reformation is often thought of and referred to as 'Catholic revisionism', so much so that Professor Dickens simply took it for granted that Christopher Haigh, one of the most prominent assailants of the older Protestant account of the Reformation, and of Dickens' writing in particular, must *be* a Roman Catholic, and when it was explained to him that he was not, and never had been, Dickens exclaimed in exasperation, 'then why does he *say* such things?'[24]

But in any case, it is one thing to change the historical emphasis in school and university curricula, and quite another to budge deep-seated inherited assumptions about national religious identity consolidated over centuries. This pervasive imaginative persistence of that older historiography has little or nothing to do with the actual state of religious conviction in the culture at large. The novelist Kingsley Amis was not noted for his Anglican or Protestant piety, but his 1976 novel *The Alteration* draws its comic power from its deployment of some of the main assumptions of the Protestant historiography that I have been discussing.[25] *The Alteration* is a distopian fantasy. It is set in a fictional 1976 England. In this world, the Reformation did not happen: Martin Luther became Pope Germanian I, and had been succeeded by Thomas More as Hadrian VII. Europe as a whole and England in particular is sunk in a theocratic autocracy, a world ruled by the pope and dominated by the clergy. England is governed by a puppet king under the thumb of the cardinal Archbishop of Cowley, made the ecclesiastical centre of England to commemorate the Holy victory of King Arthur Tudor over his rebellious brother Henry the Abominable there, and the consequent triumph of the Catholic faith. Sexual repression reigns among the laity, sexual hypocrisy among the clergy. Only in the Protestant republic of New England is there an oasis of human freedom, and there alone free thought and science have taken refuge, since both are banned as heretical throughout Europe. All this is policed by the Holy Office, headed by Tony Benn, backed up by a fearsome pair of murderous enforcers, Michael Foot and Corin Redgrave.

The Pope, John XXIV, is a crafty scheming Englishman instantly recognizable as Harold Wilson, who talks in a stage Yorkshire dialect while retaining the papal plural – 'well, we'll be buggered, don't go so fast, our lad', and who asks, as he pours the tea 'shall we be mother?' Worried about mounting world population, but shackled by the ban on contraception imposed by one of his less worldly predecessors, Pope John has been secretly testing an anti-fertility drug called 'Crick's Conductor', which Vatican agents have been adding to reservoirs in selected communities. Afraid that the consequent spate of deformed births will lead to exposure of what he's been up to, the pope decides to solve the population problem more drastically by launching a holy war against Islam: 'Eee, it'll be a right cordial to give old Abdul a sore nose. We're afraid we don't take kindly to Mohametans, all those wives,'[26] – and at the end of the book we learn this has had the required effect, with thirty million dead on the Christian side alone.

But these are comic frills. The book's central plot turns on the fate of a choirboy at Cowley Cathedral, Hubert Anvil, who has the best soprano voice in the world. Eunuch talent spotters from the Vatican have come to Cowley to hear him, and with the connivance of the abbot of Cowley and the boy's hypocritically pious father, it is decided that Hubert will undergo castration, the Alteration of the novel's title – and be taken to sing in the Sistine Chapel choir. A plot to smuggle the boy out of the country involving the New England Ambassador and the Anvil family's chaplain, who is having an affair with Hubert's mother, succeeds, but Hubert developes a freak illness afflicting the testicles, and the doctors are obliged to amputate to save his life: despite everything, he ends up after all as Europe's finest castrato singer. But along the way, Amis has shown us what the world might have been like if the Reformation had not happened. It is as if all James Anthony Froude's night-mares had been realized – superstition rampant, clergy dominant, political freedom suppressed, science and free thought forbidden, empty ritual and sterile dogmatism triumphant, in a word, England subjected to popish tyranny. At one point, Brother Collam Flackerty, secretary to the Archbishop of Westminster, an atheist and homosexual friar who believes nothing but is playing the system for personal advancement, sums the matter up.

'Go back no more than four hundred years or so. Over all the time since, Christendom has been a tyranny of a rare sort. By way of the soul it rules the minds of most and the acts of all. As effect, no wars throughout Europe but the one, a war with long breaks of peace, a war against a power that can never be crushed and can be held in only by standing in arms from

year to year: the best possible form to draw off any will to rebel or quarrel.
And in the last fifty years, Christendom has finally drubbed a power much
more awful than the Turk could ever be, one that lives on as it can in new
England among boors and savages, science, God be praised.

It was a close thing. A little longer and science would have abolished God,
and brought our world to ruin.

His friend says 'You don't mean abolish, you mean leave on one side' but
Flackerty replies:

I mean abolish, I mean deny, I mean disprove – so many centuries of
patience, hope, content, trust, constancy and certitude, so much art, letters,
music, learning, all founded upon one great lie ... But the tyranny stays. I'm
obliged, because tyranny alone can let men be safe and serene.[27]

Amis's book is high comedy, but the jokes are delivered through gritted teeth.
Distaste for Catholicism, and for everything Amis thought Catholicism stood
for, is evident on every page. The author of *The Alteration* is manifestly an
atheist, but it is equally manifest that he is a Protestant atheist, inheritor of
an intellectual and moral revulsion from popery that stretches back through
Froude to Burnet and Foxe.

Even a relatively slight comic novel by Kingsley Amis deserves to be taken
seriously. Shekhar Kapur's film *Elizabeth* longs to be taken seriously as a
remaking of England's national epic, but is inadvertently hilariously funny, a
cod-historical farrago filmed, to the eternal disgrace of the Dean and Chapter,
in Durham cathedral, and built round the coarsest possible version of the Black
Legend of Catholic tyranny and Protestant liberty.[28] The long title sequence is
set in the Mordor-like court of Queen Mary, blackened by the smoke of the
burning Protestants screaming outside, while in the gloom within, a ravaged,
ugly and hysterical queen, surrounded by velvet-clad dwarves, clutches at a
statue of the Virgin and awaits the swelling of the tumour in her womb which
will plunge England back into heresy. From the shadowed gloom and Queen
Mary's anguished wailings, the film cuts suddenly to a sunhazed meadow,
where to the sound of pipe and tabor, maidens and their squires are dancing in
pastel shades of pink and orange and spring green, and the princess Elizabeth,

young, fresh-faced, and red haired, the only hope of her people, turns to face the camera. Throughout the picture, Mary's Catholic regime is murderous, ugly, despairing, Elizabeth a beacon of selfless decency. In one more than usually historically inaccurate scene, the new Queen confronts the Catholic bishops in the House of Lords. They stand, absurdly clad in towering black mitres and copes, hard-faced, wall-eyed, implacable, like a coven of malevolent crows, and try to prevent her inventing the Church of England. Urging on them the need to abandon their allegiance to the pope, she asks:

'Can any man serve two masters, and be faithful to both?'

'This is heresy', cries one of the bishops.

'No, your grace', says the Queen, 'it is common sense, a most English virtue.'

And the film ends as she contemplates a statue of the Virgin Mary in the Galilee chapel at Durham.

'What is her power?' she asks Walsingham, 'Men were willing to die for her'.

'They have not yet found an ideal to replace her', says Walsingham.

We cut to the final sequence: Elizabeth is having her hair cut off, and with that gesture renounces personal sexual and romantic fulfilment, to become the replacement Virgin whom her people can idolize and live and die for. Protestant patriotism had replaced the charade of Catholic myth and legend.

In theological and religious terms, the Reformation wars may be over: outside the pulpits of Ballymena or Belfast, preachers rarely invoke John Foxe's interpretation of the religious upheavals of the sixteenth century. Twelve years on from its premier, Kapur's film seems crude and overstated. But its seven Oscar nominations suggests that its vulgar and sometimes unwittingly comical recycling of John Foxe's version of Reformation England has not lost its imaginative power. Academic revisionist unravelling of the history of the Reformation has not yet dislodged that more visceral and partisan version of the story.

But England is no longer a Protestant nation, even to the extent it still was when George Orwell was writing.[29] If for many the Reformation still seems a stage in the emergence of the world from cruelty, irrationality and darkness, in some quarters of the culture it is beginning to be seen in a different light. As the last traces of ideological investment in the Reformation debates evaporates among the intelligentsia, the triumph of Protestantism in this island can look less like the march of progress than a cultural calamity. I was struck by this thought a few years ago when watching the television series on the history of British art presented by the art critic Andrew Graham Dixon. For him, the Reformation was a cultural revolution reminiscent of Mao's China, one which divided the English from their religious and cultural past and set up in the English psyche a deep and troubling schizophrenia between what he chose to call 'a superstitious faith and its radical rational rebuttal'.[30]

For Geoffrey Dickens, as we have seen, that contrast had derived from and epitomized the age-old separateness of the English church and English Christianity, born independently of Rome and preserving always a proto-Protestant purity which the Reformation did not invent but merely rediscovered and restored. In stark contradiction, Graham Dixon sees it as a radical hiatus, bringing about an entirely new and culturally catastrophic separation. The Reformation, he declared:

> decisively severed Britain's links with Continental Europe. Before the Reformation the British were vigorous participants in a pan-European Catholic culture which stretched from Dunfermline to Beirut. After the Reformation, the British were the embattled inhabitants of a Protestant nation, cut off from and at perpetual odds with the catholic peoples of mainland Europe. Britain had become an island mentally and emotionally as well as geographically.

And in the TV programme he highlighted his point by a walk though the National Gallery, beginning with the Wilton diptych, a glorious English masterpiece the equal of anything painted anywhere else in fourteenth-century Europe. As the cameras panned round the glories of renaissance and baroque art, he drove home his point.

> Walking through the rest of this museum the visitor passes all that never took place in British art: there was to be no English Raphael, no Michaelangelo, no Titian, no Tintorretto, no Rubens, no Velazquez.[31]

We may perhaps be forgiven for wondering whether even if the Reformation had not happened England would have produced a pantheon of painters in quite that class: but Graham Dixon's point seems to me to stand. At the Reformation, the English did indeed found a distinctive way of being English, and being Christian: but in doing so, they were forced to walk away from much that had seemed constitutive of English identity and English religion. One of the most distinctive features of the English church between the thirteenth and the sixteenth centuries was the evolution of the glorious Lady Chapels which are so remarkable a feature of cathedrals like Winchester or Ely. Those chapels became the principal focus of daily worship in the cathedrals, generating elaborate liturgy and a rich repertoire of music and visiual art: the Eton choir book, the most complete surviving collection of the miraculous polyphony which the English veneration of Mary generated, gives us a sense of what was lost when the Reformation outlawed and destroyed that cult. Standing in the grey light of the desolate stone box which is now the Lady Chapel at Ely, an 'empty parallelogram' with its wrecked stonework and blank windows, it is hard to realize that it once contained acres of jewelled glass and the largest assembly anywhere of gothic sculpture celebrating Mary's life and legend.[32]

The Reformation, of course, brought its own glories: the creation of a vernacular bible and a vernacular liturgy had ramifications for the development of the English language and its literature which are quite literally incalculable. Whatever his own mysterious religious allegiances, it seems entirely likely that without the Reformation, there would have been no Shakespeare – and by the same token, no secular drama, no Marlow, no Spenser, no Milton.[33] However one reckons the tally of loss and gain, another and different England was hammered into oblivion in those terrible years. And there can be no denying that for the visual and decorative arts, and for the reaches of the human spirit those arts represent, the English Reformation was indeed a cultural calamity. But in a more passionate and dogmatic age than our own, men and women then were perhaps clearer and less nostalgic than any of us are likely to be about the balance of profit and loss involved in replacing one cultural and religious identity by another.

Part II

The material culture of early Tudor Catholicism

3

The parish, piety and patronage: the evidence of rood-screens

The fifteenth century in England was marked by unprecedented lay investment in the parish, and it has been rightly said that 'there is no period at which money was lavished so freely on parish churches'.[1] The wills of the late medieval laity are testimony to their practical engagement with their religion, for they are filled with bequests for the adornment and equipping of their local churches. The huge numbers of churches built, extended or altered in the Perpendicular style remain as monuments to the energy and scale of the great rebuilding which those parishioners undertook, and paid for, on the very eve of the Reformation. At the level of material culture, there is no hint of any flagging in lay commitment to the practice of Catholicism.

The nature, social location and motivation of this pious investment has increasingly interested historians. Who gave to the church, and why, and what was the balance in pious giving between devotion, conspicuous consumption and the desire for influence or prestige in the community? The answers to many of these questions can only ever be conjectural, but in this chapter I want to throw light on some of them at least by examining benefactions for one specific purpose

– the erection and adornment of the rood-screen, the partition between chancel and nave which divided the high altar and choir from the people and supported the great crucifix flanked by statues of Mary and John. These screens, the largest and most complex single piece of furniture in the late medieval parish church, were a feature of every parish in the land until the Reformation.[2] Though the crucifixes they existed to support and honour were destroyed in Edward's reign, and again under Elizabeth, hundreds of the screens themselves survived the Reformation and, in two regions especially, mid-Devon and East Anglia, many retain the supporting images of the saints with which their lower sections, or dados, were decorated. In Norfolk eighty of the surviving screens retain some or all of their paintings, in Suffolk thirty-nine and in Devon forty two. Some Devon churchwardens' accounts, such as those for the market-town of Ashburton and the Exmoor village of Morebath, preserve details of the erection of new screens and lofts, but the bulk of the testamentary evidence which would enable us to date the Devon screens and to identify the donors went up in flames in the World War II bombing of the Exeter Probate Office.[3] For Norfolk and Suffolk, however, wills containing bequests for the making or decoration of these screens survive in their hundreds, and so it is possible to establish an approximate chronology of the screens and their paintings, to say something about the character of the piety represented by them, and to establish a crude social profile of the donors.[4] These rood-screens were overwhelmingly the most important single focus of imagery in the people's part of the Church. The screens supported the main image of Christ, itself a centre of cult which was expressed in the rows of lamps which burned before it on the 'candilbeme'. They were also covered with at least one and often two rows of smaller images of the saints, on the dado (or lower panneling, from ground to waist-height) and the loft front. The screens, moreover, often formed the backdrop to nave altars maintained by the parish, guilds or individual families, at which the daily votive and requiem masses were celebrated.

The rood-screen, therefore, was a crucial focus of ritual activity and piety, of direct interest to every parishioner. Like so much else in the medieval parish church, they were the product of quite complex patterns of benefaction. Although, as we shall see, they were sometimes paid for by a single individual, on the whole their cost ruled out one-off benefactions. Most were parish projects, managed by the wardens, and documentation survives for a number

Figure 1. *The rood-screen ensemble at Ranworth is the most complete in East Anglia: along the dado the Apostles flank the entrance to the chancel, while reredos panels to north and south identify the positions of the medival nave altars, the Lady Altar (right) and altar of St John the Baptist (left). The great crucifix, loft-front and tympanum were destroyed at the reformation, but the door from the rood-staircase giving access to the loft remains, and is just visible top left: the wooden lectern in the aisle was almost certainly used by musicians in the rood-loft.*

of such projects for parishes throughout England.[5] In Norfolk and Suffolk, many, perhaps most, screens were paid for by multiple gifts, varying hugely in size and often spread out over an extended period. The East-Anglian screens are the most copious surviving source of medieval popular devotional imagery for which we have anything approaching adequate supporting documentation. Attention to these benefactions, and to the images, altars and other ritual arrangements associated with them, gives us a unique insight into early Tudor devotional preferences, and into the relation between individual pious motivation, choice and initiative, and the corporate activity and consciousness of the parish.

We need first to register the character and complexity of the rood-screen, and the extent to which it dominated the parish church. The role of the screen as a divider had very practical as well as symbolic implications. The area to the east of the screen was, in most cases, the responsibility of the rector or patron of the church, and the parish had no obligations for its upkeep or adornment. The whole area to the west of the screen, including the screen itself, was the responsibility – and the property – of the parish. This meant that it was the western face of the screen, the side the people saw, which became the exclusive focus of lay concern and benefaction, and it was on the west face of the screens that there developed an elaborate and often revealing iconography.

The rood-screen was normally a stone or wooden partition, solid to waist-height and then pierced with openings to allow sight of the high altar, and a doorway to permit access to the officiating ministers. A great crucifix, usually supported by a heavy beam, stretched along the top of the screen. In the west of England the screen opening was invariably fitted with lockable doors: in East Anglia doors were sometimes omitted. By the later Middle Ages this basic structure had been elaborated. The creation of large east windows, and of high arches between chancel and nave, left the crucifix starkly silhouetted against the light, rendering its detail invisible to the people in the chancel. To remedy this, it became customary to fill the arch behind the crucifix with a solid boarded or plastered tympanum, more or less continuous with the east wall of the nave. The solid expanse of wall thus provided behind the rood cried out for decoration, and the subject chosen almost everywhere was the doom, or last judgement. It was believed that when Christ came again to judge the living and the dead he would display his wounds, as signs of condemnation to those whose sins had caused them, as signs of mercy to all who were truly penitent. The angels who attended Christ would carry the instruments of his passion, and the association of the doom with the crucifixion was thus theologically very compelling. As the cult of images grew more elaborate, it became a customary act of parochial or individual piety to endow candles or lamps to burn, sometimes in their dozens, before the great crucifix. In the course of the Lenten liturgy the crucifix had a veil suspended before it, which was ritually drawn aside during the liturgy of Palm Sunday. To facilitate the maintenance of these lamps, and the other ritual activities surrounding the rood, a walkway or loft above the screen and below the crucifix became a universal feature of the screens. These lofts acquired a variety of other functions. In all but the smallest churches they served as a musicians gallery, organs were placed there, and they became choir lofts for the singers accompanying the liturgy. At Louth in Lincolnshire, Long Melford in Suffolk and many other great churches, the singing of the Passion during the Solemn Liturgy on Good Friday was done, appropriately, from the rood-loft at the foot of the great crucifix. More practically, the lofts were useful store-places for parish chests containing the church records and valuables.[6]

By the early fifteenth century, most churches in England would already have had a rood-screen and loft, but the replacement or enhancement of the screens as a whole, or of some of their component parts, was to continue right up to the Reformation. In preparing this chapter I examined testamentary evidence from almost 300 parishes in Norfolk and Suffolk: those wills suggest a steady increase of devotional investment in rood-screens and their images from the 1450s through to the end of the decade 1500–9, with significant further activity up to the late 1520s, halted only by the religious disturbances of the 1530s, and the general nervousness then about the implications of royal religious policy for parochial devotional expenditure.[7]

Table A: Norfolk and Suffolk parishes undertaking work on their rood-screens, 1450–1539 (sample of 280 parishes)

Decade	Parishes
1450–9	24
1460–9	12
1470–9	27
1480–9	21
1490–9	33
1500–9	52
1510–19	38
1520–9	29
1530–9	14

One of the commonest reasons for the replacement or refurbishing of the screen was the extensive re-building of churches that was such a feature of fifteenth-century England. Since it divided chancel from nave, any major restructuring of either part of the church was liable to involve alterations to, or total replacement of, the screen. The magnificent new screen erected at Mattishall in the 1450s was the consequence of the rebuilding of the nave in the 1440s and 1450s. In 1508 Robert Gardener of the Norwich parish of St Andrew directed that 'the perke (screen) in the same chirche be made at my cost in the myddes of the same accordyng to the olde werke made on both sydis'.[8] The rood-screen at St Andrews had been attracting bequests for painting only a generation before, but the church had recently been entirely rebuilt, the work being completed in 1506. In the course of that work the chancel had been enlarged and extended, and the central part of the screen evidently no longer fitted, though the parish retained the old parclose screens at the sides.

Such new screens were often an integral part of a projected rebuilding because access to the lofts was normally by a staircase either built into the masonry of the chancel walls, or housed in specially constructed turrets. Large-scale work on structural features of that sort would need careful planning and the consent of the parish.[9] Testators leaving money for the rood-screen, therefore, were frequently joining in parish projects by providing funding for particular aspects, often before the work actually began. Gregory Galion of Besthorpe in Norfolk left 30 shillings in 1507 towards the carving and gilding of the rood-loft in his parish church, provided that 'it be in makynge by the space of iii yerres after thys day', otherwise the money was to be given to a priest to say mass for his soul. Richard Clemens, a Norwich tanner, left the huge sum of £10 in 1534 for the gilding of the perke, 'at suche tymys as the Perysshennes of the same p(ar)isshe ... go forward' with the work, and the Norwich Mason Robert Mayour left 3s. 4d. to his parish of All Saints, Bere Street, to gild the rood there 'when yt ys p(er)formed'. Thomas Drake of Bunwell left. 3s. 4d. in 1533 towards the rood-screen, 'on this condicon if the parisshonors of Bunwell goo forwarde wt it and sett ytt up', and Robert Clerke of Thorndon left 6s. in 1526 to the making of the new rood-loft, 'to be paid in the iij yers that the kerver is in makynge thereof'.[10]

In all these cases private donations, great or small, were contributions to a parish project which had clearly been planned and in many cases launched before all the funding was in. Parishes could routinely count on raising funding as work progressed, since the project might take years. The contract for the elaborate screen commissioned from the carvers John Daw and John Pares for the Cornish parish of Stratton in 1531 spread the work over seven years. The Kentish parish of Hackington commissioned a screen in October 1519 from the carver Michael Bonversall of Hythe, the work to be completed by 1523. He was to be paid 20s. the foot for the work, £7 in hand and the rest on completion.[11]

The indenture between Bonversall and the parish was signed by the vicar, but in most cases such parish projects will have been managed by the wardens. As part of a general refurbishment of the church which involved extensive reglazing and pewing, the parish of Great St Mary's in Cambridge commissioned a new rood-loft in 1518. Specially appointed parish officers took collections 'of mennys goode wyll every sunday by a certeyn Roll' for a whole year, averaging 6s. 8d. a week. The wardens sold some rings from the church 'jewels' to augment funds, and as the work advanced prominent parishioners left legacies towards its cost. In 1521 Robert Goodhale, who had been church-warden in the year the project was launched, left £10 towards its cost, while 'lorkeyn', servant to William Abington, another former churchwarden, left 36s. 8d. The Cambridge rood-loft, which cost the immense sum of £92 6s. 8d., was funded, therefore, by a mixture of organized parochial fund-raising and individual pious benefaction.[12]

At Morebath on Exmoor in September 1534 the parish completed an extensive programme of renovation and pious decoration of their church. They commissioned the carver William Popyll to make a new crucifix, with statues of Mary and John, together with a carved and gilded celure or ceiling of honour. Popyll was to receive £7 in all for the work, 40s. in hand, a further 40s. at Lady Day (25 March) 1535, and the remainder when the work was complete, which was to be in time for the parish's patronal festival on St George's day, 23 April 1535. Popyll was to find and erect all the materials except the great beam on which the rood-group would rest, and the wall-plates to support it, which the parish provided and set up. The parish also made separate arrangements for the painting and gilding of the carved work, involving two other craftsmen and their assistants.[13] The new Rood at Morebath was emphatically a parish project, but in fact its funding was not handled straightforwardly by the churchwardens. The initial payment of 40s. was provided by the Young Men or Grooming Store, and the gilding of the completed carvings was paid for by the Mayden's Store. The logic of this arrangement no doubt sprang from the fact that both the Young Men's Store and the Mayden Store maintained tapers before the 'high cross', and the Young Men regularly presented their accounts to the parish on the Sunday nearest Holy Rood day. Hence the contract with Popyll and the first payment were made, appropriately enough, on Holy Rood day 1534. This was a character-istic early-Tudor mix of piety and practicalities, the spreading of financial burden within the parish, together with a symbolically appropriate devotional gesture. For all that, the parish kept a tight control of the management of the project. The workman employed to paint the figures evidently ran short of cash before the work was complete, and the Vicar unwisely advanced him 20s. from his own purse, without clearing the payment with the wardens, an action which, despite the generally good relations between priest and people at Morebath, was resented by his parishioners because it was done 'agaynst the p(a)rysse wyll'. The Vicar was eventually refunded from the funds of the Maiden Store, but in view of the tension caused by his unilateral action, he donated the money to another parish project.[14] Financial sponsorship of a parochial project by a guild, store or other sub-group within the parish was, of course, commonplace. The early sixteenth-century screen in the parish church of Thorpe le Soken, Essex, for example, had a painted inscription informing the reader that 'This loft is the bachelers, made by Alles' (i.e. funded by ales), 'exactly as at Morebath'.[15]

If guilds and stores might initiate, adopt, or partially fund parish projects, so too might individuals, and there are many examples of rood-screens being bestowed upon parishes by wealthy clergy or laity. In 1505 Robert Reydon, a gentleman and lavish benefactor of the parish of Creeting St Peter in Suffolk left money for the carving and gilding of a new Rood Mary and John. Robert Northern, vicar of Buxton in Norfolk, left £20 to his church in 1508 'toward the makyng of a new perke after the newe perke in the chapell of the ffelde in

Norwyche', and the Norwich rood-screen he here prescribed as the model to be followed at Buxton was itself the result of the lavish gift of £40 by Henry Bachcroft of Little Melton in 1502.[16] The benefactor bestowing this sort of benefit on a parish must always have had the principal say in the character and decoration of the screen he or she paid for, but such bequests needed the consent and acceptance of the parish, and the benefactor had to consult and carry the parish with them. In 1483 Alice Chester, a wealthy widow of the Bristol parish of All Saints, 'considering the rood-loft of this church was but single and no thing beauty' decided to replace it 'at her own proper cost' with something much more splendid. She proceeded with care, however,

> according to the parish entente, she, taking to her counsel the worshipful of this parish with other having best understanding and sights in carving, to the honour and worship of almighty God and his saints, and of her special devotion to this church, has let to be made a new rood-loft in carved work filled with 22 images.[17]

Consultation with the 'worshipful' of the parish must have been a necessary part of every such endowment, particularly when, as often happened, other parishioners wished to add their contributions to the main benefaction. A number of screens attributed by inscriptions to a single donor are known to have been in fact the object of many smaller supplementary donations by other parishioners. The screen at Ludham has a carved scroll on the dado with the date 1493, requesting prayers forJohn Salmon and his wife Cecily 'that gave forten pounds', but it also commemorates 'alle other benefactors', and there is surviving testamentary evidence between 1491 and 1508 for a host of smaller, but still substantial, donations of a mark or a pound towards its gilding and painting.[18] [*Colour Plate 5*] At East Harling the magnificently carved early sixteenth-century screen is covered with the armorial bearings of the dominant local gentry family, yet once again we know there was a stream of smaller benefactions from parishioners between 1499 and 1513.

Screens were expensive projects, which often attracted very substantial donations from the well-to-do. Surviving will evidence from Norfolk and Suffolk suggests that screens were rarely the focus of giving by the poorest testators, though gifts of 6s. 8d. or even 3s. 4d. are not uncommon. But even substantial donors might not get the credit of a specific ascription. At Marsham the screen was inscribed in memory of John de Norton and his wife Margaret, yet between 1503 and 1509 several other parishioners contributed significant sums of between £1 and £3 towards its gilding and painting, and at Garboldisham a screen which attracted many benefactions is similarly inscribed for William and Katherine Bole.[19] The precise dynamics of such corporate efforts under the umbrella of a single donor are mostly concealed from us, but may reflect the standing of the donors or their families in the community, their initiative in beginning the project, or their long-term and life-time benefactions to the parish, rather than the amount donated in wills towards the screen itself. At Foxley in Norfolk the screen has portraits of two donors, John Baymonde and his wife, kneeling before the saints on the screen doors.

Figure 2. *John and Hilary Baymonde kneel before the Four Latin Doctors and beg the parish's prayers, on the screen doors at Foxley.*

Baymonde left just 5 marks towards the painting of the screen in his will 1485. It is thus very much iconographically 'their' screen, yet £3 8s. 4d. does not seem an overwhelming benefaction and we know there were other donors. Five marks will certainly not have covered the whole costs of even the small screen at Foxley, but it may be that Baymonde's bequest for painting the screen was merely a death-bed addition to earlier and larger benefactions, and he perhaps initiated the project, thereby establishing his claim to the central place on the screen itself. Certainly the family were and remained major benefactors of the parish. Two generations later, in 1543, a Joan Baymonde, widow, left a range of gifts to the parish, including a surplice, altar cloths and £6 for a new cope.[20]

Many screens, then, were the result of joint benefactions by large numbers of donors. At Trunch in Norfolk the screen, which is dated 1502, attracted many bequests and donations between 1496 and 1505, and has a carved inscription in Latin along the dado, enjoining the onlooker to 'Pray for the souls of all the benefactors of this work, which was made in the year of the lord 1502, to whose souls may God be favourable. To him be glory, praise, honour, virtue, and power, and to him be jubilation, thanksgiving, and love unfailing, through endless ages. Amen'. The Latin inscription may well be the composition of the late fifteenth-century Rector of Trunch, Richard Mytton, who appears as witness to the will of the principal benefactor of the screen, John Gogyll, and who may have encouraged ailing parishioners to make bequests towards the work.[21]

Figure 3. *The Latin inscription of 1502 carved on the rail above the Apostles at Trunch celebrates the completion of a collaborative parish project, involving many benefactors.*

The benefactors of the screen at Trunch are unnamed in the commemorative inscription, an indication perhaps that there were too many of them for this to be practicable, as there were for most rood-screens erected in the late Middle Ages. Nevertheless, the injunction to pray for them pinpoints the principal motivation for their giving. Early Tudor testators liked value for money in this matter, and they preferred their benefactions to be attributed, like their tombstones and brasses, 'for a remembrance that some such of my Evencristianes as shall see and loke upon it wull of ther charite pray for or soulys'.[22] They might spell out the terms of the bargain they were striking with the community, as John Mottes of Thorpe-by-Haddiscoe in Norfolk did in 1534, when he gave a new perke 'upon condicon the towneship yerely every yere aftre my decease do kepe an obite in Thorpe to the value of vi d'. With no close relatives, a parish benefaction was Mottes' best hope of remembrance and intercession after death, but his impulse was shared by many who left loving relatives behind.[23] Some donors even had themselves portrayed on the screens they had donated, like the Baymondes at Foxley, the Bacon family at Fritton, William and Joan Groom at Burnham Norton, or the now anonymous female donor praying to St Sylvester at Houghton St Giles. The nine men and seven women crowded into a single panel at Ipswich St Matthew are probably the brethren and sisters of the Erasmus guild there.[24] Portraits of donors, however, were never common, and group portraits rarer still. But many screens with multiple donors nevertheless at least listed their names, or at any rate the names of those whose gifts rose above a certain level. The screen at Westhall in Suffolk had an inscription naming at least five donors, including one still living when the inscription was made. Similar inscriptions are, or once were, visible in Norfolk at Attleburgh, (where a former parish priest, several married couples and the guild of All Saints are named), North Burlingham, Aylsham, Wellingham, Weasenham All Saints, Wiggenhall St Mary and elsewhere. Part-donors of screens might have their particular contribution specified, as at Cawston, where donors made themselves responsible for painting single panels or 'panes' of the screen, and where William Atereth and his wife Alice in 1502 had an inscription placed asking for prayers for them 'the wheche dede these iiij panys peynte be the executors lyff'.[25]

In the same way, at Aylsham in 1507, one of the principal donors of the screen, the worstead weaver Thomas Wymer, had an inscription placed under the pictures he had paid for, informing the reader that he had 'caused this part … of this work to be gilded'. The panels he paid for included the Apostle Thomas, his name-saint, and Wymer's Christian-name appears directly under the image

Figure 4. *These eight figures arranged in pairs on the north screen at Cawston were paid for by a single donor, William Atereth, whose benefaction is recorded in a painted English inscription below the figures. Those on the south screen, by contrast (colour Plate 3), were paid for by a number of other parishioners, employing painters from several different workshops.*

of the Apostle. Such specificity sought to personalize an otherwise somewhat anonymous absorption into a parish project. So John Funber of Martham made his will on Holy Cross day 1507, requesting burial in the church there 'before the Image of the Crucyfyx and by my seete in the sayde churche', and went on to bequeath five marks 'to the payntyng of one payne of the perke before my grave'. At Eye in Suffolk in 1504 the widow Joan Busby "adopted" one part of what was clearly an already fixed programme for the new rood-screen there, stipulating that the 'Medylpane of the Newe candilbeme in which xall stan an ymage of our Lord be payntid if it may be born'.[26]

Such prescriptions for the painting of particular portions of the screens raise the question of responsibility for the iconographic schemes of the screens as a whole. To some extent this was fixed by convention. The upper part of the screen invariably carried the crucifix, often with the doom behind it, but the loft front and the dado left more room for personal devotional preference. Some screens, especially in poorer parishes, were decorated only with formal geometric or floral patterns and perhaps the names of donors, as is the case at South Walsham, but by the late fifteenth century the overwhelming majority had elaborate sequences of saints painted on the dado, and painted or carved in niches on the loft front. The choice of these figures was influenced by a range of factors – visual and religious convention, specific theological concerns, workshop styles and pattern-books, and individual devotional preference. Parish and individual commissions were often inspired by encounter with a particularly striking screen elsewhere. A parishioner in St Swithun's parish, Norwich, left money in 1520 to gild the Rood and directed that 'the same Rode have a scene after the Rode of Seint Laurence'. The parishioners of Hackington in Kent specified that their new screen should be 'made Carven & wrought in every forme of woorkemanship or better as nowe is wrought & made after the newe Rood loft nowe sett and being in the parishe Churche of the Holie Crosse of Westgate at the Citee of Canterburie'.[27] Rivalry as well as imitation played a part here, for individuals and parishes were anxious that the furnishing of their churches should reflect the community's pride and be 'aftyr the best faschone off anny her abowth'. The parishioners of Morebath instructed their carver that their new rood should be 'accordyng to the patent of Brussorde *or better*', Brushford being a village two miles away across the Somerset border. The churchwardens of Yatton in Somerset in 1446–7 rode to Easton-in-Gordano to inspect a model rood-loft with a gallery, and to enquire about costs before commissioning their own work. The wardens of Stratton similarly travelled round a number of churches in the region before commissioning a new screen for their own church: in such cases, where a satisfactory pattern was found, no doubt the same workshop was often employed.[28]

We know next to nothing about these workshops, however, though often more than one will have been involved in any particular project, presenting wardens and executors with considerable problems of co-ordination and organization. The screens in East Anglia were probably prefabricated in the workshop and assembled locally, but once erected would be painted and gilded *in situ*, and in many cases also elaborate gesso-work (moulded plaster designs) were applied. At Aylsham the figures paid for by Thomas Wymer were painted on vellum and glued onto the screen, and were markedly better than the cruder paintings next to them: it seems that here (as at Cawston) a wealthier patron could buy better work. [*Colour Plate 3*] There is a similar discrepancy on the south screen. Any one commission, therefore, involved a range of crafts and personnel. Morebath's new rood involved three separate craftsmen: William Popyll the carver, John Creche the gilder, and John Painter.

It is sometimes possible to identify the same workshop in different commissions – the same gesso mouldings of the saints can be found on the font at Westhall in Suffolk and the screens at Aylsham, Cawston and Marsham in Norfolk, for example.[29] Stylistic similarities are trickier to handle, though the paintings of St Barbara on the Norfolk screens at Ranworth, North Walsham, Filby and North Elmham are clearly related to each other in some way, as are the Apostles at Ranworth, Hunstanton in Norfolk, and Southwold in Suffolk. The demi-angels in the arches above the saints on the Ranworth screen occur again at Attleburgh and at Gooderstone, but we have no certain way of deciding whether the similarities stem from a common pictorial source, the same painter or workshop, another firm using second-hand patterns, or simple imitation. Of these screens only Attleburgh can be dated approximately from commemorative inscriptions for donors who died in 1446 and 1458: stylistically it looks just as early as the paintings on the Ranworth screen, which some experts date (improbably) as early as the 1430s.[30]

The conventions governing the choice of images on a screen were determined partly by theology, partly by decorative requirements. Theologically, the screen and tympanum as a whole was a complex eschatological image. Its theme was mercy and judgement, and the saints and angels on it would accompany Christ when he came to judge the living and the dead, and could now be recruited as 'advows' or intercessors. Spatially the loft-front and dado of the screen divided most naturally into a series of niches or panels in which sequences of saints might stand, and there were a number of ready-made groupings to hand in late medieval iconography – apostles, prophets, virgin martyrs, the orders of angels.[31] Of these the most obvious and appropriate group were the apostles, for Christ had said that they would sit on twelve thrones and judge Israel when he came again: they sometimes occur in the doom painting itself, as they do at the feet of Christ in the doom at St Thomas' s, Salisbury, and they were an obvious choice to range along the panels of the dado. They occur on some of the earliest and best of the surviving screens in East Anglia, from the early or mid fifteenth century (six only at Edingthorpe, the full set at Castle Acre, Ranworth, all in Norfolk, and Southwold in Suffolk), and they are by far the most frequently represented saints on the surviving screens in Norfolk as a whole (twenty-four sets out of eighty surviving screens) and Devon (twenty-seven sets out of forty-two). Interestingly, they are less common in the admittedly much smaller group of surviving Suffolk screens (occurring on seven out of thirty-nine screens), where other sequences, for example prophets, occur as frequently. There being only twelve apostles, and screens often having more than a dozen 'panes' or segments, the apostles regularly occur in association with other sequences, alternating with or alongside prophets or the four Latin Doctors, St Gregory, St Jerome, St Ambrose and St Augustine. These latter associations of apostles and prophets or Doctors were immensely popular all over Europe in the fifteenth century, and had a 'learned' feel to them. In many medieval representations, though only rarely on the surviving screens of East Anglia, both apostles and prophets have Latin texts, in the case of the apostles the articles of the Apostle's Creed, in the case of the prophets messianic texts from their prophecies.[32] Apostles with Creed texts survive on Norfolk screens of Mattishall, Gooderstone, Ringland,Weston Longville, and Salle, and the Doctors on the pulpit at Castle Acre have texts from their own writings.[33] The Doctors occur again on the pulpit at Burnham Norton, and as their association with pulpits suggests, even without texts their occurence alongside the apostles probably reflects the fifteenth-century Church's preoccupation with orthodoxy and catechesis. At Porringland the screen was a gift to the parish by the rector, Robert Draper, in 1473, and the apostles with the articles of the Creed on labels were part of an elaborate theological programme. This included not only prophets with messianic texts, but the Fall and expulsion of Adam and Eve from Eden.[34] This sort of learned scheme is hardly surprising on a screen commissioned by a wealthy and well-educated priest, but the replication of similar schemes, at Salthouse, Gooderstone and almost three dozen other sites in Norfolk, may have been a matter of convention and the contents of workshop pattern-books.[35] Yet there are some indications of a degree of theological self-consciousness even by lay donors. It is a curious fact that most of the surviving examples of donors portrayed on the screens they commissioned show them kneeling before or beside representations of the four Latin Doctors – at Houghton St Giles, Burnham Norton (pulpit), Fritton, Foxley, and formerly on the reading-desk at Cawston. Given the range of saints found on East Anglian screens, this can hardly be a coincidence.

In Norfolk as elsewhere Lollards seem to have made a point of reviling the four Latin Doctors, who represented the teaching of the Catholic Church, as 'heretikes, and here doctrine...bey opin heresies', and although there is no evidence of a continuing threat from Lollardy in the Tudor period, overt devotion to the Latin Doctors may have been a recognized short-hand for a self-conscious Catholic orthodoxy.[36]

Even where a single donor or group of donors funded the screen, the choice of images on them must generally have been a matter for negotiation. Dame Alice Chester agreed her choice of twenty-two images for the new screen at Bristol All Saints with the 'worshipful' of the parish, no doubt including the priest. In the same way Katherine Harston left five marks for a new banner for the church of St Mary Coslany in Norfolk in 1534, and directed that it should be painted 'with suche stories of our blessed Ladie as shalbe devysed by myne executors with thassente of the most honest of the said parishe'.[37] Parochial projects funded by private benefactions must always have involved this sort of negotiation. At Leverton in Lincolnshire in 1526 the parish accepted a legacy from William Franckysshe to fill the niches of the rood-loft with alabaster images, but his money ran to only seventeen images, not enough to complete the work. The parish paid for the remainder, and the wardens raised a levy of cheese from parishioners for the alabaster-man while he was working in the parish. Frankysshe's widow Janet oversaw the payment of his legacy, and doubtless had a say in the choice of images, but the parish was clearly also fully involved in the implementation of the project.[38]

In many cases parishes will have been content with conventional sequences, which may have been workshop standards – prophets or angels in Suffolk, virgin martyrs everywhere, or more random selections of saints arranged into a more or less symetrical scheme. At Somerleyton in Lothingland, the apparently unstructured assortment of saints on the screen proves on closer examination to consist of a series of matched 'pairs', working towards the chancel opening from the outer panels of the screen – St Michael and St George, each with their dragons, St Edmund and St Edward, both royal saints, St Appolonia and St Dorothy, 'helper' saints and virgin martyrs, the two deacons St Lawrence and St Stephen, and so on. In symmetrical schemes of this sort, where every saint has to match another of the same type, it is hard to believe that the ensemble represents anyone's strong preference. Such screens present a selection of the most popular saints of the period, and they were probably picked from a pattern-book or left to the painter of the screen. But even a conventional layout of this sort might be adapted to locality. The sumptuous screen at Ludham seems equally and utterly conventional, with paired helper and royal saints arranged on either side of the central group of the four Latin Doctors. Mary Magdalene matches Appolonia, Stephen matches Laurence, Henry VI matches St Edward the Confessor. The one local touch is the pairing of the Norfolk saint, Walstan, who had a popular local shrine at Bawburgh, with St Edmund, a pairing possible because Walstan, although the patron saint of agricultural labourers, is always portrayed crowned and wearing an ermine robe. Since Edmund, too, was the focus of an even more important East Anglian pilgrimage, the Ludham screen fits a specifically local piety neatly into a scheme which might otherwise have come straight from a workshop pattern-book. [*Colour Plate 5*] The fact that eight surviving Norfolk screens had or have images of St Walstan, all of them within a seventeen-mile radius of the shrine at Bawburgh, indicates that this adaptation to local devotional preference was a regular feature of such commissions.[39]

Certainly, the range of imagery on screens in early Tudor England show ample evidence of consumer choice at work, and of self-conscious didactic and devotional motivation on the part of the donors, sometimes resulting in what can appear idiosyncratic and even eccentric representations. In 1514, shortly after the completion of the new rood-screen at Bungay in Suffolk, Thomas Fynch left money for the making of a new altar on the north side of the church, and commissioned three images to be placed behind it – All Saints in the centre, flanked by St Ursula and St Cornelius. Ursula was a popular figure in late medieval England, but Cornelius is a saint of such obscurity that Fynch's choice of him as "advow" is hard to account for, unless perhaps he had been born or baptized on his feast-day.[40] On the screens, too, one often encounters clear signs of devotional preference by a donor. It interrupts, for example, an otherwise conventional iconographic pattern on the screen at Potter Higham in the Norfolk Broads. The screen, painted about 1501, was a small one, with room for just eight painted saints, the Evangelists and Doctors, an obvious enough choice. But the set is incomplete. There are only three

Evangelists, Matthew being replaced by St Loy, brandishing a hammer, an asymmetry impossible to account for unless one or more of the donors had a particular devotion to St Loy, patron saint of smiths and farriers.

At Cawston, too, the screen represents a mixture of convention and personal or local choice. The core of the scheme is a set of apostles, flanking the four Latin Doctors on the doors (as at Gooderstone and Salle).[41] But the wide screen at Cawston had more than the sixteen panes necessary for the scheme, and the individual testators responsible for financing clusters of images on this screen seem to have dictated the choice of additional saints portrayed. Among the saints painted at the cost of William and Alice Atereth are six of the twelve apostles, but also St Agnes and St Helena. Both these holy women were popular saints on East Anglian screens, but St Agnes was the patron saint of the parish, and the portrayal of the parish patron on screens is almost unheard of, since every parish had a carved image of its patron to the north of the high altar. But there was a guild of St. Agnes at Cawston, and maybe the Atereths were members.[42] Guild-altars might be located against the rood-screen, as they were at at Attleburgh, requiring appropriate imagery: the presence of an image of the Trinity above and behind one of the former altars, together with two named donors, must reflect the location of the altar of the Attleburgh Trinity guild, with a reredos paid for by two of its members.[43] Even where there was no screen altar, a guild might leave its mark on the iconography of screens. Devotional gestures towards the patron of guilds to which testators happen to belong are a common feature of East Anglian wills, and this perhaps accounts for the presence of the guild patron, St Agnes, on the screen at Cawston. In the same way, the badly damaged carving of angels adoring the eucharistic host on the ruined screen at Gressenhall in Norfolk is probably due to the involvement of the local guild of Corpus Christi, or of one or more of its members, in the financing of the screen. Similar patronage by members of the local guild of the Head of St John the Baptist may account for the carving of St John's head and of the *Agnus Dei* in the spandrels on either side of the doorway of the screen at Trimingham in Norfolk.[44]

One screen which certainly does depict a parochial dedication is the magnificent and relatively early screen at Barton Turf on the edge of the Broads. The church is dedicated to St Michael and All Angels, and the bulk of the screen is taken up with a glittering representation of the Nine Orders of Angels. These are stylistically so close to the angel of the Annunciation in the early fifteenth-century altarpiece from St Michael at Plea in Norwich that the same artist or workshop must have been involved.[45] To make up the twelve panes of the screen three female 'helper' saints have been added – St Zita of Lucca, who had a flourishing cult in East Anglia and who recovered lost property for her mostly female clients, St Appolonia, patroness of sufferers from toothache, which was almost everyone, and St Barbara, protectress from sudden death and from thunder, fire and explosions.[46] These 'helpers' were universally popular, all of them occurring time and again in glass and painting, including naif and 'folk' commissions like the screen at Westhall. But the Barton Turf angels carefully reproduce the standard lore about the qualities and activities of the Orders as found in the Golden Legend,[47] and that fact, and the magnificent quality and unity of the paintings as a whole, make it clear that this is no folk commission, nor a piecemeal project funded over a long stetch of time. Serious money and a good deal of sophistication and planning went into this screen, and if its subject matter suggests that it was a self-consciously parochial project, its quality and execution suggest close supervision by a cleric or wealthy patron.

In many commissions, however, donors may have chosen some images, and left others to the painter's discretion. When the Ludlow Palmers Guild commissioned elaborately carved imagery for their chapel in 1524 they made detailed stipulations about the main scenes to be depicted, and their location within the finished scheme as a whole, demanding from the carver,

> on the north side ... one substantial story according to his paper that is to be known St John Evangelist standing beneath in a godly story and the Palmers receiving the ring of him, and over him St Edward in a goodly story receiving the ring of the Palmers ... and the four Doctors of the Church with other divers Saints such as he thinketh best with two or three miracles of St John Evangelist.[48]

Here the specific and detailed requirements of the clients were sketched out by the craftsman for the guild to approve – hence the reference to 'his paper'. However, elements of the scheme clearly remained fluid. The carver was permitted to add his own selection of appropriate saints, and vaguely required to portray 'two or three' miracles of St John. Such flexibility was likely to have been a feature of parish commissions, where funding for the paintings often took years to dribble in, and where the work may well have been intermittent. The late screen at Wellingham in Norfolk, dated 1532 and inscribed for Robert Dorant and his two wives Isabell and Beatrice, for John Neell, and for other donors 'who had it painted', was clearly a project attracting a range of benefactors, by no means all of whom were named on the screen inscription.[49]

Figure 5. *The very miscellaneous iconography of the Wellingham screen, including a representation of St Michael weighing souls as well as the "Image of Pity" which formed the reredos of a small nave altar, probably reflects the patronage choices of a number of local families, some of whose names remain in the painted inscription at the top of the dado.*

The iconography of the screen is correspondingly miscellaneous. To north and south of the door are elaborate if naively painted scenes depicting St George and the dragon, and the 'psychostasis' or weighing of souls by the Archangel Michael. These pictures are characteristic sixteenth-century products, when donors seem to have developed a liking for narrative, probably under the influence of prints and book illustration. Painted scenes which are certainly based on prints, as opposed to single figures ultimately derived from niched sculpture, appear on other sixteenth-century screens in the region, such as Tacolneston, Horsham St Faith and Loddon, while several Suffolk screens had carved narrative panels of Gospel scenes, remains of which survive at Wyverstone and Gislingham.[50] At Tacolneston the source print for the panel of the temptation of St Anthony is known; an engraving by Lucas Van Leyden published in 1509.[51] But the remaining panels at Wellingham, one of them now illegible, included 'an image of pity' filling only the upper part of a panel and clearly meant to form the reredos of an altar, and some helper saints awkwardly crammed into the rectangular 'panes' and not quite filling the available space. The surviving pair on the north screen include a figure of St Sebastian, much invoked against plague in Tudor England, and a now unidentifiable crowned military saint with a chained king at his or her feet. The screen thus displays, in a variety of styles and with no apparent attempt to harmonize diverse elements, imagery adapted to the function of the screen as the location of a nave altar, paired and single figures of traditional helper-saints, and story-panels reflecting a liking for narrative scenes that was new on Tudor screens. It is difficult to believe that this hotch-potch does not in some way reflect the pattern of funding for the screen. A similar, if less pronounced, diversity of choice can be seen on another group project, the stylistically more coherent screen at Gately, with its images of the Latin Doctors, a two-panel Visitation scene, and a handful of pilgrimage saints popular in rural Norfolk, three out of four of them uncanonized – St Etheldreda, Master John Schorne, Henry VI and the mysterious 'Puella Ridibowne', who appears to have had a late fifteenth-century cult in East Anglia.[52] [*Colour Plate 4*]

By contrast, some parochial projects, though funded by a stream of donations from the 'worshipful' of the parish, were clearly planned as an iconographic whole. An example is the magnificent screen at Southwold, which was being worked on throughout the 1460s and 1470s, and which displays the Orders of Angels, the apostles and a series of prophets.[53] But even unitary schemes might display puzzling inconsistencies. The complex screen-work at Ranworth is the most magnificent in Norfolk, and the most complete for any English church.[54] Though a good many Ranworth wills survive, containing a steady stream of devotional giving, none record gifts to the screen, which cannot therefore be dated with any confidence: the testamentary silence about it suggests that it was in all probability the gift of a living single donor. The likeliest candidates are the Holditch family, who dominated Ranworth in the mid fifteenth century, and who donated a now demolished double hammer-beam roof to the church sometime before the later 1470s.[55] The screen, designed not only to support the Rood but to enclose side altars to the north and south of the chancel arch, has a fine sequence of apostles along the dado. At right angles to this dado are parcloses with paired groups of saints – bishops, deacons and the warrior saints Michael and George, each with a dragon. Above each of the altars enclosed by the parcloses is a row of four saints, to the north a mixed series of Etheldreda, an archbishop, John the Baptist and Barbara, to the south the 'holy kindred' or three Maries with their children (Jesus and six apostles) plus St Margaret. As I have shown elsewhere, this south altar was the Lady Altar, and with its troupe of mothers and children, and Margaret, patron saint of women in labour, is a votive altar concerned with childbearing and safe delivery. Its choice as the theme of this part of the screen, and the source of its distinctive iconography, is a fascinating problem in itself.[56] There were several painters involved in the Ranworth screen, but the ensemble as a whole in colour and arrangement is unmistakeably a single scheme. Yet the north altar has several oddities which suggest the presence of an element of improvization and adaptation. The figure of John the Baptist is unfinished, abandoned while the underdrawing was still visible, the demi-angel in the arch above painted out and replaced with a diapered background. Pauline Plummer, the expert who conserved the Ranworth screen in the late 1960s, has drawn attention to the fact that the beardless and apparently female figure with a leaping lamb on its knee to the left of this unfinished image of the Baptist was originally drawn wearing a mitre, traces of which can be seen in the halo. The figure also wore a pallium (the circular stole made of white wool and sent by the pope to all new archbishops) just visible now under the blue overpainting of the cloak on the left shoulder. The figure is generally identified as St Agnes, and the pallium is consistent with that, since the wool for making the pallia was blessed in Rome each year on her feast-day.[57] But the saint is wearing an under-robe unmistakeably painted to represent St John's hairy camel-skin, and round the face are the traces of a large curled beard, painted over the originally clean-shaven archepiscopal saint. So it looks as if the original figure of an archbishop was altered to represent the Baptist at the same time as the drawing of John the Baptist next to it was abandoned. [*Colour Plate 6*] The most likely explanation for these changes is that, while the screen was still being painted and after all the saints on it had been drawn, another donor gave a tabernacled figure of the Trinity, Christ, Mary or another saint to stand on the altar before these panels. The remains of the stone altars against the screen make it clear that the altar here was narrower than the present arrangement: it occupied only the space under the three panels nearest the chancel arch. The modern altar, which extends the full width of the four panels, blocks access to the rood-loft stairway, which would have been in daily use. So the tabernacled statue would have been the central and principal image above this altar. Yet it was clearly felt necessary to retain a figure of St John the Baptist above the altar, perhaps because this was the location of the St John's light, which we know burned somewhere in the church. So the figure of a seated archbishop next to the statue was adapted to represent St John. The Ranworth screen thus allows us to see the interplay between different elements of the parish's life, frozen in paint: It looks as if a carefully planned scheme, funded at least in part by the wealthiest family in Ranworth and involving an altar dedicated to St John and the location of a funded light, was adapted with some difficulty, in the course of which the patron saint was demoted to a lesser position while work was still in progress, to make way for an image presented by another private donor.

The endowment of rood-screens went on in parishes all over England into the early years of the Henrician Reformation. The wartime destruction of Devon's medieval wills means that we know very little about the pattern of endowment in the West country, but the presence on many Devon screens of narrative scenes, or elements of what Emile Male called the 'New Symbolism', such as sequences of pagan sybils to match apostles or prophets, suggests vigorous activity well into the sixteenth century.[58] In East Anglia, so far as we can judge without an exhaustive search of all the surviving wills, donations tail off in the uncertain religious climate of the 1530s, but some of the most interesting surviving screens date from the years of the Reformation Parliament. Of these, probably the latest is that at Burlingham St Andrew or North Burlingham in Norfolk.

Figure 6. *Completed after the break with Rome, the
north screen at Burlingham St Andrews was paid for by
Thomas Benet: his personal name saint, Thomas Becket,
is the defaced image on the extreme right, and his family's
patron, St Benet or Benedict, second from the left. The
Norfolk saint Withburhga is depicted at the far left, holding
her shrine church at East Dereham.*

Work began on the North Burlingham screen with a flurry of bequests in 1525
and 1526. It continued for a decade, for an inscription, now gone, recorded
the completion of the screen and commemorated the main donors in 1536.
Even then donations continued until February 1538, when William Goodwin,
of the neighbouring village of Buckenham Ferry, left 20s. to the 'gyldyng
of the Perke' at Burlingham St Andrews.[59] The donors manifestly exercised
close control over the imagery on the screen. The north side was paid for by
members of the Benet family, two of whom, Thomas and Margaret Benet,
were alive when the screen was inscribed in 1536. Accordingly, their family
patron, St Benet (ie St Benedict), appears on this screen, and Thomas Benet's
personal name-saint, St Thomas of Canterbury, appears in the prominent
panel immediately left of the chancel opening. The south screen was funded
by bequests from John and Cecily Blake, whose names were commemorated
under images of St John the Baptist and St Cecilia, while under the figure of
St Katherine, Katherine and Robert Frennys were commemorated. Apart from
name saints, the 'theme' of the rest of the imagery on the screen seems to be

local pilgrimage, with images of St Withburga carrying a model of the church of East Dereham where she is buried, St Walstan of Bawburgh, and Etheldreda of Ely.

With the last bequest for gilding being paid sometime after June 1538, when Thomas Goodwin's will was proved, the paint on the screen at Burlingham must virtually have been still wet when the Henrician attacks on imagery began. In November 1538 Henry VIII ordered the destruction of all images of Thomas Becket, and the Burlingham parishioners dutifully scraped out his image to the knees, leaving the other saints untouched, though they were later defaced, less drastically, probably in Edward's reign.[60] The destruction of St Thomas's image can hardly have been welcome to Thomas Benet, nor did it represent any widespread parochial hostility to imagery – a parishioner would leave money to gild the image of Our Lady of Pity as late as 1540.[61]

The same selective defacement of images on parish screens is evident at Ludham, where, in Henry's reign, only the papal tiara of St Gregory and the cardinal's hat of St Jerome were damaged on the screen. [*Colour Plate 5*] But however unpopular it may have been, such activity by the Henrician authorities certainly put a rapid stop to this particular sort of parochial investment. And in Edward's reign the screens were to become the particular target of reforming zeal, above all their upper portions, including the great crucifix. The roods were pulled down, the tympanum and lofts either removed altogether or painted over or covered with canvas and redecorated with the Royal Arms, and with scripture-texts condemning idolatry or enjoining obedience to the magistrate. Reworked tympanum boards of this sort survive at Wenhaston and at Ludham, and at Binham the dado remains, with texts from Cranmer's Great Bible painted over the rows of helper saints.[62] Edwardine churchwardens' accounts are full of records of payments 'for the Wrytyng on the candelbeme', 'for the Colouryng of the panes...before part of the rode lofte', 'for makyng of the frame over the Rood lofte for the (painter)', or for 'takyng downe of the thyngys in the Rood loft'.[63] The Marian authorities made the replacement of the Rood group itself a major priority, but given the burdens in cash and energy which the Marian Restoration imposed on parishes, in most places there can have been little energy or resources to spare for the brutalized images on the rest of the screen.[64] Yet given that so many of the screens were the result of widescale community endowment and benefaction, the havoc of the Edwardian period can hardly have been popular. In a well-known passage, the vicar of Morebath recorded in 1555 the return by his parishioners of items salvaged from the wreck of the rood-loft they had commissioned in 1534:

> here was resceyvyd pagynntis and bokis and diversse wother thyngis concernyng our rowde lowfth lyke tru and fayzthefull crystyn pepyll this was restoryd to this churche by the wyche doyngis hyt schowyth thay they dyd lyke good catholyke men.[65]

One screen, formerly at Lessingham but now stored in the Architectural Service Archive at Gressenhall, provides the sole surviving trace in East Anglia of a Marian iconographic scheme to replace images on the dado defaced in Edward's reign. The screen, originally painted with the twelve apostles in the last years of Henry VII's reign, was defaced under Edward. Under Mary the parishioners appear to have commissioned some decidedly clumsy pictures on parchment of the four Latin Doctors and of St Roche, and had them glued over some of the defaced apostles. The choice of new images is a revealing one. The Doctors were emblematic of a restored Catholic orthodoxy, and Roche was a plague saint much invoked in the 1550s: the small selection of masses usually included for a travelling priest's convenience in the printed breviaries of Mary's reign invariably include a Mass of St Roche and often other plague masses as well. The restoration of only five out of the twelve panels of the screen suggests that once again the Marian project was funded piecemeal by individual parishioners, a process interrupted by the death of Mary and the return of an iconoclastic protestant regime.[66]

For such attempts at restoration were short-lived. The hatchets, saws and whitewash of the iconoclasts returned in Elizabeth's reign and, though many parishes struggled to retain their lofts, the Elizabethan authorities, while ordering the retention of screens as a divider between chancel and nave, were adamant that the lofts and their crucifixes must go.[67] Along with the abandonment and destruction of stained glass, the defacement which followed marked the end of an era in English religious and cultural life. It meant the effective end of the craft of the painter in regional centres like Norwich and, in the parishes, the disappearance of the most important single focus there had ever been for corporate artistic patronage and devotional investment in the local communities of England.

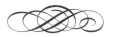

4

Salle Church and the Reformation

Figure 7. *Salle Church interior, looking East.*

The great church of Salle stands isolated in the north Norfolk fields near Aylsham: there is no longer anything which could be called a village.[1] The parish was once a rich and important place, weaving linen and hessian for the region as well as wool, but there were never enough people in Salle to fill the church. The population of the parish probably never exceeded four or five hundred, if so many, and it may already have been in decline in the early Tudor period. Fifty-four tax-payers are recorded in a lay subsidy of 1333, forty-two in the subsidy of 1544: the rector returned 150 communicants (i.e. adults over the age of about 16) in 1603.[2] So this huge building was never full, and was never intended to be full: its space was intended as the setting for elaborate liturgy and processions, involving the whole parish, but also for the smaller-scale worship in screened off family chantry-chapels and side-chapels which housed the daily and occasional activities of the guilds. In the mid fifteenth century this relatively small community supported up to seven priests, and was the focus of a complex web of religious and social rituals and relationships which have left their marks in the material fabric of the building, and in a rich deposit of documents in the diocesan, county and national archives.

In the Middle Ages the parish of Salle contained four manors, and parts of several others. It was, therefore, dominated by a cluster of great and less-than-great gentry families, some of them with country-wide interests, like the Pastons and their various alliances, others more modest in their wealth but, by the same token, more solidly rooted in the parish itself, like the Brigg family who held two manors and who built the south aisle and porch. This strong gentry presence is registered on the west front of the church, where a series of heraldic shields on either side of the empty central niche (which, a will of 1528 tells us, housed 'Our Lady of the West') contain the arms of the Brewes (who were patrons of the living, and whose arms therefore occur first), Ufford, Mauteby, Morley and Kerdeston families, all major clans with landed interests in the parish.[3]

The Brigg arms are similarly displayed on the south porch. Inside the church, there are more gentry memorials, not least to the Boleyn family, local landlords who were to rocket to fame, fortune and subsequently near calamity in the person of Anne Boleyn. Geoffrey Boleyn, whose brass is the most dominant monument in the central aisle, was probably one of the key figures in the rebuilding of Salle Church in the early fifteenth century (between *c.* 1410 and 1430).

Through these gentry, squires and squireens, the parish touched national politics, and not only at the Reformation. The nave roof once

Figure 8. *The West door, Salle with the arms of local gentry famlies, and flanking the central niche, the instruments of Christ's passions. The statues removed from the niches at the Reformation were St Peter and St Paul, the parish patrons, flanking the door, and above the arch, the Pieta, 'Our Lady of the West', near whose image many parishioners requested burial.*

had the arms of the intermarried Brewes and Shardelow families blazoned on the rafters, and Sir John Brewes, patron of the living and another of the gentry whose estate probably provided much of the funding for the building of the present church, was one of four Norfolk gentlemen captured during the 1381 Peasants' Revolt, and forced into an embassy on behalf of the rebels to the King: he was eventually rescued by the militaristic bishop of Norwich, Henry Despenser. The five-panelled altarpiece of the Passion of Christ in Norwich Cathedral is sometimes said to have been commissioned by Despenser in thanksgiving for the suppression of

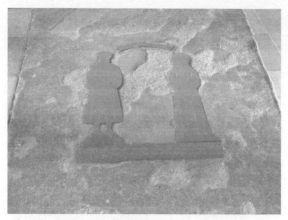

Figure 9. *The brass of Geoffrey Boleyn, principal patron of the fifteenth-century rebuilding of Salle. He was Anne Boleyn's great-great grandfather.*

the Rising, though there is no contemporary evidence for this link, and the retable may predate the Rising. But whatever its date and occasion, it bears the arms of another family with land-holdings in Salle, the Kerdistons, one of whose manors was partly situated in the parish, though their main base was elsewhere.[4]

The building itself, then, was paid for by a group of rich and not-quite-so-rich families, whose fortunes were founded on the sheep that grazed the commons and fields of Salle, Cawston and the surrounding parishes. By no means all of these families had blue blood, and the proud blazoning of their arms on the west front here at Salle, as at neighbouring Cawston, has as much of the jumpy pride of the *arriviste* as of the confidence of those born to effortless social superiority. Most had made their money in wool, not necessarily all that long ago, like Thomas Roos (= Rose), who built the north transept chapel and who is buried there under the best brass in the church. He and his wife Katherine were members of the Coventry Cloth guild (as were many other prosperous Salle graziers and wool-staplers – the Boleyns, Briggs, Founteyns, Gowers, Melmans and Seggefords). Roos, pious patron of the Trinity guild, was fined in 1425 for grazing 500 sheep on Cawston common when he was only entitled to graze 200.[5]

These wealthy men and women had an enormous impact on parish life. John Fountaine, whose brass is also in the north transept, where he and his three wives Alice, Joan and Agnes are buried, made a will in 1453 which shows his involvement or interest in every dimension of parish life. He left gifts to the High Altar, to the light before the Rood, to the guilds of the Blessed Virgin, of St Margaret, St John, the Holy Trinity and St Paul, made bequests for the building funds of eight local churches (including Cawston) and to two plough-lights and three maiden-lights in Salle – perhaps those for the parts of the parish where his land was. And to emphasize both his personal and his parochial piety, he sent a priest to Rome, to say mass in the Church of St Paul outside the Walls, the shrine where the patron saint of the parish is buried.[6] Once dead, the influence of such men was continued by the recurrence of their funeral celebrations, or 'obits' every year when candles were placed on their graves, masses and dirges sung, and alms of food, money and clothing given to the poor. John Fountaine's funeral celebrations immediately after his death lasted for seven days and will have been a prominent feature of the parish's round of worship during that time, and annually thereafter on his anniversary day – as they were meant to be.

As Fountaine's will shows, Salle had a number of plough-lights and maiden-lights, at Marshgate, Kirkgate, Lunton and Steynwade, all of which maintained lamps in the church. The maiden-lights are referred to in Latin documents as 'Puelaria' or 'trepidaria', (more or less the Latin for tripping the light fantastic) and they were regularly remembered by testators, like Alice Martyn who left 6d. to the plough-light and 'to the daunsyng lights of the maydens to eche of them 3d.'[7] Identical organizations flourished in surrounding parishes, as at Cawston a mile away, where they are specially well documented. Both plough-lights and dances were organized by streets or districts, and were gender-specific youth groups which raised money to maintain lamps in the church, and which might on occasion contribute funds towards parish projects. Maiden-lights were usually funded by collections taken at dances, plough-lights by collections made by the young men in January, when they harnessed themselves to a plough which they dragged round the district, raising money from householders on threat of ploughing up the ground outside their door.[8] Parishioners often left bequests for the

maintenance of their local plough-light, like William Kechyn, parishioner of
Sloley, in Norfolk, who left 20d. in 1506 to 'the plough light of the street ther I
dwell ynne', and 12d. 'to every of the odir vii plough lights in the same town'.[9]
Plough-lights might also be funded by ales organized by the young men of a
street or settlement. The bell-ringers' gallery in the tower at Cawston has a
carved beam, recording that the gallery was paid for by ales organized by one
such group, the plough-light of Sygate, a settlement on the north side of the
parish. We know that there were other Cawston plough-lights based on settle-
ments at Eastgate and 'the Dams', and In 1490 William Herward of Cawston
left 12d. 'to the Plowlyght of Sygate', another 12d. 'to the Dawnce of Sygate',
and 6d. 'to ich other plowlyght in Cawston and dawnce of the same town'. The
gallery inscription runs

> God spede the plow and send us ale corn enow our purpose for to make
> A(t) crow of cock of the plowlete of Sygate
> Be mery and glad
> Wat good ale this work mad(e).[10]

Wat Goodale here is not, of course, an individual, but a joking reference to the
drinking celebrations which funded the gallery.

Awareness of the existence of such groups in Salle – at Marshgate, Kirkgate,
Lunton and Steynewade – perhaps even more than the presence of the guilds,
helps modify the sense the present building conveys of overwhelming gentry
domination of the parish and its social and sacred space. It may well be that
the sons and daughters of the gentry took part in the activities of the lights and
dances, as their seniors seem to have done in the guilds, but numerically at least
they can hardly have dominated them. The popular sociability represented by
ales, dances and plough celebrations suggests a plebeian involvement in the life
of the parish, invisible now but which will have been symbolically registered in
the lights these bodies maintained at images and altars in the church.

There were seven guilds in Salle – of the Blessed Virgin Mary (the
Assumption guild), of St Thomas, of St Paul (the parish dedication), of St
John the Baptist, of St Margaret, of the Trinity, which had its altar and priest
in Thomas Roos's chapel, and of St James, which had its altar in the chapel of
the south transept, built for it by Thomas Brigg (d. 1444).[11]

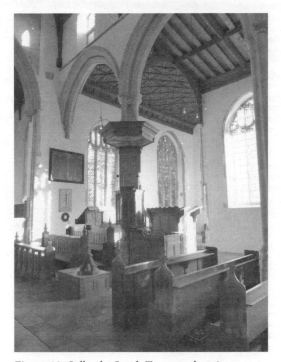

Figure 10. *Salle, the South Transept, housing the Brigg family chapel, which doubled as the chapel of the St James Guild. The pulpit formed part of the fifteenth-century furnishings, though the tester and prayer-desks are post-Reformation additions*

Brigg's initials are on bosses in the roof, his name on the outside of the chapel cornice, and the remains of his gravestone and that of his two wives, both called Margaret, can be seen in the south end of the transept, with other Brigg burials. Thomas and his wives kneel before St Thomas Becket in the upper registers of the reconstructed glass of the east window of this chapel. It was therefore very much a Brigg family chapel, partitioned from the rest of the church as Briggs' land, no doubt, was fenced off from that of his neighbours. But his chapel was also the St James guild chapel, and along with the Brigg family name, the scallop-shell of St James can be seen carved on the outside of this transept. The Briggs dominated this southern side of the church, and not just the transept. Thomas's son John is buried in the south aisle under a shroud brass, paid for, somewhat belatedly, by *his* son Thomas, who left £1 6s. 8d. in his will in 1494 'for a marble stone for my father in Salle Church'.[12] The effigy of John Brigg presents this member of one of the parish's more opulent families as the ultimate pauper, a dead man stripped and in his shroud, thrown on the mercy of his neighbours, rich and poor: the inscription runs:

> Here lyeth John Brigge under this marbil stone
> Whose sowle our Lord I.H.S. have mercy upon
> For in this worlde worthyly he lived many a day
> And here his body is buried and couched under clay
> Lo friends fro whatever ye be pray for me I you pray
> As ye me se in soche degre so schall ye be anothir day.[13]

The other Salle guilds had altars placed around the church. From the will of Robert Luce, chaplain to the Assumption guild,[14] we know that its altar, like that of the Trinity guild, was in the chapel of Thomas Roos in the north transept. One of the windows in the East wall of this transept has been cut away to house the reredos for an altar, and the piscina for the ritual ablutions of the Mass was uncovered there earlier this century. The Guild of St Margaret had its altar in the North aisle – the grave of John Ryghtwyse, who asked to be buried before the image of St Margaret in 1475, is still visible in the aisle and pinpoints the spot.[15] The guild of St John the Baptist had its altar at the east end of the south aisle, and in 1731 there were still substantial remains of a window here depicting the life and martyrdom of St John: it had a memorial inscription for John Holwey, rector of Salle between 1375 and 1401, so he no doubt left money for a window in the new church in honour of his patron saint. There were also two altars against the rood-screen, their presence indicated by the unprimed blank spaces on the figured panels of the screen dado: the other guilds may have celebrated there, or in the chapel over the north porch. The interior of the church was therefore not a single open space, but an interconnecting network of sacred zones based round altars and images, some privately owned, some the property of guilds in which many parishioners were sharers, all of them in some sense part of a shared symbol-system and set of resources, and manned by a clerical cadre financed by guild salaries, by the recurrent benefactions of the leading families and by short-term benefactions like that of Robert Pull, who left eight marks in 1510 as wages for 'a pryst that shalbe abble to synge in the church of Saul a yere'.[16] We get some sense of how these sacred spaces were viewed, at least by the chaplains, from the bequest by one of the former chaplains in 1399 of three sets of vestments 'to serve the common altars', or the bequest of another chaplain in 1456 of his missal, to be used on two of the guild altars (not ones which he had himself served while alive) in the church.[17]

The guild certificates of 1389 for the guilds of St James, St John and the Blessed Virgin survive in the Public Record Office.[18] Members of the guilds met at Vespers on the eve of their patron saint's feast-day to recite the Rosary ('the psalter of Our Lady') for the repose of the souls of dead brethren and sisters. On the feast-day itself, or the Sunday after, they had a common meal, first attending mass together and offering the priest a farthing each. Poor men and women were invited to the meal and given a farthing each in alms. The guild members attended each other's funerals and gave alms there to the poor. They paid a small pension to impoverished members, if the guild funds were able to sustain it, and they also maintained three candles to burn during services on Sundays and major feast-days before their patronal image. In addition, they paid for a large torch – a flare of wax and resin round a cluster of thick wicks – to burn at the elevation of the Host at the parish mass each Sunday. These torches were very prominent objects, and therefore a noticeable addition to the splendour and reverence of parish worship: the St John's Guild paid for a single torch weighing 12 lb, the Assumption guild maintained two, of 6 lb each. Each torch will have been held by a guild member or a clerk assisting at the mass, and their presence gives us a hint of the scale and elaboration of worship in Salle – worship in which the largesse of the gentry and of the parish guilds provided a range of ritual gestures and furnishings which reminded the community of the piety – and the importance – of the donors.

Commensality – shared feasting – was clearly an important aspect of guild life, and bequests of place-settings or 'a garnesse' of pewter to the guilds are common in Salle wills.[19] The lights maintained by the guilds were seen as parish amenities, not simply the possession of the guild itself, and bequests might be made directly to the lights, distinct from any gift to the guild.[20]

The sharing of chapels by gentry families and by the guilds at Salle was clearly a feature of the region. A similar pattern is evident across the fields at Cawston, which had guilds of the Holy Trinity, St Agnes (the parish patron), St John the Baptist, St Mary, St Peter and St Thomas. The St John guild at Cawston had a chapel on the north side of the chancel, and the St Mary guild met in the south transept chapel.[21] These and several other chapels in the church were screened off, so that the present open arrangement of the building gives, as at Salle, a quite misleading impression of unified space. [*Colour Plate 1*] The altars in all the chapels were regularly used for guild masses, but were also designated sites for temporary chantry arrangements, paid for by members of the parish elite. Richard Brown, a wealthy Cawston parishioner who was one of the donors of the rood-screen, left 10 marks in 1505, for example, to his brother John Brown, who was a priest, to say mass daily for him for a year at the altar of the Lady Chapel, where Brown asked to be buried 'afore the Image of oure Ladi of pitee'.[22] On the east wall of this same (south transept) chapel at Cawston is further evidence of the annexation of public space by private benefactors – a wall-painting of an enthroned saint, now hard to decipher – perhaps the Virgin, or St Anne teaching the Virgin to read (there is a book on the knee of the seated figure) or perhaps St Agnes, the parish patron – with two kneeling donors, left and right.

At Salle, the association of these common spaces with two of the chief parish families, the Roos and the Briggs was more emphatic, more firmly encoded in the stones which those families had raised. None, however, was a perpetual foundation: none of the families concerned had the inalienable property right conveyed by royal licence for a perpetual foundation in 'their' part of the church – and this may account for the curious presence in the transept chapels of guild as well as private altars.

Architecturally, the poor of the early Tudor parish are largely invisible: they left no monuments, they annexed no portions of the churches, at the back or sides of which they stood or sat. Where were the poor in Salle? Much depends, of course, on what one means by the term 'poor'. Salle's weaving industry will have required a pool of waged labour. There will have been relatively poor young men and women – the sons and daughters of labourers and cottagers– in the plough-lights and the dances, perhaps even in the guilds, though the guild provisions for alms to paupers makes it clear that the very poorest were likely to be 'outsiders' to the guilds, the objects of compassion rather than fraternity, as they were in society generally. Paupers feature regularly, of course, at the funerals of the wealthy, holding candles and saying the Rosary, receiving in return beef or herrings, and beer and bread, or money doles. These were normally of a penny or tuppence, but Thomas Briggs in 1494 left £20 to the poor of Salle, and in 1463 Geoffrey Boleyn, son of the founder of the building who had risen to become Lord Mayor of London, left the fabulous sum of £200 to be shared by the poor householders of six Norfolk communities, including Salle.[23] In 1532 John Norman left the residue of his goods after the payment of his specified bequests to be distributed among 'the poore needy creatures of the town of Sall', a vivid glimpse of an underclass who became increasingly prominent in mortuary benefactions in the course of the hungry and inflationary Tudor century.[24]

Like the transepts, the chancel of Salle church, donated *c.* 1440–50 by one of the fifteenth-century rectors, John Nekton, and his patrons, the Brewes family, was itself a space emphatically in the hands of a parish sub-group – in this case the clergy. It has a magnificent set of medieval stalls, all of them carved with 'misericords' on their under-side, against which the clergy rested their bottoms during the lengthy performance of the daily offices. These stalls alert us to the presence of a community of priests in the parish church, serving the various altars and guilds, as well as the parish or high altar. The rectors of Salle were wealthy men, and many of them were clerical careerists, graduate high-fliers based elsewhere, employing other priests to do their work. They were often members or clients of local families, however, and they left their mark on the church. John Nekton, who died in 1467, left legacies to Simon Boleyn, his deputy in the parish, to the parish clerk, and to the poor of the parish.[25]

Boleyn was officially called 'parish chaplain', but the need to staff guild and chantry altars ensured the additional presence of a fluctuating body of assistant clergy. None were priests of a perpetual chantry foundation, but rather stipendiaries on contract to one or other of the parish guilds, or serving in the family chantries. And quite apart from the guild and family chaplains employed long term to serve the transept altars, both clerical and lay testators in Salle contributed to the clerical presence in the parish by making provision in their wills for a small stream of priests on short-term contracts to celebrate masses for one, two or three years.[26] We have details of almost thirty such priests for the century from 1399 to 1499, and evidence of their continuance thereafter, and it is clear that the absence of perpetual foundations did not prevent them forming strong, and in many cases life-long, attachments to the parish and the parish community. The graves of several are to be seen still in the church – for example that of Simon Boleyn (d. 1482) in the central aisle, (one of several priests' graves indicated by a chalice-shaped indent in the slab), and of Robert Luce (d. 1456) in the north transept. Luce was chaplain of the guild of the Assumption: requesting burial before the altar which he had served in Roos' chapel, he spoke proprietorially of 'our' chapel – that is, the guild's.[27] Boleyn, another local man from a gentry family, as parish chaplain was in effect vicar for the absentee rector.

These men formed part of a close-knit clerical sub-culture, with strong links out into the wider community of the parish. They left money, clothing, vestments and books to each other (from surviving wills, we can trace the passage of some of these books, including professional treatises on the work of a priest, like the *Pupilla Occuli*, through successive generations of chaplains and rectors), they entered into joint ownership of property, witnessed each other's wills, loaned or gave each other pious objects, recruited likely young men from the local families into the profession, and sometimes signalled a deeper level of friendship by requesting burial near each other.[28] The font at Salle is a monument to the embedding of these chaplains in the life of the parish community. It is one of the forty or so distinctive East Anglian octagonal fonts which portray on seven of their eight sides, with considerable theological precision, the seven sacraments of the Catholic Church. The Salle font comes from a workshop which produced similar fonts for Cley and Binham, yet is unique in retaining not only its medieval canopy, but the mechanism for raising and lowering it. The font was the gift of the chaplain Robert Luce (d. 1456) and his parents, William and Agnes – no doubt he donated it in memory of them: it is inscribed for them in Latin round the step:

Pray for the souls of Thomas Luce and [Agnes] his wife and Robert their son, chaplain, and for those for whom they are bound to pray, who caused this font to be made.[29]

The chaplains of Salle left money for the poor (Simon Boleyn left 2d. each to two paupers every Friday for a year, in return for which the poor people had to say a Rosary every week for his soul), and they acted as spiritual advisors – and sometimes financial consultants – to the wealthy men and women of the parish. In return, they were promoted in their careers by their gentry friends. Many prosperous Norfolk rectors started out as guild chaplains in churches like Salle. They often formed close links with the community, which survived their promotion to parishes elsewhere, like John Crome who went on to be rector of Bale but acted as supervisor for Simon Boleyn's will, or Henry Newman, formerly chaplain of St James' guild, who went on to be rector of Pensthorp but left substantial legacies to Salle church and to the light of St James in his chapel. The continuous presence of a group of clergy in the parish with a strong *esprit de corps* no doubt brought its own tensions and challenges to the community – a number of chaplains turn up in the manorial courts for poaching the local rabbit warrens, and there may have been more specifically religious frictions too. But they were undoubtedly a tremendous resource in the parish, a source of spiritual advice and expertise, and in many cases material benefactors of the community, making gifts of books, ornaments, vestments and vessels, to instruct the laity, provide resources for the parish's other stipendiary clergy and enhance the parish's worship.

The screen at Salle was planned as part of the reconstruction of the church in the early fifteenth century. It was savagely truncated during the Reformation, the whole upper section being sawn away. The decoration on the dado, which remains, follows a common Norfolk pattern, the side-panels of the screen having the twelve apostles, the doors into the chancel having the four Latin Doctors, just like the screen at Cawston. But only two apostles survive on the panelling on either side of the doors – St Thomas and St James on the north side, St Philip and St Bartholomew on the south, with Gregory, Jerome, Augustine and Ambrose on the doors between. To north and south of the apostles there are blank white panels. This is not the work of the reformers, but the original priming paint of the screen. The explanation is that the other eight apostles were painted on parclose screens, now gone, standing at right angles to the dado, and forming enclosures blocking in two altars, which were pushed up against the blank sections of the screen.

The apostles have the articles of the Apostle's Creed inscribed over their heads, an unusual arrangement in Norfolk, where the texts normally occur on scrolls carried by the apostles. But in one form or another the Creed texts themselves are found on a number of screens in the county, such as Gooderstone (where there are also doors with the Latin Doctors), Weston Longville, Ringland, and elsewhere.[30] These texts underline the symbolism of Doctors and apostles as expressions of the teaching of the Church. Salle, like so many other fifteenth-century parishes, evidently prided itself on its self-consciously correct Catholicism.

The screen at Salle is notably more coherent as a conception than its equivalent, but probably somewhat later, match at Cawston. There too, apostles and Latin Doctors dominate, but without their Latin texts, and they are flanked by a rather miscellaneous group of helper saints – St Agnes the parish patron, St Helena, carrying a relic of the true cross in a reliquary which looks like a representation of the reliquary at one of the region's great shrines, the shrine of the True Cross at Bromholm, and the uncanonized wonder-worker, Master John Schorne. The Cawston screen, which was being built from about 1460 but which went on being painted and decorated until 1504, was certainly a commission of a type common in Norfolk, involving the cooperation, or rather the not-particularly-coordinated serial donations of a number of quite modest donors. The figures of the saints on the north and south screens are patently by different hands, a reflection of the mixed origins of the funding. We know from wills of many gifts ranging from one mark (13s. 4d. or two-thirds of a pound) to ten marks towards the building or painting of the screen. In 1505 Richard Brown left four marks to paint 'a pane in the Rode lofte', and the first four 'panes' or panels on the left were paid for in memory of a married couple, William and Alice Atereth in 1490, and the screen has an inscription in English which runs:

> Pray for the sowlis of William Atereth and Alice his wyff the wiche dede these iiij panys peynte be the executors lyff.[31]

At Salle, by contrast, there is no such evidence of piecemeal patronage. The screen's iconographic unity and the blank spaces for two symmetrically placed altars, moreover, make it look like a unitary planned commission, (there is a close parallel at Ranworth in the Norfolk Broads), probably a reflection of the domination of the patronage of the church as a whole by clusters of wealthy parishioners acting in concert, and with clerical advice.[32]

Salle was once filled with cycles and sequences of stained glass.[33] The chancel windows contained the legends of the church's patrons, St Peter and St Paul, as well as a series of bishops, popes and kings associated with the conversion of southern England – a scheme adapted from the series in the choir clerestory of York Minster. There was also a good deal of heraldic glass, dominated by emblems of the De la Pole, Beaufort and Brewes families. On the north side of the chancel are the remains of a series of figures of prophets with scrolls, and the Fathers of the church: there were almost certainly the twelve apostles also, making up a standard set symbolizing Christian teaching. In the south transept, in addition to the Brigg's window, are figures of St Jerome, St Margaret, St Catherine, St Helen and St Etheldreda. In the north aisle East window is a restored Annunciation (originally the Coronation of the Virgin in heaven) and in the north transept (Roos chapel) parts of a Visitation scene and the figures of the Virtues – Mercy, Truth, Justice and Peace, remnants of a depiction of a scene known as the 'Parliament of Heaven' in which God plans the Incarnation. Originating in the works of St Bernard, it is replicated in such early-fifteenth-century devotional classics as Nicholas Love's *Mirror of the Life of the Blessed Jhesu*, but is a somewhat rarified subject which occurs only occasionally in stained glass or carving.[34]

There are bits and pieces of prophets, cardinals and patriarchs in the tracery lights of the south aisle. But the best glass in the church is in the east and south windows of the chancel, the remains of what was once a magnificent double set of the Nine Orders of Angels. In medieval tradition, inherited from Jewish and early church speculation, the Angelic Orders were divided into three groups or 'hierarchies'. The highest division was that of Epiphany, or Revelation, and contained the Orders of Seraphim, Cherubim and Thrones. Next came Hyperepiphany, containing the Orders of Dominations, Virtues and Powers. Lastly came the Hypophany, containing Principalities, Archangels and Angels. All these Orders had distinctive functions and powers, encompassing both this world and the next.[35] Their representation in communities like Salle, alongside heraldic glass endorsing the rule of Henry VI and the greatness of the local aristocratic families,[36] may well have spoken to the parishioners of established order, hierarchy, and the given nature of social and religious reality. Like the screen, the evidence of the glass suggests a church whose iconography was determined by clerical and lay elites and planned programatically as a coherent whole: here, in contrast to many humbler parish communities, and even in contrast to Cawston a mile across the fields, order and control rather than spontaneity seems to have been the keynote.

Any parish where the Boleyn family were major landowners was bound to feel the impact of the Reformation. James Boleyn, who was Anne Boleyn's uncle, made the most of it, acquiring yet more property here and at Cawston throughout the early 1530s and 1540s, and the family held on to their status even after Ann's disgrace and execution in 1536.[37] The Henrician Rector of Salle, presented to the living in 1523 by his own father who was patron, was Roger Townsend. The family had a tradition of notable piety and hard-nosed attention to the main chance. The rector's grandfather, Sir Roger, was a succesful lawyer who had married into serious money, the Hoptons of Blythburgh in Suffolk. Sir Roger was, among other things, a moneylender. His very distinctive will of 1494 established a chantry in East Raynham served by two priests, one of whom was to engage in theological studies at Cambridge, returning each year at Easter to preach God's word to the parishioners: Townsend asked for a thousand masses immediately after his death, distributed through twenty towns, including Salle. He sought the prayers 'of all the aungells of hevyn and patriarks prophets apostles martyrs ... and all the hooly company of hevyn ...', but he also begged Christ 'for the merytes of his bitter and gloriouse passion to have mercy on me and to take me to his mercy which is above all workes, unto whom it is appropused (sic) to have mercy ...'[38]

Sir Roger's son, Sir Roger Townsend II, was an active landowner whose marriage to Anne Brewes made him lord of the manor of Stinton and patron of both Heydon and Salle parishes. Conventionally pious, heading his notebook entries with the holy names of Jesus and Mary, and steward of four monastic houses including Walsingham Priory, he was nevertheless a ruthless opportunist, and he identified himself lock, stock and barrel with the process of reform in Henry's reign. He was one of the commisioners for the Norfolk section of the 1535 *Valor Ecclesiasticus*, and a key figure in the containment of discontent with the reformation in North Norfolk: he profited directly from the suppressions, acquiring, among much else, the Franciscan house at Walsingham for himself. Unsurprisingly, he played a central role in uncovering and suppressing the Walsingham plot after the destruction of the shrine of the Holy House at Walsingham, and taking drastic and sometimes dubiously legal action against criticism of royal religious policy in the years which followed.[39] His zeal earned him the enmity of the Norfolk commons, especially through the late 1530s and 1540s, when the county seethed with animosity against the gentry who fattened on the spoils of Reformation. In 1540 it was reported that John Walker of Griston had tried to raise the county against such profiteers:

> let us kylle them, ye, evyn theyr childern in the cradelles: for yt were a good thinge yf ther were so many jentylmen in Norffolk as ther be whyt bulles ...

They should begin, he declared, with Sir Richard Southwell,

> ... and so to Sir Roger Townsende ... and so to spoyle them all ... and hernesse our sylffe.[40]

This Sir Roger had appointed his own son Roger to the rectory of Salle (and to Heydon) in 1523. As might be expected from a family with these sorts of traditions, the rector was an educated man, a Cambridge-trained canon lawyer, whose library had the latest editions of Church Fathers like St Augustine and St John Chrysostom. He was also, again as might be expected, an archetypal Henrician careerist, pluralist rector not only of Salle, Heydon and North Creake within the county,[41] but of St Mary Woolnoth in London, where he is buried. In 1538, the year of his death, he also became chancellor of the diocese of Salisbury, holding the prebend of Netherby there.[42] He was therefore intended to be a member of the evangelical establishment that Bishop Shaxton was seeking to build in Salisbury. Townsend was probably rarely resident in Salle. In addition to his various livings he was heavily involved in the Faculty Office, the administrative body which under the Royal Supremacy took over the work of the Roman Curia in granting dispensations and the like.[43] He was also active in the business side of the dissolution of the monasteries, though he appears not to have had much share in the loot, complaining in his will that although he had been often 'in attendance...for the sealing and dispatching of a great number of capacities as well of houses suppressed as surrendered, never hitherto receiving one penny for the same, whereas I have always been put in hope that I should be reasonably recompensed for my pains'. Townsend died in October 1538, before the Reformation entered its radical phase. The exact extent of his evangelicalism is hard to gauge.[44] The preamble to his will is reminiscent of his grandfather's, but also clearly confirms his sympathy with the Henrician reforms, while retaining some Catholic attitudes and beliefs. The preamble commits his soul

> to God eternall the father almyghty maker of hevyn and erthe: hys oonly sonne and my lord Jhesus Criste by whose passion dethe and the shedyng of his precious blod upon the crosse, for all mankynd and by the meryts thereof excluding all my deserving, merits or good dedis I stedfastly truste and beleve my poure soule to be redeemed from all my synnes, deth, and hell, noon of them all never to have any power over hyt but that it shall forthwith from its departure oute of this my mortall body, have the fruycion of theternal godhed, and to be partaker of the unspeakable joys of theverlasting inheritance prepared for me and all true belevers, nothyng douting but the hollye goost ... dothe and will at my most need, when deth synne and hell shall most trouble me, strengthen and so staye me in this my beleve that they shall nothyng prevaile ageynst my poure soule.

Nevertheless, he added that he trusted also that

> as at all tymes so most chefly when my soule shall departe from my body, to be partaker of the charitable prayers of all saints, both quyck and deede.

He left to each of his parishes

> a hole Bible in Englishe to be chayned at my own propre cost, desireing my parisheners that they wolde so reverently here and rede the same so they increase in the fear and love of God.

This was the 'Great Bible' required by the Royal Injunctions of 1538, a sign at the very least of Townsend's up-to-the-moment political correctness. He left £6 to be divided among the poor of his three Norfolk parishes, and £4 to 'Mr Nicols of Raynham', asking him to preach two sermons in each of his parishes. The will contains no request for masses to be said for the repose of his soul, though it seems inconceivable that these can have been omitted at this early stage in the Reformation: such arrangements for his obsequies will have been made verbally.[45]

Townsend's will still just about envisages prayers for the dead, and the intercession of the saints, but like the teaching of the Henrician Ten Articles of 1536, he does not seem to believe in purgatory – hence the reference to immediate enjoyment of the fruition of God. The rejection of purgatory spelled the death-warrant for the guilds and chantry masses which were the main occupation of the community of priests at Salle, and with the accession of Edward VI in 1547, all guilds and chantries were dissolved, and the chaplains of Salle sang no more for the dead. The Rood and the whole upper part of the screen was destroyed, the altars which filled every corner of the church were pulled down and their images and tabernacles burned, and many of the commemorative brasses, representing the roll-call of the dead benefactors of the community, were ripped up – most of those in place today were replaced in the eighteenth and nineteenth centuries, having been rescued and kept in the church chest.

These transformations of the sacred space of Salle church – the abolition of the multiple corrals for the holy which divided the body of the church – had the effect of at once making invisible, and indeed of abolishing, some of the social complexity of the parish. What happened to the local loyalties of scattered parishes like Salle when the plough lights and dances of Marshgate, Kirkgate, Lunton and Steynewade were abolished, when the feast-day meetings as well as the altars of the seven guilds became illegal, when the opportunities – and burdens – of office-holding and stock-holding within the guilds were suppressed? No guild or churchwardens' accounts survive for sixteenth-century Salle, but where such accounts do exist elsewhere we get some measure of the social transformation such changes involved. In the tiny and much poorer Exmoor village of Morebath in this period twelve men and women, including the teenage wardens of the Young Men's and Maiden's stores held office in the parish and the parish's 'stores' or light fraternities – a primitive form of guild. These twelve people were annually elected: they managed small flocks of sheep, handled donations and laid out money for ceremonial and social functions, and they presented annual accounts to parish meetings. After the Reformation, the parish elected just one person a year to office, and that person was always a man.[46]

We should not idealize: there never was a merry England, and office-holding was often a serious burden which medieval parishioners wriggled to avoid. But such office-holding, within guilds and light stores, was also an aspect of the complex social geography of the medieval parish community, and that geography was mapped out in the interior of the churches in which the guild and chantry altars were placed and in which stood the images before which the lights burned. With the removal of altars, images and lights, and the social and religious groups which funded them, the dynamics of local communities were permanently changed.

In terms of the social geography of the parish church, that, of course, left the wealthy in possession. The Reformation abolished altars, lights and guilds, and with them, the groups who paid for and maintained them. The Reformation also abolished family chantries, but not, of course, the families who maintained them. The rich, like the poor, are always with us. The Townsends, hard-faced men who did well out of the Reformation, remained Lords of the Manor and patrons of the living, for another century. The chantry-chapels of Salle ceased to function: we do not know at what point they lost their parclosing, but they did not altogether lose their semi-private function. As all the church's seating came to focus on the pulpit on the south side of the nave, they are unlikely to have been satisfactory family pews, but they certainly retained their value as semi-private family mausolea. In 1802 Edward Hase, an early nineteenth-century parish grandee, thought nothing of bricking up one of the north transept windows to provide a suitable background for his own funeral monument. He consulted neither parson nor people.[47]

Was the reformation in Salle a gentry *coup*? Without a lot more documentation than we posess, we cannot hope to answer that question satisfactorily. We have no idea, for example, how the commons of Salle at large behaved during Kett's Rebellion in the 'camping time' of 1549, though one Salle man at least, Robert Chapman, died among the rebels at Mousehold Heath, and the likelihood is that he did not march alone.[48] That rebellion, unlike the Western Rising the same summer, has been widely interpreted as enthusiastically sympathetic to protestantism,[49] and certainly the rebels ostentatiously secured Prayer-book worship and reformed preaching in their camp at Mousehold Heath, in which, famously, the future Archbishop Matthew Parker played a part. But Parker came within a whisker of being lynched by the rebels and, according to Nicholas Sotherton, this Prayer-Book conformity was policy rather than piety, adopted 'in order to have a fayre shew and a similitude of well doinge'. Sir Roger Townsend was one of those appealed to against the rebels by the Mayor of Norwich and, however Townsend's tenants in Salle behaved, the men of the neighbouring village of Heydon, where the Townsends were also patrons of the living, marched to the rebel camp carrying their church banner, a strongly traditionalist gesture reminiscent of the Pilgrimage of Grace and certainly suggesting no very strong protestant convictions.[50]

Like the Townsend family, many of the influential people of Salle were establishment figures, men and women with a lot to lose from non-conformity. Whatever their innermost convictions, most of them will have cooperated with the processes of Reformation. We should not assume that this was ever straightforward. One might benefit from the Reformation yet not endorse all its teachings. Anne Boleyn's brother, Sir James Boleyn, who died at Blickling in 1561, was Queen Elizabeth's uncle. He remembered her in his will, leaving her a gilt basin and ewer, but also 'my written book of the revelations of S Bridget, most humbly beseeching her Highness to read well and ponder the same'. We do not know whether Queen Elizabeth followed his advice and read St Bridget's detailed descriptions of the pains of Purgatory, or her blow by blow accounts of the life and Passion of Christ, but it is not routine Protestant reading matter.[51]

But there may well be in any case a sense in which the Reformation barely came to mid-Tudor Salle, except in its destructive aspects. Roger Townsend was succeeded as Rector in 1538 by William Worrison, who would remain in the benefice till his death through the remainder of Henry's, Edward's and Mary's reigns.[52] As that suggests, Worrison was a conformist who made no religious changes: the religious provisions of parish wills in the 1540s manifest no hint of reformed convictions, and even after the disappearance of the guilds and their clergy the parish retained enough clerical and musical resources in 1543 for a parishioner to specify with confidence that he would have 'Masse and dyrge by note' at his burial.[53] Sir Roger Townsend himself hardly qualifies as a convinced Protestant, and was unlikely to have been a force for radicalism in Salle. His closest allies in East Anglia came from conservative families, notably the Bedingfields, to whom he was related by his daughter's marraige, and his commitment to reform was strictly opportunist.[54] The preamble to his own will, made in May 1552, would pass superficial inspection as an evangelical document, with its emphasis on salvation by 'the merite of [Christ's] most blissed passion'. In fact, however, these phrases are directly copied from his impeccably Catholic father's will-preamble, with the references to the Virgin Mary, the saints and the sacraments removed, and a phrase on scripture inserted: indeed, it was far less insistent than the will of old Sir Roger on the doctrine of predestination. Family identity is far more in evidence here than evangelical conviction.[55]

Salle parish certainly cannot have welcomed the destructive aspects of the Reformation. Early in Edward's reign they seem hastily to have sold off more than £17 worth of silver and diverted the bulk of the money to repairs in the church, to prevent the Royal commissioners getting their hands on it, a proceeding matched in many other parishes in the region – at Cawston the parish spent £40 of the £44 2s. 6d. that they raised from the sale of the church silver on parish projects like roofing an aisle, paying for the white-washing and 'scripturing' of the Church, and repairing roads. But at Salle much remained in the church, and in 1552 a new batch of royal officials took away barrow-loads of ornaments and vestments – two chalices, nearly a hundredweight of candlesticks in silver and brass, eight elaborate sets of velvet and gold high-mass sets of chasuble, tunicles and copes, many of them black and obviously designed for use in the elaborate requiems which had been so important a part of the worship of Salle church, as well as another eleven sets of humbler vestments, the handbells used in Rogationtide processions and for calling people to prayer for the dead, and three of the five bells in the steeple.[56] One of the leading parishioners who joined the Rector, William Worrison, in signing the 1552 inventory was Arthur Fountain, a member of one of the longest-standing Salle families, whose monuments and pious benefactions were now the target of Royal religious policy. By the end of Edward's reign, Salle had been stripped of at least six generations of pious giving. The religious regime of Marian Salle seems to have reverted to traditional practice: Richard

Lockett, in May 1555, asked for 'diridge and mass', provided funds for 'my neybors to have good chere', and alms to the poor for the 'profitt of my soule': he also left 5s. to the reparation of the church, and a load of squared marble for repaving in the south aisle 'where most nede is', which may simply indicate that his seat was there, but which may represent repair-work after officially enforced Edwardian iconoclasm.[57]

From Elizabeth's reign onwards the rectors of Salle were mostly resident, and were the only priests in the parish. The living lapsed to the Crown in 1558, because the patron, Roger Townsend III, was a minor. William Warrison died in July 1558, leaving a will with a Catholic preamble, bequeathing his soul to St Mary and 'all the holly companie of heaven', but otherwise containing no religious provisions of any sort. His successor, John Crane, was duly nominated by Philip and Mary. Crane was a native of Pulham, near Diss, but he was probably related to a local Salle family – one of the stipendiary chaplains in the 1490s was a Walter Crane, and one of the signatories of the 1552 inventories, signing with a mark, was a Robert Crane.[58]

John Crane was a decidedly surprising Crown appointment in 1558, for he was a theological graduate and a preacher with a notably protestant past. As a young fellow of Christ's College in Henry VIII's reign, he had taken a prominent part in a notorious performance of Thomas Kirchmeyer's play *Pammachius*, during Lent 1545. *Pammachius* was a scurrilous satire against the papacy, and concerned a mythical pope who had sold himself, and the papacy, into subjection to Satan. Denounced by another Christ's man, Cuthbert Scot, the future Marian Bishop of Chester and a dedicated defender of conservative orthodoxy, the play, which reputedly 'reproved Lent fastinges [and] al ceremonies' had attracted the enraged attention of the chancellor of the University, Stephen Gardiner, Bishop of Winchester. With Matthew Parker's emollient assistance, Crane had been obliged to defend himself against accusations of sacramental heresy, claiming that the objectionable aspects of the original had been bowdlerized and that 'they entended not but to rebuke the popes usurped power'. Crane went on to take his BD in 1549, but it is not clear whether his subsequent career before his arrival in Salle sustained the tone of this controversial beginning. His whereabouts and activities in the earlier part of Mary's reign are unknown, though by the time of his death in 1578 he had acquired the reputation of having been 'an ernest Professor of Christ in the tyme of Queene Marie': his curate describes him as 'a trew, a constaunt and a devout follower of Christ unto his Death', which may or may not indicate that he was puritanically inclined.[59] He evidently kept his head down sufficiently to pass muster as a possible Marian incumbent, however, and above all he was unmarried. He can have had little impact on Salle in any case, for he was an absentee. Crane was a pluralist, who by 1561 was not only Rector of Salle, but incumbent at Feltwell, in the west of the county, and of Tivetshall, near Diss in South Norfolk, where he resided.[60]

It is not clear how far Crane's successor, John Thurston, appointed in 1565 and who does seem to have resided in the parish, qualifies as a convinced Protestant. In 1572 he married a local girl, Dorothy Turner, and their first son, born in 1572, was baptized Esaye (Isaiah), which looks on the face of it like a revealing indication of the reformed ethos of the parsonage. But if Thurstan was a Protestant, he was not admired by the godly: the 1586 puritan survey of the Norfolk ministry notes that he was a non-preacher, 'blinde, a leper, he was a shoe-maker, and then a masse priest'.[61] The next rector, Thomas Aldred, married a wife perhaps significantly named Faith, but was not long in the parish, since he died in 1590. His successor, Richard Wrathall, who married into one of the parish gentry families, the Fountains, is described in a legal document in 1615 not as rector but as 'Minister of the Word of God of Saull'. Like the rector of neighbouring Cawston, he was in trouble in the 1590s for persistent failure to wear the surplice,[62] and it was for him, in 1611, that Thomas Lord Knyvett, another Salle landlord and one with marked protestant credentials, turned the elegant fifteenth-century pulpit into the present dominant 'three-decker' with a prayer desk and a clerk's desk below the pulpit itself.[63] The pulpit was placed half-way down the church (not its present position) and the pewing was arranged towards it, so that everyone seated in the eastern half of the nave sat with their backs towards the now largely redundant chancel.

We know something at least of the use the pulpit was put to. In 1584, Robert Sendall, a wealthy yeoman parishioner who had occupied the lands of Nugoun's manor since 1545, made a will, requesting burial 'at my stooles ende' in the church, leaving 1d. to every poor man, woman and child who attended his funeral, 1s. each and their food and drink to the men who carried him to the grave, and 6d. each to the bellringers. He also stipulated that 'some learned man shall preach in Sawle Church at the day of my funerall and he to have for his paynes 5s of lawfull englysh money'. Sendall had been one of the parishioners named in the parish inventory submitted prior to the drastic Edwardine confiscation of 1552. He was clearly proud of the church, leaving land in fee to help maintain the building in perpetuity. He also provided for an annual distribution of 20s 'on St John's daie in Chrystmas', 'to ease and unburden the poore in Sawl'. Sendall commended his soul into the hands of 'Almighty God my maker and Jesus Chryste his onlye sonne my alone saviour by whose merites I hope to be saved', and he asked for a learned sermon, not a dirge and mass by note, at his funeral. Yet in its manifest pride in the building, attachment to his own place in it, and desire for remembrance on a festal anniversary in the form of charity to the poor, his will is reminiscent of dozens of similar surviving Salle wills made over the previous century and a half. By the 1580s Protestantism had certainly arrived in the parsonage, and at least occasionally in the pulpit, of Salle. But if the puritan survey's contemptuous dismissal of Sendall's pastor John Thurstan as a blind, non-preaching former mass-priest is anything to go by, it was a Protestantism muted and modified by continuities which had little to do with ideology. All in all, it is not clear to me whether the religion of Robert Sendall was different in kind from the religion of the pre-Reformation Briggs and Fountaines and Roos, or much the same sort of thing, working in reduced circumstances.[64]

5

The end of it all: the material culture of the late medieval English parish and the 1552 Inventories of Church Goods

When did the Middle Ages end? More specifically, how and when did the medieval parish end? At one level, of course, the question is nonsensical: the parish did not end at all. It is with us still, many of its institutions, offices and functions direct and demonstrable developments from medieval roots. Yet equally clearly, the Reformation constitutes a major watershed in the history of the parish, inaugurating or at any rate accelerating a trend towards the assimilation of previously independent parochial structures and functions into an increasingly oligarchic centralism, and putting an end altogether to some of the most fundamental energies and activities of late medieval parishioners, from hoggling and maygames to diriges for the dead. The doctrine of purgatory and the cult of intercession for the dead underlay many of the institutions and much of the funding of late medieval Christianity. Stipendiary clergy whose

principal function was the recitation of masses and diriges provided the bulk
of the clerical manpower of early Tudor England, and the vestments they wore,
the books they read and sang from and the vessels and liturgical furniture they
deployed in the liturgy, even the very buildings themselves, were for the most
part donated by or on behalf of the dead, and were often emblazoned with
their initials, names, arms and images. It would be an exaggeration, but not
much of one, to say that death staffed, furnished, decorated and dominated
the liturgical round of the late medieval parish church. The Reformation put
a stop to all of this, and with the protestant ban on purgatory and on images
the life of the parish and the appearance of the parish church permanently
and profoundly changed. If we are looking for an end-point for the medieval
parish, therefore, it must surely be found in the early 1550s and the revolu-
tionary religious upheaval of the reign of Edward VI.[1]

In the last chapter, we considered how all this played out in a single
parish. This chapter considers a decisive moment in those decisive years, by
trying to get to grips in a preliminary way with a comparatively neglected
category of document: the Inventories of Church Goods compiled by Royal
Commissioners for every county in England in the summer and autumn of
1552, as the preliminary to a massive confiscation which was carried through
from the early spring of 1553, ceasing only with the death of the king in the
first week of July. This most drastic of Reformation spoliations stripped the
parish churches of England of something like two centuries of accumulated
devotional investment by lay and clerical parishioners. It bulldozed away
much of the material culture of late medieval Christianity, and with it, the
complex indoor landscape of memory which that investment had created.

Parochial confiscations were of course potential dynamite in Tudor England.
The rebellions of 1536, which we call by the blanket term the Pilgrimage of
Grace, originated in the conviction of the Lincolnshire Commons, mistaken
as it turned out, that their church goods were about to be plundered by
the Crown.[2] The suppression of the chantries in 1547 involved the compilation of lists of recent sales of parish property by churchwardens and other
officials.[3] These enquiries were probably genuinely designed to halt the alienation or embezzlement of parish property which the uncertainties of reform
had triggered, but they understandably prompted widespread suspicion of

imminent confiscations, and, in a few cases, violent resistance.[4] In February 1549, however, the whole exercise was repeated, this time through the sheriffs and justices of the peace. To stem the flood of pre-emptive sales by which panic-stricken parishes had attempted to frustrate the feared Royal confiscations, parish officials were now expressly forbidden to alienate or sell any plate or other valuables, and duplicate copies of every inventory were to be lodged with the *Custos Rotulorum* of the Shire. Wardens were required to sign a declaration that 'we knowledge ourselves straitly commanded neither to sell nor alienate any plate, jewelles, ornaments or belles from henceforth'.[5] Ominously, the Council also stipulated that a brief summary of every inventory should be made, listing only the chief saleable valuables, in the form of the church plate and the bells.[6] In practice, many parishes failed to provide these inventories, contenting themselves with an itemized list of objects sold since the start of the reign, and an explanation of the necessities which had dictated the sales, a laxer interpretation of the Council's instructions which the Commissioners in many places were apparently willing to accept.[7] But the Council evidently took all this very seriously, and in the next two years was to intervene directly in a number of parishes to allow or prevent the sale of church goods for specific public projects, such as the improvement of the haven at Sandwich.[8]

Whatever the regime's motivation in the late 1540s, however, growing financial crisis and the demands of war ensured that the fears of the parishes of a massive confiscation were to prove prophetic. On March 3rd 1550/1 the Council decreed that 'forasmuche as the Kinges Majestie had neede presently of a masse of money, therefore Commissions should be addressed into all shires of Englande to take into the Kinges handes suche plate as remaigneth, to be emploied unto his Highnes use'.[9] This seems not to have been acted on at once, but by the end of January 1552 letters had been despatched to the *Custos Rotulorum* of every shire asking for copies of the 1549 inventories, and in mid May 1552 the first County Commissioners, six or seven to a shire, had been appointed. They were to 'take and receave a due, full and just view of all goodes, plate, jewells, bells and ornaments of every Churche or Chapell in whose hands soever the same be belongyng'. They were to make a full inventory, and to compare that inventory with 'the best of the former Inventories heretofore remaynyng with the … Churchwardens'. Any missing items were to be pursued, the Commissioners establishing how they had disappeared, in whose possession they were and, if they had been sold, who had received the proceeds. They were given draconian powers of arrest and imprisonment to secure the co-operation of local officials and parishioners.[10] In London the Commissioners implemented these instructions by presenting each parish with a set of four articles, demanding the names of the current wardens, the names of the wardens in 1547, a copy of the earlier inventory prepared by those wardens for Bishop Bonner in 1548/9, and an itemized list of everything sold between 1548 and 1552, together with an account of the use to which the proceeds had been devoted. To judge by the format of the returns, similar articles seem to have been used elsewhere, as in Surrey.

The inventories and certificates which resulted from this intense scrutiny vary hugely in value. The returns from many counties survive only in part, and for some counties, such as Westmorland and Northumberland, do not survive at all. In Cornwall and Devon most of the original inventories have perished, leaving only books containing the brief final summaries made by the Commissioners.[11] And independently of the vagaries of survival, the original documents themselves vary hugely in scope and value. The inventories for Norfolk are mostly meagre and vestigial, presenting a bafflingly gloomy picture of the poverty of the churches of what had once been one of the wealthiest regions of England, and which had been exceptionally rich in ecclesiastical art and furnishings.[12] By contrast, the inventories for Cambridgeshire, Essex, Surrey and, above all, the city of London are massively detailed, giving a very full picture not only of the medieval and early Tudor ornaments and plate surviving into the maelstrom of the Edwardine Reformation, and of the sumptuousness of provision for worship in the late Middle Ages, but detailing the sales, thefts and alienations of the years before the inventories were compiled. In the process, these inventories and associated documents provide precious information about the pace, agents and beneficiaries of reform, and of local resistances to it, which historians have curiously neglected and sometimes actively misunderstood.

The 1552 inventories were an assault on the autonomy of the parishes of England. Churchwardens were of course accustomed to compiling inventories: they were a routine element in the process of visitation, and in the handover of responsibility from outgoing wardens to their successors. So summary

check-lists of church property, listing everything from the altar vessels and
hangings to the sexton's spade were included among the papers kept in the
parish chest. But many parishes also had more elaborate lists serving, as Clive
Burgess has shown us,[13] more complex functions. Such lists itemized in detail
the wealth of the church and especially its ritual furniture, but also commemorated the donors and benefactors of the parish by linking their names to their
gifts: in the process they held up a pattern of generosity for others to follow.
Lists of this sort were a powerful expression of parochial identity and parochial
pride, a complex social map of the parish pecking-order, a recitation of the
names of the beneficent dead, and a form of exhortation to commitment
and generousity by the living. So the inventory compiled and updated at the
London city church of St Margaret between 1486 and 1511 proclaims itself
as an inventory of items embodying the collective pride and aspiration of the
early Tudor parish, 'gotten and laboured to be hadd for the same Chirche use'
by successive wardens and parsons. The list itself, which has the cost of every
item proudly displayed in the margin, is highly circumstantial.

Item A white Cope of Damaske powderd with Archangelles and the
Offeraries of the same of nedyll werke of a parte of the lyffe of Seynt
Margarett to the whiche payment of the same Cope we had of the bequest
of Richard Bowell and Elyzabeth his wyff by the handdz of Sir John Plomer
preest and Executor ... £8 and we paid the overplus ...

Item 4 stavys paynted for the Canapye with Corpus Christi uppon
theym and with 4 angellz gilt to stand uppon them by our said Master
Parson (Thomas Howghton) price 20s.

Item Of the gyft of Annes Wymarke a paxbred silver and gilt weighing
six ounces di with blewe rosez and with the salutation of our lady the wich
paxbred is geven for the soule of Sir Thomas Avelen preest.

Item a Suete of Blake velvett that is to wytt vestment, Decon and
subdeacon with a Cope of the same with Orfrays of nedle warke with the
appostolles and Prophetes of the gyfte of Robert May, John Wylson and
Johanna their wyffe on whose sowles Jesu have Mercy.

Item a Suet of Whyte damaske with Orfrays of Redde velvett with
flowres of nedle werke ... of the Gyfte of Master Henry Wayte ...

> Item we labered to be had in the same tyme 8 Corporaxis casis..on
> of theym of blew tissew, Item a noder of theym white damaske with 2
> archangellz ...[14]

All these items reappear in the 1552 inventory, but shorn now of their
particularity, and especially of their personal associations and the names of
their donors. Once again, there are prices attached to them, not now as the
measure of the piety of their donors or the eagerness to the wardens, 'labouring
to have' desirable devotional accoutrements, but as the knock-down price in a
series of auctions precipitated or decreed by Royal religious policy.

> Item solde to one unknowen ... one cope vestement Deacon and Subdeacon
> of blak velvet ... the offeras of the same of nedyll woorke with Images
> amountynge as they were sold to £9 16s.
>
> Item to one unknowen one suett of whyte Damaske vestement ... 32s
>
> Item to one unknowen one chalyce.one pax of sylver weyinge xvi oz di
> at 4/10d the oz, £4 4s 7d
>
> Item 8 banner staves 12d.[15]

There is then, something inherently amnesiac about the 1552 inventories.
They existed to depersonalize and desacralize the material framework of the
medieval system of salvation, to transform the named deposit of meritorious
giving into so much saleable lumber. And the compilers of the inventories
seem often to collude in this process of desacralization, in their apparent
dismissiveness of the once-sacred objects they describe, as in the inventory
prepared by the parish of Clapham, which included

> dyvers olde stayned and paynted clothes for the doyng of ceremonyes lately
> used in the churche.
>
> dyvers smalle ornamentes sometyme used about ymages ...[16]

A similar tone is evident in the inventory of the city parish of St Ethelburga,
where the wardens reported the sale of 'olde ... vestementes Latten waxe and
other *olde Cerymony thinges* belonging to the saide Churche', and of 'iij Copes
and other trumpery'.[17] In the same way, at St Alban Wood Street the wardens
sold off 'certeyn olde paynted cloathes hangynges of aulters and cloathes to

hange before saintes in lent *and other olde tromperie*', at St Martin Outwich they sold 'old tabernacles being defaced *and other lyke baggage*', and at St Dunstan's in the West '*certen olde trashe* of coopes and vestementes'.[18]

In some cases this language may well reflect hostility to the ritual paraphernalia of the recent Catholic past, and the inventories do sometimes reveal manifestly protestant parishes. At St Bride's Fleet Street the incumbent was the reformer John Cardmaker, and his predecessor had been John Rogers. Unsurprisingly, there was strong protestant sentiment among his parishioners. The inventory duly records sales in 1547 dictated because

> there was no money then in the Churche boxe to reforme the seid Churche of the idolatrous images and monumentes then standyng therein and to garnyshe the same Churche with Scriptures accordyng to the appoyntment and commaundement of the Kyngys Maiesties visitor:

the proceeds had been spent

> with the consent of the parishioners that yere in reformacyon of the Abuses aforesaid and in furnyshyng of the Churche accordyng to the commaundement afore seid.[19]

St Ethelburga's and St Alban Wood Street also had notably protestant incumbents in the late 1540s and early 1550s, while at St Martin Outwich the wardens proudly commented on their possession of a 'very faire Communion cuppe', and reported the disposal of 'certeyn cristal which was in the best Crosse with glasse, paynted papers and other baggage', suggesting both an appreciation of the new worship and a robustly dismissive attitude to relics.[20] But caution is needed in interpreting such phrases. St Dunstan's in the West, where the inventory also spoke of 'old trashe', was in fact a stoutly conservative parish, which retained most of its catholic ornaments and ritual equipment through all the viccissitudes of the turbulent Edwardine years: it was one of the first London churches to revert to the celebration of the Latin Mass when Mary came to the throne. In this case at least, the 'old trashe' of copes and vestments mentioned in this parish's accounts almost certainly represents a financial assessment of the market value of worn out articles rather than a blanket condemnation of vestments as such.[21]

And in many parishes there was widespread conservative feeling even when the management of the Edwardine changes had fallen into the hands of committed reformers. At St Botolph Aldgate the wardens and sidesmen reporting the selling of the Latin service-books commented 'which the people understood not'. But they were speaking for themselves, not 'the people', and in Mary's reign the leaders of reform at St Botolph's were be pursued by their fellow parishioners and made to contribute £20 to the reconstruction of the parish's catholic worship.[22] At St Sepulchre the 1552 inventory was compiled by the Edwardine warden who managed much of the deconstruction of traditional religion there, Gregory Newman, a committed reformer. But Newman certainly did not speak for the majority of his fellow-parishioners, and after Edward's death he was to be targeted both by the Marian authorities, who called him to account for the destruction of the rood loft, and by his fellow parishioners, who bided their time and then denounced him to the church courts for adultery with his protestant maid-servant. He was forced to do humiliating public penance, and, in a punishment designed to fit the crime, to contribute 20s. to the reconstruction of Catholic ceremonial in the parish church he had helped to strip.[23]

So the inventories here are a potentially extremely misleading source. The picture they provide, of local compliance with the deepening iconoclastic radicalism of the Edwardine religious regime, is very striking. It is all too tempting to read the inventories, therefore, as evidence for the early success of the Reformation in changing hearts and minds, and not simply in eliciting obedience. Even so sensitive and alert an historian as Susan Brigden, whose *London and the Reformation* is one of the best studies we have of the urban Reformation anywhere in Europe, does not altogether avoid this pitfall. Using the inventories as her main source for the purging of images from the London churches in 1547 and 1548, she writes that the Injunctions 'were carried out *with a will* in the City churches'. Soon, 'by the assent of the most part of the parishioners there' the churchwardens began to sell wholesale the ornaments and treasures of their churches, given and honoured over decades, even centuries,'old trumpery' sold within a year of Edward's accession in half of London's churches. One by one the churches were 'transformed, reformed from idolatry'.[24] Dr Brigden documented in ample detail the

religious complexity and divisions of Edwardine London, but her discussion
of the evidence of the inventories here and elsewhere gives the impression that
they represent the trace of widespread enthusiasm for reform.

This is manifestly not so. There is indeed an overwhelming and even monot-
onous emphasis in the inventories from London and elsewhere on collective
responsibility – the wardens in all these cases being declared to have auctioned
off vestments and plate with the assent 'of thenhabytantes and heddes of the
parysshe', 'of the most part of the parishioners', or by 'thassent of the hole
paryshe at a vestrie holden at the seide churche', 'with the consent of the moste
aunciente and discrete persons of the seide parische' or by 'the comen consent
of the whole parrish', 'all the hole parysshe beynge together'.[25] The point of
these references, however, is not the enthusiasm or otherwise of the parish
for the changes, but the fact that the wardens were acting legally and under
instructions. The Council's demand for the compilation of the inventories was
an offensive measure, perceived everywhere as threatening. One of the prime
purposes of the inventories was to track down malpractice and embezzlement,
and to recover alienated goods or their cash value from those who had misap-
propriated them. The commissioners minutely scrutinized the returns. Many
of the Surrey inventories are annotated 'Examined by the Commissioners and
found to be true', 'allowed by the Commissioners', 'not fully allowed by the
Commissioners but referred to be further examined'.[26] In places the parish
inventories are interlined by the Commissioners with minute details of the
colour and fabric of items deemed insufficiently clearly described. The Earl of
Oxford, who headed the Essex Commission, busied himself like a provincial
draper noting the colours of old copes, the whereabouts of black worsted and
old dornyx, of worn-out towels and disused organ pipes.[27] Under this micro-
scopic and apparently hostile scrutiny, the emphasis on legitimacy is in most
cases not so much a sign of mass enthusiasm, as a nervous insistence by the
responsible officials that they had done nothing wrong in selling ornaments
rendered redundant by officially enforced religious change, 'church candyl-
stykes and other olde thyngs past use for the church, as latyn, iron, holy water
buckett, processhon bell, auter clothes or hangynges, banner and such other'.[28]

The London inventories are especially informative here, for they provide
a mass of careful detail itemizing for the years between 1547 and 1552, the

sale or disposal of medieval Catholic ornaments. And while it is evident that some parishes, or at any rate their governing elites, were indeed enthusiastically protestant, the overwhelming majority of these inventories, even in London, suggest an essentially reactive response to the Reformation, which followed rather than pre-empted royal policy. Once again, extreme care has to be exercised in interpreting the evidence of the inventories. Dr Brigden, for example, lists St Martin Ludgate among the city churches where 'altars had been pulled down by zealous protestant parishioners 'long afore' the order came'.[29] But as Dr Brigden herself has demonstrated, St Martin Ludgate was in fact a rankly papistical parish, singled out by Edwardine protestant satirists as one of the last lurking places of Mother Mass,[30] and the alleged zeal for the removal of altars there is in fact an optical illusion. The Inventory for St Martin Ludgate does indeed indicate that the parish sold 'an olde aulter' in 1547, three years before Bishop Ridley ordered the destruction of all the altars in London, but this was not part of an enthusiastic purge of the altars from the body of the church. The altar disposed of in 1547 had in fact stood on or against the rood loft, which was removed by the parish as part of the destruction of images imposed throughout the city that year. The parish undertook no further ritual changes of any kind until 1549, when the Book of Common prayer became mandatory, nor is there any indication that the other altars in the parish church came down before 1550, when their removal was generally enforced throughout the diocese. There is certainly no hint in the inventory that anyone at all was *zealous* for these changes.[31]

At St Martin's Ludgate, as in most other parishes, therefore, the sale of medieval furniture, vestments, plate and books almost certainly represents obedience to royal and episcopal authority, i.e. dutiful or enforced conformity, rather than hostility to traditional religion or active zeal for the new. Many of the inventories make explicit the motivation for the stream of sales which had begun in the first year of the reign, and which had swollen to a torrent by 1549: almost all pleaded either necessity or obedience, or both. At St Benet Fink the wardens and swornmen concluded a long list of sales between 1549 and 1551 with the tart remark that 'we have not one foote of lande to mayntayne our churche withall for the Kynges Majiestie hathe that we had which was the Summa of £22 by the yere'.[32] The conservative parish of St Dunstan in the West prefaced a list of goods sold in 1551 on the authority of the wardens and twenty-five named parishioners with the explanation that they had been forced to raise money because 'the parish was so destitute and troubled for lacke of a house to kepe the Kinges lete and for other necessarie meatinges'.[33] The inventory for St Olave, Silver Street explained that the wardens had disposed of plate and vestments to meet the expenses of the Reformation changes and the demands of the new provisions for the poor, because the parish itself was 'lytell and powre'.[34] At St Leonard, Foster Lane, they certified that 'our churche is in such Ruyne and decaye that povertie will cause us to make shifft with such as owr plate is to buylde and Repaire the same' or else 'it will fall shortly to the grounde which is playnely and evidently to be seen of all men'.[35] Many parishes were at pains to emphasize that the proceeds of sales had been spent about the king's business, or on authorized or mandatory projects 'bestowid uppon weapons and artyllary for the king in his wars', 'uppon harneis and other weapons ... and ...for the payntyng (whitewash and texting) of the churche', 'bestowide in bowes and arrowes to serve the kinge', 'layed out for armour and artillery for the kinges affayres', 'for payntyng the scripter ageynst the rode lofte and over the awter'.[36] Many also specified both the timing and motivation of the sales: at St Olave's, Hart Street, sales had commenced 'syns that tyme of the Comyng out of the Kynges maiesties iniunccyons', at St Botolph Aldgate, they explained that they had sold nothing till 1551 except the brass and latten bowls 'whych served for the Lyghttes in the churche now extincte by our soveraigne the Kingges inuncions ... sold for the reparacions of the same churche and the rest of the money ... shalbe putt in the pooremen chest accordinge to the commandement of the Kyngges iniuncions'. At St Stephen, Coleman Street, they had replaced the stained glass windows 'as Imagerye was contrarye to the Kinges proceedinges'.[37] In a pattern repeated, *mutatis mutandi*, all over the country, the parish of East Ham in Essex sold the wainscoting which had stood round the images in 1547, to help with the costs of 'making up the broken places in the church where the ymages stode' and whitewashing the interior. They then sold nothing at all till 1551, when 'the churchwardens ... with the whole paracheners agreed to sell such things as remayned superfluous and unoccupied' to pay for the costs of reformation.[38]

There is a striking difference, too, between the comparatively small number of inventories revealing parishes which had made a clean sweep of their

medieval furnishings, retaining or newly acquiring only what was essential
for the decorous performance of the new rites, and the majority, which held
on to many objects now outlawed or redundant. Inventories pared down to
little more than the mandatory 'comely' communion cups, a communion
table and its carpets and linen towels, a surplice, bible, prayer-book, psalters,
homilies, Paraphrases, poor man's box and a register book, mark many parish
churches as thoroughly and deliberately reformed – in London these included
All Hallows, Honey Lane; St Bride, Fleet Street; St Lawrence, Pountney; St
Martin, Pomery; Holy Trinity, Queen Hythe; St Alphege, London Wall; St
Giles, Cripplegate, and a dozen or so others. The overwhelming majority of
parishes, however, despite massive sales and alienations, especially after 1549,
retained many items of their medieval furnishing, though now in storage not
in use. In 1552 even a small and relatively poor city parish such as St Andrew
Hubbard retained fifteen highly ornate corporas cases, ten copes, including
some of sumptuous cloth of tissue, or embroidered velvet, and one retaining
the patronal image, and fourteen chasubles and sets of vestments for priest,
deacon and subdeacon. The wardens of All Hallows, Bread St, sold no fewer
than 39 sets of mass vestments in 1549 and 1550,[39] but many parishes seem to
have sold only what was essential to cover the costs of expensive reformation
changes. The inventories of conservative city parishes like St Nicholas Cole
Abbey, St Martin Orgar, St Mary Woolnoth or St Magnus Martyr, whose
rector was Maurice Griffiths, future Marian bishop of Rochester, retain dozens
of copes and vestments, as well as crucifixes, monstrances, pyxes, paxes and
censers. Their abundance gives an overwhelming sense of the lavish provision
of late medieval city parishes, and in the midst of the iconoclastic fury of
Edwardine London, their simple retention represented not merely thrift,
but something of a deliberate stance. The vestments at St Martin Orgar were
embellished with images of St Martin, St Helena or St Katherine, the vestments
and banners at St Nicholas Cole Abbey with their serried ranks of images of
Christ, the Assumption of the Virgin, the archangels Gabriel and Michael, the
Annunciation, St Margaret, St Katherine, St Erasmus, St Dunstan (displayed
alongside the Fishmongers' arms) and their patron St Nicholas. None were in
use in 1552, of course, but all were illegal, even in storage.[40]

And if some inventories characterized the now redundant ritual furniture of

Plate 1 *The chancel arch at Cawston retains the silhouette of the great crucifix destroyed, along with the rood-loft, under Edward VI.*

Plate 2 *The fifteenth-century church of Sts. Peter and Paul, Salle, from the south.*

Plate 3 *The two apostles on the left of the south screen at Cawston were painted direct on to the wood, and are crudely executed. The other more sophisticated figures, painted on vellum and glued to the screen, came from a superior workshop, presumably at greater cost to different donors. The defaced figure, far right, is the uncanonised saint, Master John Schorne.*

Plate 4 Early Tudor popular devotional taste: *the two central figures on the North (left) screen at Gateley are St Elizabeth and the Virgin Mary, an allusion to the recently introduced feast of the Visitation. They are flanked by St Etheldreda, whose shrine was at Ely, and the mysterious uncanonised "saint", 'Puella Ridibowne'. On the south side, 'St' Henry VI (3rd from right) and Master John Schorne, (far right), were also uncanonised "saints", whose shrines in St George's chapel, Windsor, nevertheless drew many pilgrims. They alternate with Sts Augustine and Ambrose, two of the Four Latin Doctors: the other Doctors, Sts Gregory and Jerome, may have appeared on the screen doors (now lost). The placing of male and female saints on opposite sides of the screen perhaps reflects the seating arrangements in the church.*

Plate 6. Devotional gazzumping: the incomplete figure, (second from right), behind the north altar at Ranworth, dedicated to St John the Baptist, was a picture of the patron saint, but was abandoned at the drawing stage, probably because a large statue of some other saint was donated to stand in its place. The painter therefore transformed the already completed figure of a saintly archbishop, second from left, into the patronal image of the Baptist.

Plate 5. The carved inscription on the dado rail of the lavish screen at Ludham, dated 1493, commemorates John Salmon and "all other benefactors", though gifts for painting and gilding it were still being received in 1508. The popular uncanonised Norfolk "saint", Walstan of Bawburgh, appears third from right. St Gregory's papal tiara and St Jerome's cardinal's hat (first and second left) were gouged away under Henry VIII, an officially enforced anti-papal gesture.

the parish churches dismissively as 'old trash or suchlike trumpery', many list them in circumstantial detail which recalls their former use 'our Ladyes coote of gryne satten a brdges with her sonnes coote', 'the little gospell that hanged aboute our ladye neck', 'the sylver nayles that were on the chest the whiche theye caryd the sacrament in on[e] Palm Sundaye', the banners and cloths 'that longeth to the Sepulture and for good Frydaye', 'a broche which stode upon the Image brest that was borne about upon Easter daye gylt', 'a chaplet uppon our ladyes head with a sapher with dyverse other stones and perles', the two and a quarter yards of cloth of gold that had gone round the Easter sepulchre at St Dionis Backchurch, 'sore dropped with wax', an incidental detail which vividly evokes the blaze of light from the watch-candles round the buried image of Christ in Holy Week, or, simply but tellingly, 'one old vestment for the feryall dayes'.[41] Even an alienated stock of money might encode a memory of now outlawed pieties, like the 8s. in the hands of a parishioner of Little Totham in Essex, 'that was the mayeing mony the which was certified to the mayntenyng of the sepulchre lyght'.[42]

Nevertheless, despite all these echoes of a ritual past still vividly present in the minds of the compilers, the inventories were the devastating record of the abrupt and effective suppression of Catholic *cultus*, and they bear witness to the toll of the Edwardine years on the material and ritual framework of Tudor christianity. The special target here was of course images. All the statues and altarpieces in London seem to have been removed and defaced within a year of Edward's accession, but the Edwardine purge extended far further, to the '142 feet of old glass' disposed of at St Dionis Backchurch in 1549, part of a sale that year which realized for the parish the immense sum of £125 14s 5d. A striking feature of the London inventories in particular is the evidence for the wholesale destruction of brasses in the late 1540s and early 1550s. At All Hallows London Wall in 1551 they sold 30lb of metal 'which was taken upon the grave stones and other monumentes', at St Alphege the year before 'all the olde latten that was uppon the graves', at St John Wallbrook 'the pyctors of plate uppon the stones in the Churche', at St Mary Aldermary the 'plattes that ware over gravys stonys', sold to a pewterer for £3 13s. 4d. Since the average sale price of old latten was 3d. the pound, they must have prised an immense number of brasses out of the floor of St Mary Aldermary.[43] Most of these brasses were sold to founders and pewterers and melted down, though some churches, like St Magnus Martyr and All Hallows Bread Street obediently removed them from the floor, but stored them in the parish chest or in the vestry. At All Hallows the Great they still had four and a half hundredweight of brasses 'taken of grave stones' in 1552, piled in the now redundant rood loft.[44]

Who were the buyers and beneficiaries of all these sales? In the first place, of course, very often, the parishioners themselves. At St Saviour's, Southwark, four of the five wardens who presided over the massive sale of vestments, hangings and plate in 1550 were also major purchasers. The other largest buyer, John Whitwode, who spent £72 4s. for the parish's best copes, high-mass vestments and the altar-hangings from the Lady Altar, was one of the six named 'enhabytantes and heddes of the parysh' assenting to the sales.[45] In 1552 at St Mary Magdalene Milk Street £29 18s. was raised by a sale 'in presence of the whole parsh unto theym that wold geve most', and such parish auctions must have been a very familiar occurrence all over Edwardine England.[46] The original donors or their families were sometimes given first refusal on such sales, as they were at All Hallows Bread Street in 1550, when Master Pargeter bought back for 18s. 'the new crosse banner cloth that his mother gave'.[47] Wardens might run foul of the parish in such transactions, as John Whitepayne did at St Dunstan's-in-the-West when, apparently without charge and certainly 'without the assent of the parisshe', he returned to the widow of the wealthy merchant tailor Henry Dacres the magnificent velvet copes and vestments bequeathed to the church by her husband.[48]

But if many parishioners might bid for velvet, satin or linen, for old cupboards, candlesticks or bells, the surge in sales of precious and base metals, the hundredweights of outlawed parchment books, the bales of velvet, silk and brocade created a market of its own which specialists, and some parishes, were swift to capitalize on. At St Mary Somerset in 1550 the wardens sold the copes and vestments to parishioners only after getting a preliminary 'vew made and price sett' by John Rooke, embroiderer, of London. But many tradesmen themselves eagerly entered the market and the London goldsmiths, founders, pewterers, tailors, saddlemakers, pursemakers and embroiderers had a bonanza, not merely in the sales within the city, but much further afield.

The same purchasers crop up repeatedly in inventories within the city and the home counties – Thomas Thaxton, founder, into whose furnaces at Lothbury much of the memorial brasswork of London and the home counties disappeared, Clement Killingworth, pewterer, Robert Madder, broderer, Robert Donkin, tailor, Thomas Muschamp, Fabyan Withers, William Southwood, John Reynolds and Robert Fryer, goldsmiths. All these recur again and again, the goldsmiths both as purchasers of chalices, crosses, cruets, pyxes, and monstrances, and as suppliers of silver-gilt communion cups for the new worship. Reynolds served with Fryer as churchwarden of St Mary Woolnoth, a conservative parish which disposed of very little of its Catholic furniture till 1552. Unsurprisingly the two goldsmith wardens were then among the chief purchasers.[49] Similarly, Muschamp served as warden of his conservative parish of St Christopher le Stock in 1551 and 1552. The parish had retained most of its vestments and a basic complement of catholic vessels, but there had been a steady sale of goods through the reign to fund the reformation changes although, interestingly, not in 1549–50, 'for that hit was not nedefull'. Muschamp himself was the principle purchaser, buying over £70-worth of the parish plate in the course of the reign.[50]

These transactions reveal religiously conservative men doing well out of religious revolution, and their pragmatism of course offers a vital clue to what might otherwise seem the baffling success of religious changes to which few had much prior ideological commitment. All the participants in such transactions, whatever their motivations, whatever their religious reservations, were participants in, and beneficiaries of, the process of Reformation. And for every named profiteer there were dozens of busy tradesmen turning an ill wind to personal good, as parishes noted sales to 'two men that dwelled in Southwarke which went about to by sich thyngys', 'to one that came about to enquire to bie latten … but what he was he cannot tell', to a 'boke bynder in Powles church yard', or, as the wardens of Pagelsham in Essex noted simply, 'at Bartholomew fayr'.[51]

The roaring trade in rare and base metals, precious cloths, linen, wax, precipitated a rash of thefts: I have dealt with these elsewhere, and will not repeat myself here,[52] but it is worth registering the staggering scale of the problem. Of the 115 Surrey parishes for whom a usable inventory survives, no fewer than 48 reported that they had been robbed, several of them repeatedly, of items ranging from seriously valuable chalices and crosses, down to to relatively cheap bibles and books of common prayer. The situation was bad all over the country: the commissioners for Hertfordshire compiled a special report on thefts, including a long section on irrecoverable goods with the heading 'things done by men dead'.[53]

The most predictable feature of the 1552 inventories is the picture they offer of the splendour and lavishness of the suppressed worship of late medieval and early Tudor Catholicism. A less obvious aspect of the inventories is the light they throw on the unexpected complexity and richness of the emerging pattern of Reformed worship, as patterns inherited from Catholic ritual customs were imposed on or adapted to the liturgy of the Prayer Book. The London and Surrey inventories make clear the dramatic internal reordering of the churches, the norm everywhere being whitewashed walls and the 'scripturing' of the interior, especially the rood loft, its images removed and the structure covered by canvas screens often made from sown-together altar cloths and hangings. At Wandsworth the parish paid £3 12s 6d to pull down the loft and 'set up the scriptures, that is to saye the creacion of the worlde, the comyng of our Saviour Christe, the Beatytudes, the ten commaundementes the xij articles of our belief and the Lordes Prayer the judgement of the world the Kinges Majesties armes'.[54] At Battersea, they bought 'half a hundred of gold foyle to peynte the name of jesus with'.[55] The altars had gone, and had been replaced by communion tables set east and west in the choir or in some cases the body of the church, surrounded on four sides by long 'forms' with kneelers, what the wardens of St Mary Rotherhithe called 'a framed table with settylles rounde abowte yt for the mynystryng of the holy communion', forming a supper-space emphatic in its Protestantism.[56] We encounter a few churches, mostly outside London, where the communion plate was of wood, or glass, or pewter. But such starkness was rare: we should not, for example, imagine these long tables (the covers for the table at St Benet Gracechurch Street were more than sixteen feet long)[57] as being puritanically draped in black and white. Instead, they were resplendent in multi-coloured covers and carpets adapted from restitched chasubles, tunicles and copes, canopies or altar-hangings.[58] At St George Botolph Lane they had 'a carpytt off pourple velvett and clothe of goldlde', and another of red and green damask 'to cast apon our Communyon Table', at St Martin Pomery ' a fayre table cloth of gold made of aultor Clothes for the communyon table', at St Benet Gracechurch Street 'three carpetes for the communion table, one of blew clothe of golde an other of red velvet with roses and staves and the thyrde of blew silke with lyons of golde'. In some churches these covers were of ascending degrees of splendour allocated for seasonal use. At St Martin Ludgate they had a carpet for the communion table of green bawdkyn for 'worke dayes', another of red velvet for ordinary Sundays, and one of crimson velvet 'for hye dayes'.[59] The 1549 Prayer-book had prescribed the wearing of copes at the communion, and most churches retained copes for this purpose: the persistence of older ways of employing vestments of appropriate colour or splendour is evident in the revealing list of five differently coloured copes retained at All Hallows Bread Street, which included one of black velvett 'to syngge the comunyon at the berriall of the ded'.[60]

Singing, including the singing of polyphony, was also a striking and perhaps unexpected feature of Edwardine worship, attested to in the inventories not merely in the psalters prescribed for every church, but by the many prick-song books for the new English services which occur there, and by references, like that at Bletchingley in Surrey when the communion table was being made, to additional expenses for 'fower seatts and dooble deskes for the syngyng men to syt in and to laie ther boockes'. There were also references to surplices for the choir.[61] Most churches also had richly coloured hearse cloths or palls adapted from old vestments. A few were what we should expect of a hearse-cloth, like the one at All Hallows the Great, of black velvet 'with dede mens heddes',[62] but most were richly coloured, and many retained Catholic emblems and decorations, like the 'herse cloth of gold called our Ladyes clothe' at All Hallows Bread Street, or the hearse cloth of tawny velvet 'the borders embothered wyth Jesus' at St Botolph Aldgate, or the hearse cloth of cloth-of-gold with borders of blue velvet 'with our Lady St John and Saynt George theron' at St Benet Gracechurch Street: they had another for children's funerals of blue damask 'with the five woundes theron'. Many churches had hearse-cloths in graded degrees of splendour, for children, adults and, humblest of all, 'for the power and for servantes'.[63]

The compilation of these inventories proceeded through the summer and autumn of 1552. Though the commissioners had no powers of confiscation, it was clear to everyone that a confiscation was imminent. In Essex, Hertfordshire, Norfolk and Cambridgeshire, but not, interestingly, in London, the Commissioners reserved most of the surviving goods 'for the King's use', but allocated, reserved or allowed to the wardens 'for the administration', a few items, generally a communion cup, a quantity of linen for the table, and often a cope or vestment, almost certainly to be made into a carpet rather than worn. Where there was more than a single chalice the church was usually given the smaller and less valuable, but where this was too small to serve as a communion cup for the expected number of communicants, another item of plate might be allowed, to help make a larger cup. At Lawling in Essex they had a tiny chalice of just four ounces, but had bought a large glass, worth 2d, to serve as a communion cup. The Commissioners reserved the chalice to the King's use, and left the glass for the administration of Holy Communion.[64]

In all this, the Commissioners were pursuing parishes ruthlessly for details of the disposal of every napkin and brass candlestick over the previous four years. But they themselves were being pursued. The Privy Council dispatched a series of letters urging the Commissioners on, rebuking them for weakness in accepting protestations of ignorance about the 1548–9 inventories, and in general demanding that they should be 'more diligent about their charge and to send their certificate with spede'.[65]

On 16 January 1553 the Council at last ordered the general confiscation of all church goods except the barest provision for worship according to the 1552 Prayer Book – a cup or chalice, an 'honest and comely' covering for the communion table, the necessary book and psalters, a surplice. Everything else, including any church stocks not needed for urgent repairs, was to be collected up. Linen and other cloth of little value was to be 'distributed and given freely to the poore people'. More valuable vestments and hangings were to be sold for the benefit of the Crown. The most precious tissue and cloth of gold vestments were to be parcelled up and sent to the Master of the Wardrobe, the plate to the master of the Jewel House. New Commissioners were named for the whole country to implement the confiscations. These orders caused consternation. The Commissioners for the Weald of Kent at first refused to proceed, and had to be coerced. Several Commissions stalled for months before proceeding to the sales, and in Kent, as the Commissioners later explained, 'the parishioners perseyving that the churche goodes shuld be taken from them did sell part of their plate and ornamentes of their churches awaye before we sate in commyssion and did bestowe the money therof upon reparacions of the churches'.[66]

But by now the parishes of England were accustomed to compliance to royal demands. There were no repetitions of the disturbances of 1536 or 1549, though in April the Privy Council ordered an investigation of the parson of a Reading church

for the wordes bespoken by hym to his neighbours, whereby he dyd comforte them to kepe a good porcion of theyr churche plate, saying that a tyme wolde come that they shold have nede of it, and the old ceremonies be restored to the churche againe.[67]

To minimize this sort of resistance, the Commissioners for Kent, and probably elsewhere, auctioned all but the most precious items locally – 'sold in grose to dyverse persons moost comenly to the parishioners of the parishes where the ornaments came from ...'.[68]

Sales limped on into June 1553. But Edward VIth died on 6 July, and his Catholic sister Mary – after the ten tense and uncertain days of the reign of the unfortunate Queen Jane – was duly proclaimed. Till her claim was securely established her attitude to the confiscations of church goods was uncertain and probably undecided. She urgently needed money, and on 17 July her Council wrote to the Mayor of Norwich ordering him to open (in the presence of witnesses) the chests containing the church goods still in the city, and to send the money and plate they contained to the Court.[69]

By the autumn, however, the Marian regime had decided on a policy of modified restoration. All the money from the confiscated church stocks would be retained by the Crown. Undefaced plate and precious vestments would be restored, all church goods whatever still in regional depots would go back to the churches of origin.[70] But all this was easier said than done. The crown had confiscated thousands of chalices and patens, cruets, crosses and censers. Much of this plate had been melted as soon as it arrived at the Jewel House, and the ownership of items that remained was often contested. One London observer noted on 5 September that 'there is no news but candlesticks, books, bells, censers, crosses and pipes'. Parishes needed to bustle to secure their goods before they disappeared ot were claimed by another parish. St Mary Woolnoth's wardens sent a fast boat up river to Westminster to collect their ornaments, and paid Arthur Stourton, the Royal Receiver, for searching 'divers parishes' for two of their confiscated tabernacles.[71] The Edwardine Commissioners for the Counties were now ordered to assist in the process of identifying the goods they had sent to the Wardrobe, and to deliver them to the parishes of origin.[72] A more Solomonesque solution was devised for the restoration of plate, so much of which had already been melted down. The Crown ordered the restoration of patens to the churches from which they came, but the few undefaced chalices which survived in the Jewel House were to be returned not to the parishes from which they had been taken, but instead distributed to 'the biggest parishe churches within the said countye'. Nineteen such chalices were redistributed in Somersetshire.[73]

All this was a recipe for strife, recrimination and frantic and sometimes vindictive litigation in the Ecclesiastical Courts. The Crown was squeezing the Edwardine Commissioners for reparation for their part in the confiscations, though interestingly they were allowed substantial expenses claims for their troubles. Parishes were pursuing wardens, incumbents and patrons who had embezzled or alienated goods, and the Marian church courts enforced reparation by the individuals concerned or their executors.[74] There were golden opportunities here for personal and collective vendettas: we have already noted the troubles of Gregory Newman at St Sepulchre's, London, but worms were turning all over England as the agents of the Edwardine reform found themselves denounced and pursued as profiteers and sacrilegious thieves.[75]

The accession of Elizabeth I in 1558 ensured that what the Edwardine spoliation had left undone would now be completed. The Royal Visitation of 1559 initiated a process of ritual suppression and iconoclasm which would continue for years. But not of confiscation. The 1552 inventories are the most concrete documentary trace of the most invasive central intervention in the English parishes ever, a dismantling of the machinery of medieval Christianity which left those parishes permanently changed. Though the whole episode at one level reveals the resourcefulness and resilience of the parish community, coping with, and occasionally outwitting, the Royal Supremacy, nothing would ever be the same. After such knowledge, what forgiveness?

For at least two centuries parishioners had worshipped in buildings which were a dense forest of symbolic reminders of the dead, and of their living kindred, in which ritual objects and the organization of sacred space located the parishioner within a community that articulated itself through time as well as through physical and social space. The parish church was a forum within which the parishioner's standing in the community could be perpetuated and recalled for his own benefit and, after his death, that of his living affinity. After 1553 that would be true only for the very wealthy, who could afford a monumental tomb.

In 1517 John Garrington, of Mondon in Essex, made a will leaving a set of vestments to match the church's best cope, and a cross-cloth for the parish's best cross. He left 6s 8d to each fraternity in the church and a flock of thirty ewes to maintain two tapers before the Sepulchre, the light before the Rood, the High Altar, the Trinity and Our Lady in the chancel, for 'as long as the world doth stande'. Garryngton's world, the world in which these perpetual dispositions made sense and had some hope of enduring, came to an end just thirty years later. In 1547 the wardens obediently put out the lights Garryngton had endowed in perpetuity, sold the candlesticks they had stood in for 21s, and disposed of the remaining wax for 6s. The parish told the 1552 Commissioners that they had paid some of this money to a plumber to mend the roof, and had used the rest to repair a window. Five parishioners signed the Mondon inventory, and duly received back from the Commissioners a single chalice, a cope, a vestment and an alb (to be turned into coverings for the communion table), all that remained of the formerly lavish furnishing of a richly endowed church. The five parishioners involved in the whole transaction included Henry Garryngton, Thomas' son.[76] Perhaps someone can tell me what we ought to make of that.

III

Two Cardinals

6

John Fisher and the spirit of his age

Catholic piety conventionally explains the scarlet robes that Cardinals wear as a sign of their readiness to shed their blood for the sake of the Christian gospel. This is an edifying thought: but as a matter of fact, in the whole millennium-long history of the cardinalate, only one member of the Sacred College has actually ever suffered martyrdom. That man was John Fisher. Bishop of Rochester from 1504, he was created Cardinal in May 1535, in the same consistory as the great Catholic reformer Gasparro Contarini, and his appointment was in part intended as papal confirmation of the universal recognition of Fisher as the greatest Catholic theologian in Europe, without any rival the most formidable and influential writer against Luther and the early Protestant Reformation. But the Pope mainly acted in the hope that Fisher's elevation would deter Henry VIII from killing him for his more localized opposition to the Royal Supremacy and Henry's divorce and remarriage.[1] This was a catastrophic, but perhaps a characteristic, Roman misreading of the local situation. Although the king's loves were notoriously fickle, his hatreds were implacable. By 1535 he had identified Fisher as an intolerable irritant, one of the most resolute and influential opponents of his religious and constitutional proceedings, and a man whose very integrity and reputation for unworldly holiness and deep learning made his offence all the harder to bear.[2]

So it is ironic that, far from mollifying or intimidating Henry, the Pope's well-meaning gesture hastened the bishop's trial and execution, along with that of his companion Thomas More. Fisher never received formal notification of his elevation, and he never wore the scarlet robes which Catholic tradition identified with the colour of spilled blood.

The road that led Fisher to the headman's block on Tower Hill, and a traitor's or a martyr's death, depending on your point of view, was an unexpected and circuitous one. Only with hindsight has it any hint of inevitability or destiny about it. Until the late 1520s Fisher's must have appeared, and indeed was, an uncomplicatedly successful establishment figure, the pet of the royal family, court preacher, royal confessor, favoured mouthpiece of English Catholic orthodoxy, a phenomenally successful fund-raiser for his beloved University of Cambridge, and the darling of the intellectual elite in, and far beyond, England. He was a classic case of the scholarship boy made good. He was the eldest of four children from a shop-keeping background, his father a moderately successful mercer in the Yorkshire wool-town of Beverley.[3] Fisher's father died when young John was only ten, but his mother remarried happily, more children came, and the bishop would remain all his life a strong family man. Despite a career entirely outside Yorkshire, at Cambridge University, and then as bishop of Rochester, he was to remain close both to his own surviving siblings and to his step-brothers and sisters. His half-sister, Elizabeth White, would settle as a Dominican nun at Dartford Priory in Fisher's own diocese of Rochester – one of his last and in some ways most revealing writings was a devotional tract composed for her while he was a prisoner in the Tower.[4] Fisher thought it his duty to support his family: he gave closed scholarships at his College of St John's to two nephews, loaned money to their families, devised family annuities chargeable to St John's, and his brother Robert became MP for Rochester and the bishop's steward.[5]

All this may sound as if there might be more than a faint whiff of sleaze about it, but in Tudor England a successful public man like Fisher would have been expected to look after his relatives in this way, and no contemporary, even his most hostile protestant opponents, thought worse of him for doing so (though he *was* criticized for filling his College with other Yorkshiremen, a much more serious matter). It was clearly a close and loving family, and his relatives reciprocated his loyalty when he fell from favour. Elizabeth would remain a staunchly committed nun even after the abolition of the religious life in England, and his younger brother Robert, and their half-brother Edward White, visited and supported him at some cost and danger to themselves in his last imprisonment.[6]

But until 1527, when he was in his late fifties, Fisher was unquestionably the darling of the Tudor establishment. He came up to Cambridge in the mid 1480s, and by 1491 had been elected to a Fellowship at Michaelhouse, in effect a combined chantry foundation and seminary for academic priests presided over by another Yorkshireman, Fisher's admired and beloved teacher William Melton.[7] Fellows of Michaelhouse had to be priests, and although Fisher was below the canonical age, he was ordained the same year. He evidently felt no call to the parochial ministry: given his university commitments he would certainly have been an absentee, serving any cure through a vicar. He was to hold a succession of livings as part of his revenues as a bishop, but he never served a parish. This was standard procedure for academic clergy, and was the normal way in which their studies were supported. Fisher never questioned the practice, and clearly considered that he was sufficiently discharging his pastoral ministry by devoting himself to the study of theology and the promotion of the interests of his university. By 1494 he was Senior Proctor, then the key administrative officer of the University.[8] The late fifteenth century was a time of academic expansion and experiment in both Oxford and Cambridge: the medieval residential system of hostels was giving way to the establishment of colleges, much more close-knit and controlling institutions, and Fisher was almost certainly involved in the arrangements for the establishment of Jesus College by the saintly bishop of Ely, John Alcock, also a Beverley man. Alcock suppressed the run-down convent of St Radegund in order to help fund his new college, and Fisher would follow suit with similar suppressions when, as the Queen Mother's executor, he came to establish St John's College. Reform was in the air, and though Fisher was an academic to his bones he was no ivory-tower dilettante. There was a pastoral edge to his academic engagement, for he thought that the purpose of theology was the service of the Church through the more adequate proclamation of the word of God, and he emphatically believed that the training of holy and learned secular priests as theologians and preachers was far more urgent a pastoral and religious priority than propping up slack, easy-going and over-funded monastic houses.

His opportunity to do something practical about this ideal of an educated and preaching secular priesthood came in 1495, when University business took him to Court and to a momentous meeting, which he recorded with his own hand along with a note of his expenses, in the University Grace Book – 'pransum eram apud dominam matrem Regis' – 'I had lunch with my lady the king's mother'.[9] The Lady Margaret Beaufort, three times married and now a widow religiously vowed to chastity, was a formidable old battle-axe, passionately committed to the well-being and ambitions of her successive families, and with her full share of Tudor imperiousness and even ruthlessness.[10] But she was also a devout Catholic, intent on making a good end. She collected clever young priests as a hobby and was evidently bowled over by the lean, learned and plain-spoken young Yorkshire don from Cambridge. When, some years later, she renewed her vow of chastity before him, she told him that she had been 'verily determined to owe my obedience' to him as her spiritual director from that very first meeting. In due course, she would communicate her admiration to her son the King, and Fisher would become, in a sense, the family chaplain. Such a royal fan-club was heady stuff for an uncourtly lad from the provinces, but Fisher took it in his stride, and friendship with Lady Margaret was all the easier because he seems to have recognized in her a genuinely holy woman. Long after her death he would tell a European readership that 'once she had adopted me as her confessor and her moral and spiritual guide, I learned more of what leads to an upright life from her rare virtues than I ever taught her in return'.[11] Since he regularly heard her confession, and since he was not much given to flattery, we have to take this testimony very seriously. When he came to preach her month's-mind sermon he produced what was in effect a portrait of a saint, and among his lost writings was said to be a biography of Lady Margaret, which may have been meant as the first step in a canonization process.[12]

However that may be, Lady Margaret was determined to attach Fisher to her entourage, and by 1498 she had winkled him out of Cambridge and established him within her household as chaplain and, by 1500, as her principal confessor. But Cambridge was never far from Fisher's thoughts, and he set about turning this royal connection to good advantage for his projects of University and clerical reform. A stream of benefactions now began to flow from the court to the University. In 1497 Lady Margaret took the first steps towards establishing chairs in Divinity at both Oxford and Cambridge, (they materialized formally in 1502, with Fisher as the first incumbent of the Cambridge chair) and a preachership at Cambridge alone – the duties of the preacher, who was to be a BD or DD and a fellow of a Cambridge College, were not only to preach within the University, but in London and five other places associated with Lady Margaret, including the Cambridgeshire town of Bassingbourne.[13]

But this was just a rehearsal for the major projects that Fisher had in mind. The Queen Mother had made conventional and lavish dispositions for the establishment of a chantry for her soul at Westminster. Fisher persuaded her that this was an unimaginative and wasteful use of her money, and that she should transfer her benefaction to the foundation of Colleges in Cambridge. First, in 1504, she endowed Christ's College, a lavish new seminary created out of a run-down chantry-cum-grammar-school, God's House, providing for a Master, twelve priest-Fellows, and forty-seven scholars (a total foundation of sixty).[14] Her second and final project, watched over at every turn by Fisher and completed by him with his own money and that of other donors after her death in 1509, was the establishment of St John's College. Institutionally similar to Christ's, it had the added dimension that at least a quarter of the Fellows were to be engaged in preaching in the parishes in English, and had an elaborate programme of humanistic study as part of the curriculum, offered to the University as well as to the College. There were to be lectures in secular disciplines like mathematics and medicine, but above all in theology and the biblical languages – Greek, Hebrew and, later, Syriac and Aramaic. With Fisher's close personal involvement and oversight St John's was to become the leading centre of humanism and of modern theological studies in early Tudor Cambridge, indeed in England.[15]

As all this suggests, Fisher never severed his connections with the University. Cambridge had instantly recognized that having their own man in the royal household was a golden opportunity, and they cashed in on it. In 1501, the year in which he took his DD, he was elected Vice-Chancellor and when, in 1504, Henry VII appointed him Bishop of Rochester, quite explicitly as an act of reparation for all the worldly and secular-minded men he had formerly appointed to bishoprics, the University elected Fisher as Chancellor. He would be re-elected annually till 1514, when he himself advised the University to hitch its wagon to the rising star of Wolsey. Wolsey declined the honour, however, at which point the University recognized reality and its own luck, and elected Fisher for life.[16] It was accepted practice to have as Chancellor a successful man of affairs who could drum up support, financial and political, for the University: Fisher had already proved himself a past master at this. And so as Bishop of Rochester he would oversee the establishment of Christ's and the creation of St John's. In 1511 he used his influence to bestow a different but equally momentous kind of benefaction on Cambridge by attracting as lecturer in Greek grammar the greatest humanist of the age, the Dutch biblical and patristic scholar Desiderius Erasmus.[17] Erasmus didn't in fact stay in Cambridge long, but this was designed as a flagship appointment, and his presence gave a tremendous impetus to the renewal of theology represented by renaissance study of the Bible and early Fathers in the original languages.

Fisher, himself trained in the traditional scholastic methods of medieval theology, was in the forefront of this patristic revival in England. He had been steadily accumulating what Erasmus considered to be the best private library in England, perhaps anywhere in Europe, and his shelves groaned with the latest editions of the Fathers, the newest biblical commentaries and lexicons. Like Thomas More he was an ardent supporter of Erasmus' controversial edition of the Greek New Testament, and in his forties learned Greek and the rudiments of Hebrew, so as to be able to draw on this modern scholarship and the theological treasure it unlocked. He never acquired much Hebrew, but he often quoted from Erasmus' New Testament in preference to the Vulgate, and he was to make effective use of his Greek in his writings against the protestant reformers.[18]

For Fisher this commitment to the humanist revival of letters or, as we would say, modern classical scholarship, presented no conflicts with his own formation as a scholastic theologian. In the often rancid theological conflicts of the time he instinctively, though not invariably, sided with the *avant garde* among humanist biblical scholars. But for Fisher this was a matter of making intelligent use of new resources, not of overturning old orthodoxies. Fisher himself saw no necessary conflict between the latest learning and the intellectual traditions of late medieval Catholicism. The statutes of St John's College provided for a Hebrew lecturer, but stipulated that if there were insufficient takers for the Hebrew course, the professor should instead give lectures on the theology of Duns Scotus, provided that the barbarous style in which Scotus and his commentators had written was recast in more elegant Latin.[19]

Fisher's appointment as Bishop of Rochester moved him from the University to the national stage. It was in fact the poorest bishopric in England, worth a mere £400 a year, and almost everyone appointed to it moved on after a few years to wealthier bishoprics. Fisher, however, would remain bishop there for thirty years, till his death. The earliest life of Fisher, written in Elizabeth's reign, says that he was offered other great sees, specifically Ely and Lincoln, but that he refused them, being content to be the husband of one wife, and to serve the poor in his poor diocese.[20] This may or may not be true. But in 1516 Fisher himself said that the Lady Margaret would have liked to have promoted him to a better bishopric, but 'when she saw her approaching death would frustrate this desire' she left him some money to enable him to pursue his educational objectives. I think myself that this suggests that Fisher would not have been averse to a move had it been offered, and that rings truer to me than the edifying notion of Fisher holding out against promotion. Fisher seems to have had no scruples about the normal career moves by which able clergy accumulated promotion and multiple ecclesiastical posts. Priests whom he loved and respected, like Melton, had shown him the way here. In his own appointments in the diocese he certainly showed no particular squeamishness about the financial side of clerical life, and lavished livings held in pluralism on his key officials. Nicholas Metcalf, Fisher's chaplain and first master of St John's, had a staggering accumulation of livings and dignities, several of them given to him by Fisher. So I doubt if Fisher would have thought it wrong to have moved to another see, especially had he been offered Ely, with its proximity to Cambridge. Fisher's *entrée* to the royal family was through the Lady Margaret: with her death in 1509, it may be that his moment in the spotlight of royal favour had passed. He was probably never entirely comfortable in Henry VIII's court, and his savage preaching about the vanity and empty show of the Field of the Cloth of Gold makes it clear how uncongenial he found the flashy ethos of the new king's reign.[21] We have it on

Cardinal Pole's testimony that in the 1520s Henry routinely bragged that in the Bishop of Rochester his kingdom possessed the brainiest, best-read and holiest bishop in Christendom, but it would be entirely in character for Henry to have trundled out this trophy bishop as required, and otherwise to have left him to read his Greek and Latin and say his prayers in the damp and down-at-heel seclusion of the bishop's palace at Rochester.[22] And of course, once the divorce got under way, Henry rapidly came to detest Fisher as a bitter enemy, the one and only bishop he could not bend to his will.

Certainly he was a model bishop, almost uniquely among Tudor bishops resident in his diocese for ninety percent of the year, and conducting personally most of the functions which other diocesans of the time usually farmed out to auxiliary bishops. Fisher conducted all his own visitations (a rarity among Tudor bishops) and almost all the ordinations in his diocese. We know of forty-two ordination ceremonies in Rochester during his episcopate, of which he carried out thirty-nine in person – compare that with Bishop Longland of Lincoln, who performed only three out of 103 ceremonies in person, or bishop Tunstal of Durham, who performed only two out of forty-two. He was an assiduous visitor of the poor in Rochester, and fed large numbers of the poor with food from his own table.[23] In 1531, at the height of his opposition to Henry VIII's divorce, an attempt was made to kill him by poisoning his soup. Always very abstemious, Fisher didn't eat the soup that day, but sent it to his servants and the poor at the door, several of whom died while all the rest sickened, thereby disclosing the murder attempt. Henry VIII would not have been sorry to see Fisher dead by this date, but he had a horror of poison and anyway couldn't be seen to condone murder, so he had Fisher's hapless cook boiled alive.[24]

Fisher took a close interest in the standards of clergy in the diocese, appointing, as one might expect, a higher proportion of graduates than did other bishops, and taking a close interest in the religious houses in his diocese. He took a close interest also in heresy, of which he had a horror, but, interestingly, no-one was burned in the Rochester diocese for the entire period of his episcopate.

Being a bishop, and a bishop in the coastal region of Kent, involved Fisher in State responsibilities – welcoming and offering hospitality to ambassadors on their way to or from the continent, entertaining foreign dignitaries and members of the royal family, entertaining the effective day-to-day ruler of England, Cardinal Wolsey. In June 1522 Fisher was host to Henry VIII and the Emperor Charles V, on their way to Gravesend. Fisher hated this aspect of episcopal responsibility: attacking the worldliness of the clergy in a speech in synod in 1519 – he probably had Wolsey especially in his sights – he declared that

> sundry times when I have settled and fully bent myself to the care of my flock committed unto me, to visit my diocese, to govern my Church and to answer the enemies of Christ, straightways hath come a messenger for one cause or other sent from higher authority by whom I have been called to other business and so left off my former purpose. And thus by tossing and going this way and that way, time hath passed and in the meanwhile nothing done but attending after triumphs, receiving of ambassadors, haunting of princes' courts and such like: whereby great expenses rise that might better be spent many other ways.[25]

But it was the Reformation crisis which made Fisher a European rather than merely a national figure. His first publications had been sermons. His magnificent series on the penitential psalms, preached before the Lady Margaret, published in 1508 by Wynkyn de Worde, became an instant best-seller, running through seven editions in Fisher's own lifetime. He was the obvious choice to preach the sermons at the funeral of Henry VII and the month's mind of Margaret Beaufort in 1509. All this established him as the best English preacher of his age, but his real fame came in his fifties and it was as a polemical theologian that the range and depth of his learning fully showed itself. His first polemical writings were directed not against a Protestant, but against the French Humanist scholar Jaques Lefèvre d'Etaples, who published in 1518 a book arguing that St Mary Magdalene, one of the most popular saints of the Middle Ages, was not in fact a real person but a composite, created by confusing three different figures in the Gospels, the sinful woman who wiped Jesus feet with her hair, Mary of Bethany the sister of Lazarus and Martha, and the real Mary Magdalene, a former demoniac who was the first witness of the Resurrection.[26] Scholars now would unanimously agree with Lefèvre, but Fisher feared that this demythologizing would erode popular piety – the Magdalene was a powerful symbol of penitence and the sacrament of penance – and he also thought that it challenged the ordinary magisterium of the Church, which had sanctioned devotion to the saint. So in 1519 he published a harsh and powerful critique of Lefèvre's thesis as heresy, with the title *De Unica Magdalena*. A flurry of pamphlets ensued, much to the distress of humanists like Erasmus, who felt not only that poor old Lefèvre was undeservedly getting the rough edge of Fisher's tongue, but that the whole cause of modern scholarship in theological matters was being undermined by this squabble: given Fisher's proven commitment to humanist scholarship, Erasmus believed they should be singing from the same hymn-sheet.

The Magdalene debate turned out to be just a dress rehearsal for Fisher's real work as a polemical theologian. From 1521 he would be engaged in a far more momentous debate, a struggle for the soul of Catholic Christianity. As the Magdalene controversy had shown, Fisher had a horror of heresy, but his writings against the Reformation were the result of royal policy, not his own initiative. Henry VIII had distinguished himself as the first royal opponent of Luther: his *Assertio Septem Sacramentorum* of 1521, at least partly his own work, was a milestone publication in the Catholic response to Luther's teaching, and it earned Henry the title *Defender of the Faith* from a grateful Pope Leo X. Henry now consolidated his role as champion of the church by mobilizing the theological faculties at Oxford and Cambridge against Luther. Over the next seven or eight years a stream of officially backed publications, sermons and lectures by the nation's intellectual elite marked Henrician England out as the most self-consciously Catholic country in Europe.[27] This stream of court-sponsored polemic was inaugurated at a ceremony in St Paul's churchyard in London in May 1521, presided over by Cardinal Wolsey (the King had a bad cold) at which the papal bull against Luther, *Exsurge Domine*, was promulgated, and Luther's books were burned by the barrowload. Inevitably, as England's premier theologian and best preacher, Fisher preached at this ceremony, and his sermon was subsequently published in Latin and in English.[28] Aimed at a popular audience, it was important as the first Catholic publication to identify the core of Luther's teaching as threefold – the doctrine of justification by faith alone, the appeal to Scripture alone, and the rejection of papal authority. The sermon was the first of a stream of increasingly substantial works by Fisher – the *Convulsio Calumniarum*, a brilliant and stupendously learned defence of the tradition of Peter's ministry and martyrdom in Rome, the 200,000 word *Assertionis Lutheranae Confutatio*, attacking Luther's defence of the propositions condemned by the Bull *Exsurge*, the *Defensio Regiae Assertionis*, supporting Henry against Luther's counterattacks, the *Sacri Sacerdotii Defensio* against Luther's insistence on the priesthood of all believers and denial of the sacramental priesthood in *De Abroganda Missa Privata* and, finally, what is probably his theological masterpiece, *De Veritate Corporis and Sanguinis Christi in Eucharistia*, directed against the German-born Swiss reformer Oecolampadius.[29]

The impact of all these works was immediate and international. The vast *Confutatio* is a difficult work to read now because of its repetitiousness and relentless handling of minutiae. But it was and remained the most encyclopaedic and comprehensive Catholic response to Luther, and was used as a quarry by every major Catholic theologian from Eck, Erasmus and Cochlaeus, to Robert Bellarmine at the end of the century. Cochlaeus translated several sections of it into German, and had them published separately as pamphlets. The Latin was endlessly reprinted – the *Confutatio* ran through twenty editions in the course of the sixteenth century, more than any other work of Catholic theology, and Fisher's handling of Luther on Justification was enormously influential in the debates at the Council of Trent. The *De Veritate*, though it had fewer reprints, was almost equally influential, quoted and cribbed from by every Catholic who wrote or lectured on the Eucharist from Melchior Cano to Juan Suarez. Most importantly, it was the principal source for the theological discussions of the Eucharist at the Council of Trent, and underlay the Council's teaching on the subject. Though Fisher employed his training as a scholastic theologian in it, the *De Veritate* was distinctive in its profound knowledge of the Fathers, and in its sweeping away a good deal of contorted and misconceived late-medieval argument by an insistence on the identity of the sacrifice of the Mass with the one perfect offering of Calvary.[30]

By 1525, therefore, Fisher was on his way to becoming the most famous Catholic theologian in Europe, and stood correspondingly high in Henry VIII's favour. It is tempting to think that there had never been much love lost between Henry and Fisher, and as characters they were very obviously chalk and cheese, Fisher a man of self abnegation, prayer, deep reflection, Henry a seething cauldron of egoism and passion, who weighed every issue exclusively in terms of its relationship to himself. And certainly King and Bishop had had their difficulties – Fisher had to sweat blood to prise the Lady Margaret's bequests to Cambridge out of Henry, and he had bested the King in 1523 by opposing a clerical grant to Henry for a war in France.[31] But in the early 1520s Henry was prepared to forget all that, because Fisher the famous was a tremendous feather in Henry's cap, as it were an Olympic gold medalist in theology and catholic orthodoxy for Henry's England. And so the king displayed his regard for the Bishop of Rochester by publicly walking with one great bear-like arm around the old man's neck, for Henry always the ultimate accolade, which was granted also, and for much the same reasons, to Thomas More. Several of Fisher's books appeared with the Royal Arms on the title-page, a declaration that he was, in effect, theologian by appointment to the Establishment. Many years later, Cardinal Pole recalled this period and how, as a young man recently returned from his theological studies in France and Italy, he was quizzed by his cousin King Henry about Fisher's European celebrity.

> Yt was almost the first question he asked me, whether yn all the unyver-sities I had byn, and yn all the cities and places where lerned men and good men might be best knowen, I had founde such a lerned man as the same Bysshope of Rochestre.[32]

All this, however, was to unravel dramatically and, for Fisher, fatally, because of the King's marital problems. The divorce question is much too complicated to go into here in any detail, but the essentials are these. Henry's Queen, Catherine of Aragon, had been first married for less than five months to Henry's elder brother Arthur: both bride and groom were teenagers. On Arthur's death, in order to maintain the diplomatic link with Spain, a papal dispensation for Henry to marry his brother's widow had been granted. A complicating factor was that Catherine later swore, both within and outside the seal of the confessional, that she had slept no more than seven nights in Arthur's bed, and that the marriage had remained unconsummated and was therefore null. I think it is quite inconceivable that Catherine was lying about this, but it was a hard matter to be certain about, and naturally supporters of the King then, like some recent historians of the divorce, chose not to believe her. Though a son was born to the new marriage in 1511, he died within a month, and all except one of Henry and Catherine's children, their daughter, Mary, miscarried or died in infancy.

By 1524, Henry was desperate for a male heir, and in any case tiring of his ageing and never very good-looking wife. He determined to get rid of her, and his court clergy came up with a biblical text to ease his conscience, Leviticus 20.21: 'He that marrieth his brother's wife doth an unlawful thing: he hath uncovered his brother's nakedness. They shall be without children'. Ignoring the fact that Catherine was his brother's widow, not his wife, and that they *had* a child, Mary, Henry took this text to mean that the marriage with Catherine was not only cursed, but null and void, the Pope not having the authority to dispense from a divine prohibition. Unfortunately for him, there was a rival text in Deuteronomy 25.2 stipulating that if a man's brother died childless, the surviving brother *should* marry the widow and have children which could be counted as children of the first marriage. This so called Levirate law seemed to opponents of the divorce, including Fisher, to blow the King's scruples clean out of the water.

Few of Henry's bishops were entirely comfortable with his desire to shed the Queen and marry the pushy and crypto-protestant court lady, Anne Boleyn, but Henry was both terrifying and very, very dangerous when opposed, and popes had been pliable about royal marital problems in the past. So most of the the clerical establishment, from Cardinal Wolsey to the Archbishop of Canterbury, Archbishop Warham, swallowed their misgivings and set about moving heaven and earth to get an annulment from Rome.[33]

From the start, Fisher absolutely opposed these proceedings. Henry himself had broached the matter with him as a case of tender conscience in 1527, protesting that he loved the queen and wanted nothing better than to stay with her, but was fearful he was living in sin: Fisher drily told him that he could rest easy, his marriage was perfectly valid. Fisher's impatience was obvious. In the first place, he thought Henry's scruples at best neurotic, at worst a bluff, and he inclined to the bluff hypothesis. As he wrote to one of the Queen's supporters:

Kings usually think that they are permitted to do whatever pleases them, because of the magnitude of their power. Therefore it is good for those

kings, in my opinion, to submit themselves to the decrees of the church …
lest perhaps they kick over the traces and do what they like, so long as they
can weave together some appearance and pretence of right.[34]

The interpretation of scripture was of course Fisher's specialism, and he
had no patience with Henry's conveniently fundamentalist reliance on the
Leviticus text. But above all, he saw that the issue turned in the end on the
question of papal authority. The marriage with Catherine had been validated
by a papal bull. If the marriage was null, the Pope's authority was null. Long
before there was any question of a separation from Rome, Fisher saw that
the divorce question raised the same issues of Church authority over which
he had been battling with the Lutherans. He began a series of books – we
would call them pamphlets – to prove the validity of the marriage: Fisher
himself lost count but thought there had been eight in all. They could not, of
course, be published in England: some were smuggled abroad via the Spanish
ambassador and published there; others circulated in manuscript; a couple
were sent to Rome to stiffen resistance in the Curia.[35]

Fisher's opposition was a very serious matter for Henry. Here was the best
theologian and one of the holiest bishops in Europe pouring out arguments
against the divorce. Fisher's reputation for sanctity as well as learning, over
which Henry had gloated when it had served as a trophy for the Tudor
monarchy, was now a standing reproach. Matters came to a head in June
1529, when a legatine Court convened by Wolsey and Cardinal Campeggio,
sent from Rome for the purpose, met to hear the case at Blackfriars in
London. It was a fiasco, partly because the Queen refused to recognize the
Court, knowing she couldn't get a fair hearing in Henry's England. And from
the word go Fisher, acting as one of the Queen's official advisers, made his
position painfully clear. In the preliminaries, Archbishop Warham declared
that all the bishops had consented to the case being referred to Rome. Fisher
stopped the proceedings to insist that he had never consented to any such
thing, since he considered there was no case to answer. An unseemly wrangle
ensued, in which the King himself joined. Fisher held his ground even against
Henry, however, and it was clear that there had been an attempt to cover up
the fact that Fisher rejected the divorce proceedings, and perhaps even to

forge his signature. At last the King turned away angrily declaring 'Well well it shall make no matter: we will not stand with you in argument, for you are but one man'.[36] But everyone knew that Fisher's principled and now very public resistance amounted to much more than one opinion among many. Henry's rage knew no bounds when Fisher made a speech next day declaring that he was prepared to lay down his life for the marriage, just as John the Baptist had laid down his life over the marriage of Herodias. The clear implication here, lost on nobody and certainly not on the king, was that Henry was Herod to Fisher's John the Baptist: from now on Fisher was a marked man.[37]

Fisher's stand against the King at Blackfriars revealed an aspect of the man hidden till now. However skilful he had been at charming money out of the wealthy and powerful for good causes, when a point of principle was at stake he threw tact and calculation to the winds. In contrast to Thomas More, whose opposition to the divorce and the schism which followed from it was wrapped to the very end in a lawyer's caution, Fisher increasingly appeared almost to court danger. In order to put pressure on the Pope, Henry now turned on the English Church, and the Reformation Parliament which met that same year introduced a series of bills attacking the clergy and eroding the revenues and liberties of the Church. Fisher was appalled, and in the House of Lords denounced these measures – 'all is to the destruction of the Church'. He declared the new spirit of anticlericalism to be the fruit of apostasy – 'Now with the Commons is nothing but down with the Church, and all this meseemeth for lack of faith only'. This explosive accusation was seen as an attack on the liberties of Parliament, and the Duke of Norfolk angrily told Fisher 'the greatest clerks be not always the wisest men'. The Commons lodged a formal complaint with the King who forced Fisher into a humiliating climb-down.[38]

From now on every move Fisher made was watched and he was the target of a mixed policy of wheedling and bullying, besieged by former friends and colleagues like the bishops of London, Lincoln and Durham, urging him to be sensible and sign up for the Royal Supremacy, and the victim of dire and direct threats from Cromwell. When the anti-clerical legislation was passed in 1531 he and two allies, Bishops Clerk of Bath and Wells, appealed to the Pope and were briefly imprisoned. Someone tried to poison him that same year and, at one point, the tiles above his head were shattered by a bullet as he sat in his library reading. He believed, probably correctly, that the shot had been fired from the Boleyn house, directly across the river from his palace in Hackney marshes.[39] He compounded his danger by taking a keen interest in the prophecies of a visionary nun, Elizabeth Barton, the so-called Holy Maid of Kent, who claimed to have had a series of divine revelations that if Henry persisted with the divorce proceedings, he would die or be deposed. The nun and a group of her clerical supporters, several of them protégés of Fisher, ended on the scaffold, executed for treason, and Fisher himself was arrested in 1534 and found guilty of misprision of treason, imprisoned, and heavily fined.[40] In contrast with More, who kept Elizabeth Barton at arm's length, there is no doubt that Fisher believed in the nun, and he even sorted out an old score by checking with her heavenly informants that there was indeed only one Mary Magdalene and not three, as he had maintained against Lefèvre. His support for the nun was symptomatic of his connections to a wide network of those opposed to the King's religious policies. Rochester clergy were active in resisting royal measures in Convocation, his protégés at St John's led resistance to the Reformation in the University, and Fisher worked actively but in vain to stiffen resistance among his brother bishops. As he told the former colleagues who pressed him in the Tower to accept the Royal Supremacy, 'The fort is betrayed even of them that should have defended it'.[41]

His growing conviction that the English religious and political establishment would offer no effective resistance to Henry led Fisher to treason. In 1533 he sent a secret message to the Emperor, Charles V, urging him and the Pope to intervene. He was appealing here to the belief that the Emperor was God's and the Pope's policeman, charged with deposing or disciplining Christian kings who broke their coronation oath by attacking the Church. A papal and imperial Crusade against England was not a very realistic scenario, and had he ever known of it, it would have provided Henry with ample justification for killing Fisher.[42]

In the event, however, Fisher was executed for his refusal of the Royal Supremacy. Through 1534 he languished in the Tower, kept in darkness and damp, in the hope that he would either die or cave in, as all his brother bishops had caved in. Even at this late stage, Henry desperately needed Fisher's surrender. Religious conservatives everywhere would have been shaken if he had capitulated, and many would have followed suit. Archbishop Cranmer characteristically suggested a subterfuge. He thought that if Fisher and More could be persuaded to sign the act of succession, which simply accepted the children of Anne Boleyn as heirs to the throne, this might then be presented as if they had also signed the preamble to the Act, which affirmed that the King was Supreme Head of the Church. But Henry was determined that Fisher should surrender absolutely, with maximum publicity, or die, and the award of the Red Hat in May 1535 was the last straw. The bishop was formally tried on 17 June, and beheaded on 22 June. His head was boiled and placed on a spike on Tower Bridge. Disconcerting rumours spread that instead of decaying it got more fresh and lifelike as the days pass. But in any case it was not allowed to remain there long. Thomas More, the other great symbolic dissident, followed Fisher to the block on 6 July 6, and the same spike was used to impale his head: Fisher's head was tossed casually into the Thames.

That remains a powerful symbolic act, because Fisher has always suffered from his pairing with More, has always been ousted in public attention by the more genial and witty figure of his companion in martyrdom. We see the bishop through the eyes of Holbein, in that vivid but daunting drawing in which Fisher's gaunt and bony face gazes steadily beyond this world, towards the heaven he had set his heart on. The portrait is all of a piece with the earliest biography's description of the emaciated old man stripped for execution.

> There was to be seen a long, lean, and slender body, having on it little other substance than skin and bones, in so much as most part of the beholders marvelled much to see a living man so far consumed, for he seemed a very image of death, and as it were death in a man's shape using a man's voice.[43]

That was Fisher, old, sick and after months of harsh imprisonment. The living man, though, was something different. If he was a saint, he was no plaster saint, no 'image of death', but a lover of community, a cheerful host, insistent on keeping a good table, though he ate very little himself. He was a man of the library, but not a solitary. When work was finished and he had no guests to entertain or business to transact, he liked to sit chatting with his chaplains, a continuation perhaps of the companionship of Hall and High Table among his colleagues in Cambridge. He had a sense of humour, even if it was sardonic and biting in the Yorkshire manner. He was fond of hare-coursing, and kept greyhounds, he loved books and accumulated one of the best libraries in Europe. And he had charm. He spent a life-time among the great and the not so good, admired by everyone, a successful man at the top of his chosen tree. His martyrdom in the cause of the unity of Catholic Christendom has led to his being seen as a conservative figure, backward-looking, a man of the Middle Ages. But he was conservative only in the sense that More was conservative, recognizing in the unity of Christendom and its inherited faith a protection against the new and, as he thought, idolatrous claims of the early-modern state, the claim of secular authority to sovereignty even over men's consciences.

Fisher helped to define the Tudor age. He set his stamp decisively on much that was best in the development of the modern university, he enthusiastically embraced the latest in learning and in literature, provided it did not contradict the faith of the Church. He was a man at ease with power and the powerful, but miraculously uncorrupted by either. From the obscurity of the poorest bishopric in England he established himself as the most famous bishop in Christendom, and as Catholic Christendom's best thinker. It was his ill fortune that he found himself in his maturity confronted by a religious revolution which could not be argued away, and at the mercy of a king whose principal rule of conduct was the satisfaction of his own appetites and will. He had many friends among the bishops, some of them close – humanists like Stokesley of London or (especially) Tunstall of Durham, who had worked side by side with him on the research for his defence of the Eucharist.[44] But one by one, they parted company from him, succumbing to the threats of their implacable royal master, renouncing the Pope and, with the Pope, the unity of Catholic Europe. That growing isolation was the measure of Fisher's courage, a measure by which all of his brother bishops proved so notably lacking. Maybe absolute integrity is destined always to fall foul of absolute power.

7

The spirituality of John Fisher

John Fisher's place in the history of English spirituality, like his place in the history of English humanism, is obscured by problems of definition. So austere a figure challenges expectations derived from the identification of the cause of the return *ad fontes* with Erasmus. Historians have therefore been tempted to describe his relation to the movements of the early sixteenth century in terms of contrast, rather than participation. Whether the polarities employed are those of 'medieval' as opposed to 'Renaissance', or 'unreformed' as opposed to 'reformed', the temptation is to opt for a single all-purpose descriptive category. C. S. Lewis, in what remains the most helpful brief account of Fisher as a religious writer, succumbs to temptation on both scores. Fisher, he claimed, 'is almost a purely medieval writer, though scraps of what may be classified as humanistic learning appear in his work', but 'he matters less as a literary figure than as a convenient representative of the religion in possession at the very beginning of the English Reformation. He was a bishop and died for his faith: in him we ought to find what men like Tyndale were attacking.'[1] For a mere historian to quarrel with Lewis about a matter of literature might seem as foolhardy as the attempt to anatomize the spirituality of a saint. Yet one may well feel that in Lewis's easy contrasts something has been omitted. It does not seem very useful to characterize any one figure as 'representative' of so complex a reality as late-medieval English religion. To do so in Fisher's case in particular is to risk missing what is distinctive about his use of the resources of the religious tradition he inherited. If it is true that he can be understood only in the context of late-medieval piety, he neither appropriated nor deployed with equal readiness every element in that background. His choice of genre and theme, and his distinctive range of imagery reveal a sensibility resolutely his own even when apparently at its most conventional. We must not be mesmerized into thinking that in Tudor England the devil had all the best tunes, that only the revolutionaries possessed individuality.

Nor should we willingly accept Lewis's stark contrast between 'medieval' and 'humanist'. It is certainly true that neither Fisher's preaching style, his choice of themes, nor his use of scripture show much overt sign of humanistic innovation; every devotional piece he wrote can be paralleled in earlier writers. But both in theme and treatment many of them can be paralleled among his younger contemporaries also, and in many later writers too. Separating the 'medieval' from the 'Renaissance' elements in the works of Thomas More presents similar problems and has become a sort of parlour-game for historians and literary critics, without greatly advancing our understanding of him. There is nothing in the religion of Fisher that could not be found in Colet or More: since any definition of English humanism that excluded them would be highly problematic, we should beware of excluding Fisher from the charmed circle on religious grounds, without closer scrutiny. Humanist and medieval religious ideals are not so readily or so starkly contrasted as has been assumed.[2] Moreover, much that seems most medieval in Fisher's work can be paralleled in the devotional literature, both Catholic and Protestant, of Elizabethan and Jacobean England. If one concedes that, by and large, his attitudes and convictions found a more natural and congenial home in the Counter-Reformation than within Protestantism, that should not obscure the fact that Fisher's works look forward as well as back. It makes almost as much sense to read them in the light of the Baroque as of the Gothic imagination.

It is easy to see why Lewis opted for Fisher as a figure representative of late-medieval Catholicism, which Lewis characterized primarily in terms of its world-denying and ascetic dimensions.[3] It is, certainly, as an ascetic that Fisher is most readily approached, whether in the gaunt and troubled Holbein sketch at Windsor, or the 'very mortified and meagre personage with a crucifix before him' in the portrait at St John's, or in contemporary accounts of 'his face hands and all his bodye, so bare of flesh as is almost incredible, which came the rather (as may be thought) by the great abstinance and pennance he used upon himself many yeres together, even from his youth'. When he was stripped for execution he seemed 'a verie ymage of death and as it were death in mans shape using a mans voice'.[4] Fisher himself cultivated the thought and the image of death: when he said mass 'he always accustomed to set upon one ende of the altar a dead man's scull, which was also set before him at his table as he dyned or supped'.[5] Mortification was the keynote of his devotional life. When the king's commissioners came to make an inventory of his goods at Rochester after his arrest in April 1534, they found in his private oratory a locked coffer, in which they assumed valuables were stored. On forcing it open, however, they found a 'a shirte of heare, and two or three whips, wherewith he used full often to punish himself'.[6] None of this is surprising, and represents the conventional stuff of early Tudor devotion. We are all familiar with Thomas More's similar austerities, with the help of which an elaborate hypothesis of sexual repression has been constructed. Lewis found the literary expression of this 'morbid' sensibility in Fisher's utterances on the body as 'stincking flesh', 'dirtie corruption', 'a sachell full of dunge', and in his undiscriminating disparagement of sex. Fisher believed that the 'flesshe that before hath ben polluted by the foule and fylthy pleasure of the body, feleth moch more unclene mocyons than dooth the fleshe which alwaye hathe ben clene and chaste'.[7] And perhaps most revealingly of all, Lewis argued, the essentially negative character of the religious tradition represented by Fisher appeared in the horrifyingly vivid evocations of purgatory scattered through his works, a purgatory conceived not as a place of hope and renewal, as in Dante, but as a torture-house designed to exact retribution from a sinful humanity. It is no wonder that given such a vision of mankind and its destiny the reformers 'felt that they were escaping from a prison', a theme taken up from Lewis by subsequent historians.[8]

All this, however, is to start at the wrong point, to isolate as distinctive of 'medieval' religion in general, and of Fisher's spirituality in particular, features which assume a false prominence because of their distance from twenty-first-century sensibility. Fisher did have an almost wholly negative view of sexuality, a view he shared, for example, with Colet and probably most other early Tudor churchmen. In Colet's case, however, it is difficult to decide whether his repudiation of the body is part of a common medieval inheritance, derived from Augustine, or from his neo-platonic background and part, therefore, of a widespread, though often ignored, tendency in Renaissance anthropology to devalue the physical.[9] Moreover, this loathing of the body and its functions is not peculiar either to Catholicism or to the Middle Ages. It is vigorously present among the reformers. John Bradford's immensely influential *Meditations,* a standard text among the Protestant godly well into the seventeenth century, denounced the body as

> but a prison, wherein the soul is kept ... foul and dark, disquiet, frail and filled up with much vermin and venomous vipers, (I mean it concerning our affections), standing in an air most unwholesome, and prospect most loathsome, if a man consider the excrements of it by the eyes, nose, mouth, ears, hands, feet, and all the other parts.

And so 'no Bocardo, no little-ease, no dungeon ... no sink, no pit' is so evil a prison for the body 'as the body is for and of the soul'.[10] Bradford, as much as Fisher, believed that 'sensual gratification' left behind 'a certain loathsomeness and fulness', even when come by 'lawfully' within marriage.'[11] If we are to consign Fisher to some pejorative 'medievalism' on the score of his views about sex and the body, we shall be obliged to send along with him a high proportion of religious writers on the subject before the twentieth century. In any case, if we wish properly to understand both the extent and the limits of Fisher's 'medievalism', we will do well not to isolate its more obviously negative aspects, but to consider his relation to the whole religious inheritance of early Tudor England.

The first thing to be said about Fisher's relation to his religious inheritance is that he was very much at home in it. The pattern of his piety was, in the very strictest sense of the term, conventional. Christ and his cross stand at the heart of Fisher's perception of God and the world, but they never beckon, as they do in Erasmus, away from external observance and the religion of the masses. In sacraments and sacramentals, for Fisher, we touch the reality of Calvary. It is by

theffusion of the moost precious blode of cryst Ihesu upon a crosse plente-
ously for all synners, wherby satysfaccyon was made to god the fader for
the synnes of all people, whiche receyve the vertue of this precyous blode
by the sacramentes of crystes churche & by it made ryghtwyse.

So in the sacrament of penance the sinner

gooth awaye ryghtwyse, not by his owne ryghtwysnes, but by the ryghtwysnes of cryst Ihesu.

The Church has nothing of its own to give, its ceremonies have no power
in their own right, but 'there is a prevy & hyd vertue gyven unto them by
the meryte of the passyon of Ihesu cryst & of his precyous blode'. So great
is the merit of Christ in the sacraments that 'as ofte as ony creature shall use
& receyve ony of them, so oft it is to be byleved they are sprencied with the
droppes of the same moost holy blode, whose vertue perseth unto the soule,
and maketh it clene from al synne'.[12]
It is in the context of this absolute confidence in the sacramental efficacy of
the work of Christ that Fisher's often formidable utterances on good works, his
continual insistence on the need for penance, and his evocation of the horrors
of purgatory should be seen. He says most about purgatory in the sermons
on the Seven Penitential Psalms, which he preached as chaplain to the Lady
Margaret Beaufort in 1504. These sermons represent an extended meditation
on the sacrament of penance in its three parts – contrition, confession and satisfaction. It would be easy to compile from them a selection of passages to bear
out the suggestion that Fisher's scheme of salvation was indeed a prison house
for the spirit, that his God is one determined to exact from a guilty mankind
the last measure of retribution: 'For truly over our hedes hangeth a swerde ever
movynge & redy by the power of God, whose stroke whan it shall come shall be
so moche more grevous that we so longe by our grete & manyfolde unkyndnes
have caused almyghty god and provoked hym to more dyspleasure.'[13] But such
a picture would be a parody of Fisher's teaching as a whole. The God of the
Penitential Psalms is for Fisher above all a God of mercy and compassion,
bearing with human failures, ever ready to respond to human repentance: 'The
mercy and goodnes of almyghty god shewed upon synners is mervayllous grete

whiche the more that they call unto theyr owne mynde and expresse theyr owne trespasses, so moch the more he forgeteth & putteth them out of his mynde ...'

For Fisher the sacrament of penance is not the expression of an essentially fearful and works-bound theology, but the form the divine graciousness takes in liberating us from the need to endure the consequences of our own sins: 'By the vertue of contrycyon our synnes be forgyven, by confessyon they be forgoten, but by sattisfaccyon they be so clene done away that no synne or token remayneth in any condycyon of them, but as clene as ever we were.'[14] Certainly he emphasizes effort, and the need to do good works. Christ bought our salvation on the cross, 'but know this for a certayn, he nether bought this inherytaunce for the, ne made promyse thereof, but with condicyon ... The condition is the performance of good works.'[15] Yet good works are themselves the gift of God, the miraculous fruit of God's life-giving grace:

> From the eyen of almyghty god whiche may be called his grace shyneth forth a mervaylous bryghtnes lyke as the beme that cometh forth from the sonne. And that lyght of grace stereth and setteth forwarde the soules to brynge forth the fruyte of good werkes. Even as the lyght of the sonne causeth herbes to growe & trees to brynge forth fruyte ... O mervaylous mekeness of almyghty god shewed unto synners when they fle unto hym, whiche is so redy to comforte and graunte them helpe.

Every stage of the process of repentance is due solely to the grace of God:

> Thou arte sorry for thy synne, it is a gyfte of almyghte god. Thou makest knowledge of thy synne wepynge and wayling for it, it is a gyft of almyghte god. Thou are besy in good werkes to do satysifaccyon, which also is a gyfte of almyghte god.

If his vision of purgatory is indeed that of a prison, it is sin, not God, who is the gaoler – 'who that is in thraldome of synne is in full shrewd custody'. Yet in the last resort the escape route is not through human striving, but through a humbling of oneself to the mercy of God, as those prisoners do who 'sometyme undermyne the walles and crepe under them out at a strayte and narrow hole ... and soo come unto the lyberte of grace'.[16] The grim evocations of purgatory are designed to stir an unspiritual people, content with lipservice to the notion of repentance, to avail themselves of this 'lyberte of grace', the divine mercy which would spare them the avoidable consequences of sin. 'Many there be that wayle & be contryte & also confesse theyr synnes, but scant one amonge a thousande can be found that dooth dewe satysfaccyon.' And, since satisfaction is the principal evidence of sincere and lasting repentance, it is 'to be drad leest any prevy gyle or decyte remayne in the soule, that is to saye it is not very contrite and truly confessed'.[17]

The effects of such penance in Fisher himself present at first sight a daunting picture of austerity and gloom. That, however, was not his own perception of the matter. Since true penitence and due satisfaction were gifts of God, they were a source of joy: 'the penytent hath more swete Ioye & gladnes inwardly in his soule than any other creature lyvynge may have in all the pleasures of this worlde. For in the Church we live under a newe lawe, not a lawe of fere & drede but a lawe of grace and mercy'. The Christian life was to be lived as a balance of 'hope with drede and drede with hope' so that we may neither 'truste in god without his fere, nor drede hym without hope', neither 'lyfte up by presumpcyon nor caste downe by dyspayre'.[18] That balance is to be found even in unpromising places. Throughout his writings Fisher emphasizes the value of penitential tears, real, salt and heart-rending, and he himself was accustomed to weep when he said mass. Here again he is wholly at one with his contemporaries, for the Sarum Missal, like the Roman Missal till recent times, contained a votive mass for the gift of penitential tears. However, for Fisher, such tears were a sign not of mankind's fearful moral activism, the attempt to placate an angry God, but evidence of the recreative work of the Spirit within us:

> The spiryte of god shall gyve so grete infusyon of grace to them that be penytent that the waters, that is to saye theyr wepynge teres shall flowe & be haboundaunte. Upon these waters the spyryte of almyghty god may flye and goo swyftely, which was fygured in the begynnynge of scripture, by the sayenge of Moyses, *Et Spiritus domini ferebatur super aquas*.[19]

With tears as the gift of the Spirit we are firmly in the popular devotional world of the late Middle Ages, the world of the Mater Dolorosa and St Mary Magdalene, of St Brigid of Sweden and of Margery Kempe. It was part of

Fisher's confidence in the Church that he never questioned its devotional ethos, nor made any hard-and-fast distinction between official and unofficial piety. His first venture into theological controversy, *De Unica Magdalena*, was essentially an attempt to preserve popular devotion to the Magdalene from the corrosive scepticism of academic criticism. In defence of this traditional piety he invoked not merely the scriptures, fathers and popes, but the miracles of saints and the revelations of St Brigid.[20] His receptivity to the Nun of Kent was entirely of a piece with this ready acceptance of the thoughtworld of late-medieval popular Catholicism, an acceptance evident also in his frequent references to miracles and incidents from the lives of the saints culled from sources like the *Legenda Aurea*.[21] It was reflected more significantly and more deeply in his very choice of genres. The works on which an assessment of his spirituality must be principally based are traditional not only in content but in form. The sermons on the Penitential Psalms illustrate this admirably. These seven psalms were an invariable feature of the most popular devotional manuals for layfolk, the Primers, and were probably the portions of scripture most familiar to lay people. The astonishing popularity of Fisher's sermons reflects not only the quality of the works themselves, but the appeal of their subject matter.[22] John Longland also preached a famous (and immense) series of sermons on these psalms, and some of Savonarola's sermons on them circulated in early Tudor England.[23] Fisher's virtuoso funeral oration for Henry VII reflects a similar instinct for, and ease with, popular and liturgical piety. Rhetorically, the sermon is a *tour de force*. In it Fisher uses the opening psalm of the *Dirige*, again one of the most widely used of early Tudor devotions, for three distinct purposes: first to express his vision of the sinner's hopes; secondly to fulfil the classical pattern of mourning orations, in commendation of the departed, exhortation of the hearers to compassion and sorrow for the dead, and the provision of comfort; and thirdly to articulate the prayer of Henry himself *in extremis* to a merciful God. The virtuosity involved in sustaining all these objectives in a single, tightly structured sermon demonstrates with particular force the unselfconscious ease with which Fisher was able to appropriate the devotional forms of his own time. The skill with which Fisher places in Henry's mouth the words of the psalm also demonstrates what he had in mind when he says elsewhere that Christian people should use the psalms as 'lettres of supplycacyon and spedefull prayers'.[24]

The piety recommended in the funeral sermon for Henry VII is no less revealing, for it is the emotionally charged 'affective' and churchly piety of the world of Margery Kempe. In describing the last days of Henry VII, Fisher is most impressed by the king's extravagant devotion, the 'mervaylous compassyon & flowe of teres', weeping and sobbing, 'by the pace of thre quarters of an hour' with which Henry received the sacrament of penance. Two days before he died, the king desired the blessed sacrament to be brought to him and, though he was too weak to receive communion when the monstrance was brought to his bed,

> he with such a reverence, with so many knockynges & betynges of his brest, with so quycke & lyfely a countenance, with so desyrous an herte made his humble obeyaunce therunto, & with soo grete humblenes & devocyon kyssed not the selfe place where the blessed body of our lorde was conteyned, but the lowest parte the fote of the monstraunt, that all that stode aboute hym scarcly myght conteyne them from teres & wepynge.

In all this Henry features as a type of the penitent sinner whose assurance comes from the ministrations of Holy Church, the prayers of the saints, the mute eloquence of monstrance and image. After describing Henry's devotion to the crucifix on the day of his death, 'kyssynge it, & betynge ofte his brest', Fisher asks, 'Who may thynke that in this maner was not perfyte fayth, who may suppose that by this maner of delynge he faythfully beleved not that the eare of almyghty God was open unto hym & redy to here hym crye for mercy'.[25] There is no hint of irony here, despite the fact that the sermon operates at a variety of levels, and that the insistence on Henry's role as the penitent sinner is very deliberately used by Fisher to criticize the corruptions and sinfulness of his reign. For all Fisher's distrust of the pomp and the politics of the powerful, Henry's religion is here taken at face value, because it is Fisher's own religion that is being described.[26]

Similarly in the month's mind sermon for the Lady Margaret, it is her exemplary and entirely traditional piety that is commended: Fisher praises her devotion to the daily Office, her pious reading and translations, her zeal for special saints – Nicholas, Anthony, Mary Magdalene, Katherine – her daily hearing of 'four or fyve' masses, the 'stations' or visits she made to privileged and indulgenced altars and shrines, her recitation of the rosary, her devout confessions and houselling, her hair shirt and other mortifications, her generosity to Christ in the person of the poor, her readiness to go as a washerwoman for the troops on any future crusade. The educational foundations for which now she is chiefly remembered, and with which Fisher himself was so intimately and passionately involved, are produced primarily as evidence that she had true faith, for her preachers were to 'publysshe the doctryne & fayth of cryste Ihesu' and her colleges 'to maytayn his fayth & doctryne'; they are mentioned in the same context as her chantry foundation in Westminster, where three priests were to 'praye for her perpetually'.[27] The works addressed to Fisher's half-sister, Elizabeth White, an enclosed nun at Dartford, are equally traditional in form and content. The *Spiritual Consolation* is a dramatic monologue placed in the mouth of a sinner 'sodainly prevented by death', and is designed to act as a *memento mon* and an incentive to timely repentance. Not surprisingly, it contains some of Fisher's bleakest writing about the human condition, but despite some passages with a superficially autobiographical ring to them,[28] it is essentially a formal exercise in the tradition of the rhetorical *memento mori,* of a sort that persisted on both sides of the Reformation divide throughout the early-modern period.[29] *The Wayes to Perfect Religion* is both more attractive and more interesting. The idiosyncratic conceit with which it opens, 'a comparison betweene the lyfe of Hunters, and the lyfe of religious persons', is not one of Fisher's most persuasive pieces of writing, but the work as a whole is a good example of what is arguably the most influential single genre in medieval English devotional writing, the treatise of counsel for a religious sister. The most famous representative of this genre is the *Ancren Riwle,* but other examples abound, notably in the works of Richard Rolle and Walter Hilton.[30] Fisher's work is closest in spirit to Rolle, and concludes with a series of short ejaculatory prayers to the name of Jesus, a devotion which for Fisher, as for many of his English contemporaries, had a special attraction, and whose main English source was Rolle himself. The work also contains Fisher's most eloquent and lyrical celebration of the beauty of Christ, and of the world that he has made 'Behold the Rose, the Lillie, the Vyolet, beholde the

Pecockes, the Feasaunt, the Popingaye: Behold all the other creatures of this
world: All these were of his making, all there beautie and goodliness of hym
they receyved it.'[31] Such sentiments should modify our perception of the 'life-
denying' aspects of the tradition Fisher is held to represent.

Fisher's appropriation of the rich and varied tradition of late-medieval
piety is a creative one. If it is true that he is utterly at home in the devotional
world he inherited, his deployment of its forms suggests not a plodding
and dogged persistence in well-tried tracks, but a deliberate and confident
redirection of traditional materials: some of his best and most characteristic
effects are achieved by manipulating classic and even hackneyed devotional
topoi. The Good Friday sermon on the crucifix, one of his most moving
works, is a sustained demonstration of this. Affective devotion to the passion
of Christ, to the crucifix, the *imago pietatis* and related emblems stood at the
heart of late-medieval religion. In his sermon Fisher presses almost every
form of this devotion into service in what remains nevertheless a carefully
controlled and shapely 'spiritual' exegesis of Ezekiel's scroll, written with
'lamentation and song and woe'. The central conceit is that Christ is the scroll,
that the crucifix is a book, of which the upright and cross-bar are the boards,
Christ's flesh and skin the parchment, the scourge-marks and thorn-pricks
the writing, his five wounds the illuminated capitals, and so on. The conceit
has a venerable ancestry in English devotion, ranging from the ubiquitous
notion that images in general are 'laymen's books', to more specific precedents
such as the Middle English combinations of devotional verses and symbolic
passion images known as the 'Charters of Christ',[32] or such devotional writings
as Rolle's *Meditations on the Passion*: 'More yit, sweet Ihesu, thy body is lyke
a boke written al with rede ynke.'[33] Fisher daringly extends this image over
the whole sermon, but prevents its fundamental artificiality from obtruding
by ringing the changes continually on the ways in which the central image is
unfolded. One of the most eloquent passages in the sermon invites the sinner
to 'read' the message of the sufferings of Christ displayed in the crucifix.

Seest thou not his eyes, how they bee fylled with blood and bytter teares?
Seest thou not his eares, how they be filled with blasphemous rebukes, and
opprobrious wordes? Seest thou not his mouth, how in his dryghnesse they

would have filled it with Asell and Gaule? … O most unkinde sinner, all this he suffred for thy sake.[34]

The details in this and similar passages are drawn from such compendia as Ludoiph the Carthusian's *Vita Christi*, the pseudo-Bonaventuran *Meditationes Vitae Christi*, Nicholas Love's version of which was the most popular English book of the fifteenth century, and from the passion narrative in the *Legenda Aurea*. All three are ultimately indebted to St Bernard, and it was Bernard who originated the form which Fisher is using here, an adaptation of the *planctus Christi*, in which the sufferings of the crucified, usually placed in the mouth of the dying or dead Christ himself, are used to shame and urge hard-hearted sinners into repentance and compassion for the Lord who has endured so much for them.[35] The *planctus* dominated the passion piety of late-medieval English men and women, in such well-known lyrics as 'Wofully araid' and Hawes's 'Se ye be Kind'.[36] It had a direct liturgical source in the *Improperia* or 'reproaches' sung on Good Friday during the ceremony of 'creeping to the cross'. Fisher draws on all these resources, learned, devotional, and liturgical: much of the force of the sermon turns, for example, on his appeal to the visual impact of the crucifix which dominates the solemn liturgy of the day. Yet even these visual appeals to 'see' and 'behold' the crucifix, are filtered through the literary, devotional tradition. When, at the central point of the sermon, Fisher urges the fearful sinner to 'beholde earnestly the maner how thy saviour Iesu hanged on the Crosse', it is only at once to invoke a classic devotional passage from St Bernard:

> Who may not bee ravished to hope and confidence, if he consider the order of his body, his head bowing downe to offer a kisse, hys armes spreade to embrace us, hys handes bored thorow to make lyberall giftes, his side opened to shewe unto us the love of his harte, his feete fastened with nayles, that hee shall not starte away but abyde with us. And all his bodie stretched, forcesing him self to give it wholly unto us.[37]

This passage would have been familiar to most of Fisher's hearers, and to all of his readers. It occurs in countless devotional poems, in the passion narrative in the *Legenda Aurea,* and in such fifteenth-century treatises as *Dives and*

Pauper. The passage was often used emotively rather than theologically – to arouse sympathy for, and loving trust in, Jesus. The appeal was to the will and emotions rather than to the intellect. Fisher loses none of the emotional warmth implicit in the Bernardine exhortation but, characteristically, he inserts some intellectual spine, and uses the text as the point of departure for an extended and theologically rich discussion of the atonement.[38]

The sermon similarly presses a whole range of highly charged popular devotional images into theological use, without sacrificing their emotional resonance. In every case the familiar image is developed beyond its predictable lines to force the hearer to enter more deeply into the meaning of the passion. The proximity to the cross of the Magdalene, conventional type of the convert prostitute, provides Fisher with an opportunity to reflect on the nakedness of Christ, and the way in which he takes on and absorbs the shame of human sexuality.[39] St Francis and his stigmata become a metaphor for the self-exploration of the converted sinner, and his assimilation to Christ, by reflection on the Passion. And the special privilege of the saint in receiving the outward tokens of conformity to the crucified becomes the occasion for a striking and moving insistence on the universality of Christian discipleship. The stigmata, Fisher admits, are a 'singular gyfte', 'not common to be looked for of other persons'. But whoever will dwell on the meaning of the cross may, like Francis, come to a 'great knowledge of both Christ & of him selfe'. A man

> may easily say and thinke with him selfe (beholding in his hart the Image of the Crucifixe) who art thou, and who am I. This everie person both ryche and poore, may thinke, not onely in the church here, but in every other place, and in hys businesse where about hee goeth. Thus the poore laborer maye thinke, when he is at plough earying his grounde, and when he goeth to hys pastures to see hys cattayle, or when hee is sittyng at home by his fire side, or els when he lyeth in hys bed waking and can not sleepe. Likewise the rich man may do in his business … and the poore women also, when they be spinning of their rooks, or serving of their pullens … It is an easy thynge for any man or woman to make these two questions wyth them selfe. O my Lord that wouldest dye for me upon a Crosse, how noble and excellent arte thou? & agayne, how wretched and myserable am I?[40]

That passage raises in an acute way the question of the extent of Fisher's 'medievalism' as opposed to his 'humanism' with which this chapter began. The picture of farm labourers meditating on the Passion at the plough, or of business men in their counting-houses and poor women at their spinning similarly engaged recalls the alert reader at once to one of the most familiar passages in Erasmus, that section of the *Paraclesis* where, quoting Jerome, Erasmus foresees the day when labourers at the plough will sing passages from scripture, and all, even the Turk, may have ready access to the word of God.[41] The similarities between the two passages point up the contrasts. Erasmus wants to distribute bibles: Fisher sees in the crucifix a more universal book, which can be read by those who are no clerks:

> Thus who that list with a meeke harte, and a true fayth, to muse and to marvayle of this most wonderfull booke (I say of the crucifixe) hee shall come to more fruitefull knowledge, then many other which dayly study upon their common bookes. This booke may suffice for the studie of a true Christian man, all the dayes of his life.[42]

These sentiments would not be out of place in the first book of the Imitation of Christ, and indeed are by no means remote from Erasmus's own teaching. He too wanted men and women to meditate the cross and, long before Fisher's sermon was preached, had devoted a section of his seminal work, the *Enchiridion Militis Christiani*, to saying so. But in that work he expressly repudiated as a way of doing this the very pattern of medieval passion piety which Fisher here so triumphantly celebrates and renews. We must 'exercise' ourselves in the cross, according to Erasmus,

> not after the commune manner / as some men repete dayly the hystory of the passion of Chryst / or honour the ymage of the crosse ... or at certayn houres so call to remembrance Chrystes punysshment that they may have compassyon and wepe for hym with natural affection / as they wolde for a man that is very iuste, and suifreth great wronge unworthely.

This, he insists, 'is not the true fruyte of that tree: nevertheless, let it in ye meane season be the mylke of ye soules, which be yongelynges and weyke in Chryst'.[43]

On that note of condescension Erasmus waves away not only popular superstitions and more respectable para-liturgical devotion, but also the whole Bernardine and Bonaventuran tradition of passion piety, as 'mylke for yonglynges'. The dismissal is rooted, at least in part, in Erasmus's neoplatonic distrust of the physical and merely external. Its consequence, however, is the creation of a two-tier image of the church, in which there is a spiritual elite who experience true devotion, and 'yongelynges and weyke in Chryst' who grub about in the foothills. For all his undoubted clericalism, this stratification is completely absent in Fisher's devotional world. The crucifix speaks as eloquently, and as demandingly, to the unlettered and the simple as to scholar, prelate or clerk. As he says elsewhere,

> let no creature thynke in hymselfe & saye, I am not within holy ordres, I am not professed to any religyon. All we be crysten people, take hede in what degre we stande, what state is it to be a crysten man or woman, the least crysten persone the poorest & moost lowe in degre is nygh in kynrede to almyghty god, he is his sone and his heyre of the kyngdome of heven, broder unto Jhesu cryst and bought with his precyous blode.[44]

This, of course, was Erasmus's view also, but in practice Erasmus's vision of the Church entailed an elitism of the educated. He viewed the popular religious culture as intrinsically crude and misleading, a jumble from which the spiritually discriminating would select only what is wholesome. Before this discriminating elite could become the Christian democracy, therefore, the elaborate and resonant symbol-system of late-medieval Catholicism needed to be stripped to something more austerely textual. Fisher would wholeheartedly have endorsed Erasmus's biblicism: his own preaching demonstrated his profound immersion in scripture, and it was to 'a little booke in his hande, which was a New Testament lying by him', that he turned for support and guidance in the last minutes of his life.[45] But the scripture for Fisher was in no way at odds either with the tradition and ritual of the Church or with popular devotion. For Fisher, the real sickness of the Church was not that it had a corrupt piety, but that it had not enough piety. He sought, therefore, not the stripping and simplification of Christian life by the critical use of the scriptures, but the increase of traditional piety by any means, including and above all scriptural preaching, but equally drawing on all the other resources of the symbolic and sacramental world of medieval Catholicism. Given the long-term problems of Tudor literacy, and the richness and vividness of Fisher's manipulation of that symbolic and sacramental system, it does not seem obvious that his was an intrinsically inferior or less hopeful religious strategy than that of Erasmus. Certainly we are not dealing here with any straightforward contrast between 'medieval' and 'Renaissance', but between a man who retains a commitment to, and confidence in, the symbolic structure of Catholicism and one who does not. We shall return to this issue in due course.

In arguing for the essentially positive and creative relation of Fisher to his religious inheritance I have, of course, been conceding and documenting Lewis's contention that he was a medieval figure. My point, however, is that to conceive that relationship as 'representative' is to obscure the dynamic element in Fisher's work: if he never challenges the bounds of the religious conventions of his day, he is rarely content simply to repeat what he has inherited. If he is 'medieval', he is so in the same sense that Hieronymus Bosch is medieval, simultaneously original and a man of his time. Indeed, the comparison with Bosch can be pushed some way, for there is much in Fisher's writing that reminds us of the painter's work. The famous and terrifying vision at the opening of the sermon on Psalm 51, in which Fisher portrays the condition of mankind, perched in the rickety bucket of mortality over a pit of ravening demons, held up only by a thin cord in the hand of a God we have striven to make our enemy, could come straight out of a Bosch altarpiece. So too could the passage in which Fisher describes the man who has allowed himself to despair, and so has fallen into the 'depe pyt desperacyon', 'whose mouth is stopped up with a grete stone', and where he is gradually 'dygested & incorporate in to the substance of the devyll even as mete when it is dygested … For amonges all synnes desperacyon is the thinge that moost maketh us devyllysche.' And, indeed, the Bosch-like image of the soul devoured and digested by despair allows us to see Fisher's imagination actually at work, weaving a vividly concrete and complex image out of simpler elements. The sermon on Psalm 129 (Vulgate numbering) opens with an account of the whale devouring Jonah, develops by way of the devil in I Peter 5:8 seeking whom he may devour, and so produces the image of the sinner digested by the demonic sin of despair.[46]

There are, of course, ways in which Fisher's 'medievalism' narrows and limits him. For all the attractive human warmth of his portrayal of the piety of the dying Henry VII, it is impossible not to be struck by its character-istically late-medieval overdependence on *feeling*. True devotion must be tangible, felt along the pulse, it must give rise to sighs and weeping, whether of joy or of penitence. This sort of emotionalized piety was to be passed on into the Reformation by Cranmer and others in such writings as the General Confession in the *Book of Common Prayer*. Its limitations are most obvious in a hysterical exponent like Margery Kempe, but they are uncomfortable even in so austere a figure as Fisher. The weakness is perhaps at its most striking in Fisher's Latin treatise, *De Necessitate Orandi*.[47] Once again this is a work in a clearly recognizable tradition and genre. Composed probably for a *dévot* readership, it is a treatise on mental prayer drawing heavily on the English mystical tradition of Walter Hilton and the *Cloud of Unknowing*. Its basic teaching is that prayer at its highest is a convergence in wordless and imageless love on man's highest good, the God who draws us to himself, beyond the created order. Fisher is indebted, in phrase and thought, to Hilton and to the teaching of the pseudo-Denys, in the warmed up and derationalized form in which it was current in late medieval European devotion. The writings of the Victorines and of St Bernard also lie behind those passages in which Fisher uses the Song of Songs as the medium for his discussion of the soul's union with God. The work has rightly been praised by Surtz for its insistent emphasis on the prevenient grace of God, and the gratuitousness of salvation. Throughout it, Fisher stresses the overwhelming abundance of God's love for us, stirring us to prayer before we even think of praying, enticing us to contemplate the splendour of his light, to taste his 'sweetness' and, in an erotic image rare in his English works but given extended scope here, to kiss the indescribable delights of his lips.[48] There is no doubting the depth of feeling in such passages, and the treatise gives us an unrivalled and rather startling insight into the nature of Fisher's own prayer.

The fervid language of spiritual kisses, full of sweetness, ardour and delight, which is characteristic of this work is not, of course, the sign of personal aberration, but represents a convention deriving from Richard and William of St Victor and, above all, from St Bernard. In English piety it can be traced back to the *Ancren Wisse,* but its chief English exponent was Richard Rolle of Hampole, the Yorkshire hermit and mystic whose cult was such a powerful force in England in the fourteenth and fifteenth centuries.[49] Rolle's works and influence were propagated in Fisher's day chiefly by the Carthusian order, with which Fisher, like More, had close connections, and in this treatise he draws heavily on his fellow-Yorkshireman's teaching. But it is here that a disturbing limitation appears. Both Hilton and the author of the *Cloud* had criticized Rolle, or his disciples, for excessive reliance on feeling and emotion in prayer.[50] Fisher, in following Rolle, shows no awareness of these dangers. For him, the chief aim of prayer is to nourish and maintain the fervour of charity in the soul. By 'fervour' he seems to mean an emotionally experienced ardour and heat. This 'prayer of the heart' is worth more than any number of vocal prayers, though these have their place: anyone who feels such fervour in prayer should cast aside his vocal prayers and follow the promptings of the Spirit, 'with weeping and sighing'. Moreover, since this fervour is the object of prayer, there is little point praying when it has fled. When this happens, for example through weariness, we should 'at once give over' our prayer, contenting ourselves with what we have already 'acquired' from it, and go about our other business.[51] Fisher is at pains to distinguish the sweetness of prayer from the sweetness of the senses: nevertheless, this unqualified linking of persistence in prayer with a particular mental and emotional state, and his apparent tendency to make the experience of these exalted feelings the pinnacle of prayer, contrasts dramatically with Hilton's more sober teaching that we should 'beware of fervours' and 'thou shalt never pray the less when grace of devotion is withdrawn ... But then it is most acceptable and pleasing to God.'[52] Fisher's guidance is, by the standards of the fourteenth-century masters, over-concerned with affective experience, even soft-centred. He has taken up the weakest part of Rolle's teaching and failed, in transmitting it, to register the warnings of Rolle's wiser successors. It is impossible, on this score, to acquit him of what a modern historian of medieval spirituality, with characteristic Dominican rigour, has branded as 'devotionalism'.[53]

But Fisher is rarely in this way the victim of his background: his use of medieval categories and devotional conventions almost invariably extends our perception both of them and of him. In Fisher the devotional repertoire of the late Middle Ages is alive and well, putting out new branches and bearing new fruit, and he is in no sense a backward-looking writer. Perhaps the most intriguing example of this vitality of old devotional motifs in Fisher's life and writing is that of the head of John the Baptist. The Baptist is an obvious scriptural paradigm for the pious mind seeking to 'place' Fisher in the divine scheme. Name apart, the Bishop of Rochester himself is a sufficiently Johannine figure, emaciated and clad in hair-cloth, calling a generation to penitence. Had there been no closer similarities than these, even a moderately imaginative biographer might have invoked the comparison. In fact Fisher himself was intensely conscious of rather more pressing parallels, and drew attention to them. In the section on marriage in his treatise in defence of Henry VIII's *Assertio Septem Sacramentorum* Fisher had declared how much the death of John the Baptist weighed with him to establish the sanctity of marriage. John had rebuked Herod for his adulterous and forbidden union with Herodias, showing that the violation of marriage was a worse sin than many more obvious potential targets of prophetic wrath.[54] This controversial point was thrown off in 1524 as no more than an aside. Within five years, however, it had begun to assume for Fisher a far more existential urgency. In June 1529 he spoke before Campeggio's legatine court in defence of the marriage between Catherine and Henry. He startled his hearers by declaring his readiness to die in defence of the marriage, as John the Baptist had lain down his life, for that saint 'regarded it as impossible for him to die more gloriously than in the cause of marriage'.[55] There was more to this remark than met the eye; the king's supporters thought they detected an insulting comparison between Henry and Herod, and, as we have seen, the king himself deeply resented the implication of Fisher's speech.[56]

The subsequent confrontation between bishop and king, and Fisher's ultimate fate, made the elaboration of the biblical comparison inevitable. Fisher's earliest biographer devotes much space to it, and in one of the earliest revisions of that early life of Fisher it is claimed that Anne Boleyn, playing both Herodias and Salome to Fisher's John the Baptist, sent for his head after his execution, and mocked and abused it, cutting her hand on one of the teeth, a wound which, of course, never healed.[57] The story is patently false, and might have been left there had not Fr Bridgett, Fisher's first modern biographer, noticed a curious item on the inventory of Fisher's belongings made by the king's commissioners in 1534. In the long gallery of Fisher's palace the commissioners noted 'A St John's head standing at the end of the altar'. Bridgett was excited by this object. We know Fisher customarily to have placed a skull before him when he said mass or sat at table. Had this head of John the Baptist taken the place of that skull? 'This emblem of royal tyranny and saintly constancy Fisher kept ever before him when offering the Holy Sacrifice. Had God given him any presentiment of the kind of death by which he should glorify him?'[58]

We need not suppose so. Carved and painted heads of St John the Baptist, usually in alabaster and normally including, below the head on its salver, a small representation of Christ as Man of Sorrows or Lamb of God, were almost certainly the most common devotional objects in fifteenth-century England, far more so than crucifixes or images of the Virgin.[59] Their precise symbolism is obscure, but it was probably in part eucharistic, and a number of Corpus Christi guilds used them as emblems. But they were already old-fashioned by the 1520s, occurring less and less frequently in the inventories of the goods of pious lay folk in this period.[60] Fisher's retention of one on his altar shows a characteristic conservatism rather than a visionary precognition of his martyrdom, though clearly the crisis of the divorce may well have sharpened his sense of the appositeness of the old image.

However that may be, there is one final piece of evidence which prevents us from dismissing as mere pious fancy the idea that the motif of John the Baptist provides an aid to understanding the mind of Fisher. The evidence is at first sight unrelated to the divorce, since it long pre-dates it, but it does bear directly on Fisher's perception of Henry, and throws at least a sideways light onto the meaning of the Baptist's image for Fisher. It occurs in Fisher's sermon on the Field of the Cloth of Gold, preached on All Saints Day 1520 but unpublished till 1532. The sermon is justly famous for its magnificent treatment of a favourite Tudor theme, the vanity of human glory and greatness.[61] Fisher is therefore showing once again his mastery of a traditional mode, and the sermon is indeed unrivalled in the building up of its effects. The treatment of the Field of the Cloth of Gold begins colloquially, and proceeds to magnificence:

> I doubte not but ye have herde of many goodly syghtes which were shewed of late beyond the see, with moche ioy and pleasure worldly. Was it not a great thynge within so shorte a space, to se three great Prynces of this worlde? I mean the Emperour, and the kyng our mayster, and the Frenche king. And eche of these thre in so great honour, shewing theyr royalty, shewyng theyr rychesse, shewyng theyr power; with eche of theyr noblesse appoynted and apparrayled in ryche clothes, in sylkes, velvettes, clothes of golde, & such other precyouse arayments ... such daunsynges, such armonyes, such dalyaunce, and so many pleasaunt pastimes ... soo ryche and goodly tentys, such Justynges, such tournays, and such feats of warre.[62]

But at length, Fisher tells us, many 'had a lothsomes and a fastydyousnes' of such pleasures, and longed to be at home, for, 'by the reason of them, great money was spent, many great mennes coffers were emptyed, & many were brought to a great ebbe of poverty'. Covetousness and envy were the moral fruits of sumptuousness, and many 'for these pleasures were the worse, bothe in their bodyes & in their soules'. This generalized moralizing about the courts of kings is given unforgettable particularity and vividness by Fisher in his well-known description of the dust storms that enveloped the parched English camp and enshrouded all its finery.[63] For the glory of humanity is counterfeit, borrowed from other creatures to cover 'the wounde of shame'. Take away the 'glystering garment, take away the clothe of golde ... & what dyfference is betwyxt an Emperour and another pore man?'[64] This begins to be trenchant, and unlikely to please a king to hear or read, but Fisher pushes it further. Kings are not merely mortal as other 'pore men'; they are in perpetual danger of dazzling themselves to damnation. It is at this point that we begin to hear resonances of the Baptist theme, for now Fisher introduces King Herod:

> The Actes of the Apostels tellyth of Kyng Herode, that he in ryche apparrell shewed hym self upon a tyme unto the people & they for his glystering apparrell & goodly arncyon, magnyfyed & praysed hym soveraynely as though he had been a god: but almyghty god ... stroke hym with a sore

sykenesse, whereupon he dyed Kynges & Emperours, all be but men, all be but mortall.[65]

The introduction of the figure of King Herod into a discourse on the fragility and vanity of human glory is by no means arbitrary: the surprising of a boastful and vainglorious tyrant Herod by sudden death is the theme of one of the most vivid of the *Ludus Coventriae* cycle of mystery plays. The Herod being referred to here, however, is not John the Baptist's Herod, but Herod Agrippa, the third of the Herods mentioned in the New Testament. Fisher was of course aware of this, but the three Herods, all of whom feature as enemies of Christ and his Church, were commonly conflated (as the three Marys of *De Unica Magdalena* were), and Fisher is certainly here drawing on that common fund of imagery.[66] Yet the image of Herod in his sermon has a pointedness lacking from even the most vivid occurrences of the theme in the medieval tradition as a whole, for Fisher is not talking about kings in general, but 'I mean the Emperour, and the kyng our mayster, and the Frenche kynge'. And lest anyone should fail to notice, Fisher now develops his sermon in a startlingly blunt way. The whole discourse to this point had concentrated on contrasting the transient glories of earth with the eternal glory of heaven. From things, Fisher now turns to persons. In heaven, among the saints, we shall see a more glorious court than that of the Field of the Cloth of Gold. Above all, we shall see

> the excellency of that Gloryous Trynytye, the Father, the Son, and the holy Ghoost. These thre, though they be thre dyvers persons yet they be but one God perfitely knyt togyder in a perfyte amytye, in one love, in one wyll, in one wysdom, in one power inseparably. The thre Prynces of whom we spake of before, were nat so: but they had dyvers wylles, dyvers councels, & no perdurable amyty, as after that dyd well appere. These Prynces were mortall and unstable, and so theyr wylles dyd chaunge & nat abyde.[67]

The directness with which the political manoeuvrings of Henry and his fellow monarchs are made the anti-type of the wisdom and 'amytye' of heaven adds a dramatic prophetic aspect to the introduction of the figure of Herod which would otherwise be lacking. The whole sermon breathes a profound distrust of the framework of politics which in Fisher goes beyond moralizing generalities to attach itself concretely to named individuals. Here maybe is the genesis of the identification of Henry with Herod, and, by extension, of himself with the Baptist, which would have a long afterlife in Tudor England:[68] the subconscious movement towards a full identification of his role with that of the Baptist during the divorce crisis becomes more explicable.

Indeed, it is possible that we have here more than the subconscious origins of the parallel, but actually its fullest public expression. This sermon was preached in the autumn of 1520. It was not published, however, until 1532 when it was printed by William Rastell, who was Thomas More's nephew and publisher and, like his uncle, a staunchly pro-papal Catholic. The timing of the sermon's printing has the appearance of an opposition publication. For why should Fisher publish a sermon preached a dozen years before at just this juncture? The inevitable outcome of the divorce proceedings was by now evident to all, and the king's onslaught on the Church, which Fisher prominently resisted, was well under way. Professor Scarisbrick has drawn attention to the vigour of Fisher's attempts, in 1532, to mount a theological critique of Henry's anti-clerical measures, as well as to encourage political opposition. The Nun of Kent was at the height of her influence and had long since been predicting the king's death or dethronement if he divorced Catherine and remarried. Fisher had undoubted sympathy for the Nun, and had at least an open mind about her prophecies. It is difficult to believe that these facts were irrelevant to his decision to permit the publication of this sermon against the presumption of earthly kings, with its story of the grisly end of Herod who had set himself over the Church and usurped the place of God. The sermon may have been revised for publication:[69] but even if the outspoken criticism of monarchs and the Herod passage were there in 1520, their publication at this precise point can hardly have been anything but deliberate. Thus a series of medieval devotional commonplaces on the theme of transience and the vanity of earthly rulers has been drawn into an unforgettable and complex cluster, in which Fisher's own self-perception, and the crisis confronting the English Church in the early 1530s, play a concealed but real part. The resulting work is different in power and quality from the conventional materials out of which it is made.[70]

My main contention in this chapter is that if we are to describe Fisher's spirituality as 'medieval', we must not allow that label to conceal from us the breadth of vision and imaginative creativity with which it is imbued. Whatever Fisher's limitations as a spiritual guide, his religion was not the played-out and backward-looking thing that the term might be taken to imply. His religion gives no grounds for regarding its replacement by a more dynamic and 'modern' protestantism as inevitable. In that sense it is provincialism to see Fisher's religion as a thing of the Middle Ages, for most of its central emphases had a long and vigorous future ahead of them in the Counter-Reformation. And, if we can point to his tendency towards 'devotionalism' as a weakness of the late medieval tradition, that very tendency to 'emotionalize' piety was not done away by the reformers, but was entrenched by them in the charter document of the English Reformation, the *Book of Common Prayer*. If Fisher is to be judged medieval, so too must Cranmer.[71]

But even this statement of the case does not take us far enough. We may call Fisher 'medieval', provided that we do not imagine that in doing so we rule out his claim to be also a Renaissance figure. Professor McConica has reminded us of the rootedness of Thomas More's personal religious outlook in the devotional atmosphere represented by the Charterhouses of London and Sheen, and by the Bridgettine house of Syon.[72] At Sheen the English tradition of Rolle and Hilton was dominant. The monks at Syon were deeply schooled in a corpus of fourteenth- and fifteenth-century spiritual classics which included some works by Rolle and Hilton, but which was more notable for the many continental influences such as the *Dialogues* of St Catherine of Siena, and the *Imitation of Christ* and other works of the *Devotio Moderna*. In the early sixteenth century the community at Syon in particular was dedicated to making this essentially monastic and ascetical piety available to a wider audience of devout lay people. The monks chiefly involved, John Fewterer, Richard Whytford, William Bonde, and Richard Reynolds, were graduates, theologians and linguists, and all of them well acquainted with the new classical learning. The libraries they brought with them to Syon contained not only the medieval devotional classics Ludolf the Carthusian, Bernard, Bonaventura, and the rest – but also a wide range of Renaissance writings and translations. Works by Ficino, Valla, Erasmus, Poggio, Platina, Pico della Mirandola, Petrarch, Lefèvre, Reuchlin, Savonarola, Linacre, Colet,

More himself, were there, as well as a comprehensive range of Greek and Latin Fathers and pagan classics in recent editions.[73]

The spirituality of these men was precisely that of More and of Fisher, whose friends they were; like them they were to be prominent in opposition to the king's religious policies, most famously Reynolds, the martyred 'Angel of Syon'. The majority of them were Cambridge graduates and former fellows of colleges. Most were from Pembroke, but there were products of Fisher's colleges, John's, Christ's and Queens' too. Their reading closely matches that represented by the explicit citations and the influences evident in Fisher's works. Like him they held together a loyalty to the affective piety of the Middle Ages with an openness to the resources of the new Humanism, and a concern for religious reform and lay religious formation. Their religion, like that of Fisher, was unselfconsciously traditional, yet they laid out many of the lines along which later Tudor devotion, Catholic or Protestant, would develop. Their most authoritative historian has argued both for their 'modernity of outlook' and 'fervently humanistic' scholarship, and, at the same time, for their pronounced theological and devotional traditionalism. Perhaps the most characteristic member of this group was Richard Whytford, the 'poor wretch of Syon'.[74] Certainly the most important Tudor devotional writer before Becon, Whytford, a product of Queens' and friend of Erasmus, was the protégé of Fisher's friend and former patron, Richard Fox, who had founded the first humanist establishment at Oxford, Corpus Christi College. It is entirely of a piece with the devotional attitudes of this group that so explicitly humanistic a venture as Corpus should take its name from the liturgical mystery which lay at the heart of medieval piety. Whytford's publications include translations of the rule of St Augustine and of St Bernard's *De Praecepto:* they also include a treatise which in both title and content anticipated much of the essence of later English devotional developments. *Werke for Housholders* was a manual for lay folk designed to provide a piety suited to others than 'such persones as ben solytary and done lye alone by them selfe'. Its method and its tone were to be taken up and developed further by the reformers, more specifically by puritan devotional writers.[75]

It would not be difficult to present these men as essentially 'medieval' figures. William Bonde's *Pyigrimage of Perfection (1526)*, John Fewterer's

Glasse or Myrrour of Christes Passion (1534), and Whytford's *Pype or Tonne of the Lyfe of Perfection* (1532) are all attempts to distil the essence of the affective and ascetic tradition of monastic devotion: they are as full of devotional topoi and conventional imagery as the works of Fisher which we have examined.[76] And just as much as Fisher they resisted the tide of religious change. Whytford was deeply troubled by the spread of heresy, and polemic against the Reformation invades even the most tranquil of his devotional writing.

Yet this is only half the story. If these monastic conservatives were deeply committed to the transmission of the sacramental, churchly and ascetic piety of the late Middle Ages, it was also their intention to transmit it to an ever-widening lay audience, using all the resources of the press, and in the vernacular. They were concerned not merely with the transmission of the tradition, but with its renewal. And, just as much as Erasmus and Colet, they were conscious of the ills of the church; their monastery was famed for its reformed and austerely observant character. Fisher wholly shared this reformist outlook, and an important and too-little recognized element in his writings is his scarifying and pessimistic assessment of the moral and spiritual state of the Church of his own times. A number of writers on Fisher have drawn attention to the passage in which he contrasts the patristic period, when there were 'no chalyses of golde, but ... many golden preestes', with the modern age, when things are reversed. It is, of course, a commonplace, taken from Gratian, furiously debated between More and Tyndale, and used, as Fisher used it, to castigate and lament the state of the contemporary Church, by Savonarola, a figure in whom Fisher was interested and with whom he had much in common.[77] It is only one of many passages in which Fisher, like Savonarola and like Colet, lamented the decay of piety and the corruptions of the clergy. One such passage, in which Fisher denounced the spread of hypocrisy and 'feigned piety' in the Church, was considered too disturbing for a lay readership a hundred years on into the Counter-Reformation, and was omitted from the 1640 translation of the *De Necessitate Orandi.*[78]

In such a reformist yet traditionalist context, Fisher's educational foundations with the Lady Margaret and his openness to the work of men like Reuchlin and Erasmus need not be seen as in any sense at odds with his conservative and churchly piety. A correct perception of the importance of this Bridgettine circle liberates us from the crude polarities of 'medieval' and 'Renaissance', 'traditionalist' and 'reforming'. Neither protestants nor 'Erasmians', they were nevertheless participants in a new stirring within Tudor Catholicism. McConica has rightly contrasted the piety and the anthropology of More and the Bridgettines on the one hand with that of Erasmus on the other. Their vision of humanity and the Church was less optimistic, more deeply Augustinian than his and, maybe, more cloistered. The regimen of hair-shirt and discipline, even when toned down and vernacularized by publicists like Whytford, would never have attracted large numbers of practitioners. Yet every bit as much as that of Erasmus, the religious vision and the practical piety of these men has a claim to be considered a manifestation of Renaissance, for they too, and Fisher along with them, sought the renewal of the Church and of a more vital lay piety with the aid of biblical preaching, humanistic learning and the press. The imposition of an 'Erasmian' straitjacket as the only legitimate wear for any figure claiming humanist credentials serves unnecessarily to narrow the meaning of humanism, and to confuse analysis.[79] And, indeed, if one of the principal marks of Christian humanism was its concern to renew the faith of the Christian people as a whole, it could be argued without excessive paradox that on this matter at least Fisher's credentials can claim comparison with those of Erasmus. For, whatever the limitations of his ascetical austerity as a popular piety, Fisher's instinctive and creative empathy with the symbolic world of early-sixteenth-century Catholicism gives to his work a depth and resonance, and a multitude of points of contact with the piety of the simple and unlettered, about which Erasmus wrote much, but understood very little.

8

Archbishop Cranmer and Cardinal Pole: the See of Canterbury and the Reformation

Two Archbishops of Canterbury led the English Church during the most tumultuous twenty-five years of the sixteenth century. Both were reformers, dedicated to the renewal of the Church, both were long-term survivors in a murderous age of religious hatreds, both were taciturn men who hid their opinions from all but their closest intimates. But there the resemblance ends: they came from radically different social classes and they adopted diametrically opposed stands on the great dividing issues of the Reformation. Thomas Cranmer, the older of the two, probably needs little introduction. The key figure in the shaping of the English Reformation, his successive versions of the Book of Common Prayer gave the reformed Church of England its distinctive liturgical and devotional ethos and, just as importantly, some of its long-term doctrinal ambiguities.[1] And his death by fire at Oxford in March 1556, at the time an event surrounded in moral and political ambiguities would, in John Foxe's retelling of it, become an iconic moment in the English Reformation and the retrospective discrediting of the Church and regime which had condemned him.

Reginald Pole, by contrast, is probably not much more than a name to most people. Yet, in their overlapping lifetimes, he was the more famous of the two, a European figure who was a prince both of church and state, being Henry VIII's cousin and grandson of George, Duke of Clarence. As a young man he was groomed by Henry VIII for high office in the English Church, and received a magnificent humanist education at Henry's expense, first at Oxford and then at Padua and Venice.[2] Exiled from England for his opposition to the English Reformation, Pole became the lynch-pin of the incipient Italian Reformation, the centre of a circle which included some of the finest spirits of the time – his circle included Michaelangelo. Many of this group, including Pole himself, accepted the doctrine of Justification by Faith, and two of his protégés, Peter Martyr and Bernardino Ochino, became prominent Protestants and enjoyed Cranmer's patronage.[3] Pole presided over the opening sessions of the Council of Trent, but he was devastated by the Council's rejection of Justification by Faith alone. Nevertheless he reconciled himself to the Council's teaching, and he was offered the papacy by acclamation during the conclave of 1549–50. In 1554, the year after Queen Mary's accession, Pole returned to England as Papal Legate to restore the country to Catholic communion, and it was under his jurisdiction that Cranmer was tried and burned.

Though their lives crossed and recrossed, there is no evidence that the two men ever met, and Cranmer is very unlikely even to have registered on Pole's radar at all during the 1520s. But the pattern of both their lives was decisively set by the great cause which was troubling all England at the end of the 1520s: Henry's urgent desire for a divorce from Catherine of Aragon. Theological opinion about the divorce was fluid to begin with, and Pole himself was involved in securing the University of Paris's official support for Henry's cause in 1529, part of the consultation of selected theology faculties across Europe designed to pit the magisterium of the theologians against that of the Pope. Ironically, the notion of consulting the universities had been Cranmer's suggestion in the first place, a suggestion which probably first brought him to Henry's notice, with momentous consequences.

Understandably, Pole would later play down his role in promoting the divorce: he was to claim that his primary purpose in going to Paris was precisely to avoid being drawn into the campaign, and he protested to Henry himself in 1536 that 'may God be my witness – I cannot remember anything at all in my life that was more painful to me than that famous legation offered to me at your command when I was residing in Paris'.[4]

There was wishful thinking here. At the time, Henry himself made no secret of his delight in having his learned cousin's support.[5] Pole's own final despatch from Paris in July 1530 dismisses the 'crafts and inventions' by which the adversaries of the divorce in the Paris Faculty had sought to 'embecyll the hole determination', and the phrasing hardly suggests any misgivings about the King's cause. At any rate, Henry's court gave most of the credit for the successful outcome of the mission to Pole's 'politic and wise handling',[6] and he returned home in 1530 in high favour with the King.[7]

We need not suppose that deliberate deception was at work here. At this point in the King's proceedings, opinion on the divorce was fluid, and the issues were not as clear as they subsequently became: Pole would not be alone in moving from acquiescence into opposition of the divorce. For Pole returned to an England in which the underlying theological and moral issues involved in the King's divorce were becoming clearer. They crystalized around the question of papal authority, itself a fraught and uncertain theological question, and men were increasingly forced to take sides. Known opponents of the divorce found themselves marginalized or removed from the centres of power. Lord Chancellor Thomas More himself was excluded from key policy-making sessions of the Council. The ideological basis for the doctrine of Royal Supremacy was being put in place by teams of scholars, including Cranmer, so that by August 1530 the Papal Nuncio was being told that 'they cared neither for Pope or Popes in this kingdom, not even if St Peter should come to life again'. In opposition to all this, supporters of Queen Catherine gathered round Thomas More and Bishop Fisher, expressing their rejection of the divorce *and* the incipient Royal Supremacy perilously in sermons and in dissenting writings circulated more or less clandestinely.[8]

Pole was still fond of Henry, and grateful to him for his education. He was also temperamentally a very cautious man, so he kept his views to himself. But his mother had been Princess Mary's governess, and there were deep loyalties on both sides. His intellectual formation and pious temperament drew him naturally to the devout Catholic humanism of More's circle. Everything in his family background and intellectual formation, therefore, inclined him towards support for Catherine, and for More's and Fisher's position. Matters came to a head between him and Henry in November 1530, when the Archbishopric of York became vacant by the death of Cardinal Wolsey. Pole, still only 30, was summoned by the King to York House and offered the Archbishopric. The price for this preferment, however, was to declare himself publicly for the divorce. On his own account, Pole went into the interview intending to give an accommodating answer. In the event, his carefully prepared speech deserted him, and to Henry's fury he revealed that he felt unable after all to support the divorce.[9]

Pole was later to claim that Henry had become so enraged during this interview that he had reached convulsively for his dagger. Pole's modern biographer discounts the incident as fiction. But whatever did or did not happen at York House, Pole certainly was expected to succeed Wolsey at York, and his failure to do so was generally attributed to his refusal to support the divorce. Nevertheless, Pole was anxious to avoid a final breach with his dangerous cousin. So he later sent Henry a careful memorandum, explaining in detail *why* he thought the divorce was a bad idea, urging the King to set aside the opinions of the universities, and to 'commit his great cause to the judgement of the Pope'. This memorandum, however, carefully avoided doctrinal issues, concentrating on the political and prudential arguments against repudiating Catherine, including the danger of alienating European Catholic powers and rousing the common people, who loved the Queen.

As Pole's credit with the King sank, Cranmer's had risen. By the summer of 1531 this hitherto obscure Cambridge don had become the key royal advisor on the divorce. So Pole's memorandum was passed to him for comment. Cranmer briefed his patron, Anne Boleyn's father, on his opinion of Pole's letter: since the memorandum itself hasn't survived, Cranmer's account of it is our sole guide to its contents. On Cranmer's account, it was a powerful and perhaps dangerously persuasive performance, 'of such eloquence that, if it were set forth and known to the common people, I suppose it were not possible to persuade them to the contrary'. Nevertheless, Cranmer identified and rejected utterly the central premise of the memorandum, that Henry should submit the whole matter to papal judgement: in this appeal to papal authority Pole was begging the whole question, and missing the point of the consultation of the universities, which had been designed to make them undermine the verdict of the papacy on the matter, so, Cranmer wrote, 'me he persuadeth in that point nothing at all'.[10]

Henry was not persuaded either, and by the end of 1531 mounting pressure on anyone who stood out against the divorce had become intense. So at this point, Pole thought it prudent to retreat abroad once more. With some difficulty, he obtained Henry's permission to return to his studies in Italy. The King, now it was clear that Pole would not come on side in favour of the divorce, was doubtless glad to be rid of this high-profile royal dissident, whose deafening public silence about Henry's great matter threatened to become a serious embarrassment.

The silence would last for four more years. It would end only at Henry's insistence, an insistence he probably came to regret. Pole's departure to Italy in January 1532 was the start of a twenty-two year exile: it was also the commencement of a glittering ecclesiastical career which would see him a cardinal within four years and which, in 1550, would bring him within one vote of the papacy. And the trigger for all that was Pole's decision to speak out at last about Henry's actions. It was not his own choice. Early in 1535 one of Pole's former employees, the humanist writer and thinker Thomas Starkey, who had returned to England, passed into Cromwell's service.[11] He soon became the Henrician regime's chosen line of communication to Italy in general and Pole in particular. In February, Starkey began to nag Pole for an unambiguous statement of his views on papal supremacy and the standing of the King's first marriage. The King wanted him, he told Pole, to write 'truly and plain, without colour or dark of dissimulation'. Explicit support for the divorce and the break with Rome was the price Henry now demanded for Pole's education. It was also the condition of any return to England.[12] He must speak on the King's behalf, or take the consequences of silence.

Pole was a secretive and cautious man who, so far, had shied away from confrontation. But by now, More and Fisher were languishing in the Tower awaiting execution: one of Starkey's letters in this exchange contained an attempted justification of Henry's brutal execution of the Carthusians of Sheen and of the saintly Richard Reynolds of Syon. These were all men who shared Pole's humanist intellectual and religious priorities, and he knew and revered them.[13]

Pole despatched his treatise of the primacy and the divorce, *De Unitate,* to Henry on 27 May 1536. While still working on it, he had kept the book's content secret from all but his most intimate friends. His own household were under the impression that the book would be everything Henry desired, the prelude to a triumphal return home. But they were also aware that the writing of the book had triggered a spiritual and intellectual conversion experience for Pole: in the writing, they reported, their master had crossed some kind of spiritual Rubicon. As his servant John Frier reported, Pole had abandoned classical study for that of theology 'despising things merely human and terrestrial. He is undergoing a great change, exchanging man for God'.[14]

This was certainly so, and the change focused on his understanding of the providential role of the papacy in the life of the Church. When Pole began the book he shared the widespread conviction that papal primacy was a venerable human construct, an administrative convenience devised for the good order of the Church. As he wrote, however, he became convinced that it was in fact of divine origin. Interestingly, this shift in understanding was due just as much to his discernment of the finger of God in recent events as in his study of ancient texts, though he had certainly immersed himself in the patristic evidence for papal primacy. But it was Henry's ruthless execution of the opponents of Royal Supremacy that triggered Pole's change of heart.

Under an impassive exterior, he had been traumatized by the executions of Fisher, More and the London Carthusians, especially that of More whom he knew and considered the wisest and best of living Englishmen. He became convinced that these deaths for the unity of the Church round the See of Peter, the first such deaths in Europe, constituted a direct message from God, written in blood, an unequivocal assurance that papal primacy was a matter of divine and not human law. Pole became correspondingly convinced that Henry, who had once seemed the ideal Renaissance Christian prince, had made himself a tyrant, who would stop at nothing to gratify his gross appetites. Those who flattered and served him, like Cranmer, were jackals to a lion out of control.

The resulting book, written with a pen dipped in vitriol, can seem wordy and repetitive to modern readers. But it made an effective case against

Henrician apologists like Richard Samson, Bishop of Chichester, and offered a formidable theological defence of papal primacy. It was also a savagely frank personal attack on the King, as a tyrant who had separated his people from the unity of Christendom, all for the love of a worthless harlot. Pole berated Henry's demonic usurpation of the authority of the priesthood in general and of the successor of St Peter in particular, and he denounced especially his murder of God's prophets, More and Fisher. The book contained an address to the Emperor Charles V, urging him to abandon plans for a crusade against the Turks, and instead to liberate England from a tyranny greater than the Turk.[15]

This aggressive polemic circulated only in mansuscript until 1539, but it caused an immense stir in reforming circles in Rome, and was the trigger for Pole's elevation to the Cardinalate at the end of 1536. Almost immediately, Paul III despatched him on two disastrously unsuccessful missions, first as legate to France and the Low Countries in 1537 to assist the Pilgrimage of Grace, and then in 1539 to the Court of Charles V at Toledo to persuade the Emperor to a crusade against Henry.[16] There are signs that an effective lobby had been launched at Henry's court on Pole's behalf in the immediate aftermath of the arrival of his book at court in the spring of 1536: the committee appointed by Henry to scrutinize *De Unitate* consisted mostly of Pole's friends, notably Thomas Starkey and Cuthbert Tunstall. But with the outbreak of the Pilgrimage, all that became an irrelevance. In the face of a major threat to the entire Tudor regime, Pole was now written off by Henry's court as 'Master traytour Pole'. His former dependents and friends scrambled to distance themselves from him, and he became the target for a series of botched assassination attempts. And within two years, Henry, unable to reach him, instead executed his brother, Lord Montague, and his mother, the aged Countess of Salisbury, on conspiracy charges.[17]

While all this was going on, Cranmer's religious development had moved in exactly the opposite direction. Pole's reverence for the Petrine office grew, but by contrast Cranmer's earlier conventional respect for the papacy evaporated. By the early 1530s, the Pope had come to seem to him a demonic figure, the great corrupter of Christianity, usurper of the authority not only of the King but of Christ himself. While Pole was toiling over the composition of *De Unitate*, Cranmer was regaling conservative Canterbury congregations with the information that 'these many years past' he had been praying for the downfall of the Bishop of Rome: in February 1536 Cranmer preached for two solid hours in London's great open air pulpit at Paul's Cross, to prove that the Pope was the Antichrist.[18]

Cranmer's devotion to the Divine Right of Kings is of course well-known: at the coronation of Edward VI he assured the infant king that no bishop, church or ceremony could make or unmake him, because a rightful king was directly anointed by God. The king was Christ's vice-gerent and vicar on earth, subject only to the judgement of God and therefore above all earthly restraint.[19] Notoriously, during his trial this extreme veneration for royal authority would trap Cranmer into maintaining the preposterous view that as Emperor of Rome in the Apostle's time, Nero was also supreme head of the Church of the Apostles. This extraordinary devotion to the monarchy has long been seen as the key to Cranmer's religious thought. But Diarmaid MacCulloch has suggested that in fact Cranmer's hatred of the papacy came first, leaving him with an authority vacuum, which he filled with veneration of the monarchy.[20]

Pole, by contrast, was an aristocrat, who felt that his own Plantagenet blood made him at least the equal of any Tudor whatever. He thought that the best kind of monarchy was elective, not hereditary. He believed that kings were answerable to their subjects, or to the emperor, if they did not rule well. In spiritual matters, kings were subordinate to priests: only the Pope was Christ's vicar on earth.

Both men were aware of each other's beliefs: Cranmer is reported to have composed an answer to Pole's *De Unitate*, though it has not survived, while in March 1536 Pole was relaying to his horrified Italian circle reports of Cranmer's pulpit rantings against the Pope as Antichrist.[21] In Edward's reign, Cranmer was to become the patron and friend of Pole's former friends and clients, Bernardino Ochino and Peter Martyr Vermigli, and they no doubt gave him a good deal of inside information about their former patron. But Pole and Cranmer's paths would not cross again directly until they converged, fatally for Cranmer, almost twenty years on, in the reign of Queen Mary.

For with the accession of Queen Mary, Cranmer's work crashed in ruins, and England was once more restored to Catholic communion and papal juris-diction. Having taken part in the plot to exclude Mary from the throne, Cranmer was convicted of treason, but given his pivotal role in the Protestantizing of England, it was inevitable that he should also be tried for heresy. The process against him, alongside Ridley and Latimer, opened at Oxford in September 1555. Ridley and Latimer were burned together on 16 October: but Cranmer's case dragged on for months longer because his unique status as *Legatus Natus* meant that only the Pope could degrade or condemn him.[22]

Pole was not directly involved in any of these trials, but he kept a close eye on the proceedings at Oxford. Having learned from his agents there that Cranmer seemed less defiant than Ridley or Latimer, he told King Philip that if the Archbishop could be induced to recant, his example would do much good.[23] So a week after Ridley and Latimer's executions, Pole sent Cranmer an immense letter in Latin, the second half of which was in fact a treatise, *De Sacramento*, refuting Cranmer's eucharistic beliefs and defending the Church's tradition.[24] The first half of the letter was more personal, picking up some issues from the trial, blaming Cranmer above all others for egging Henry on to the divorce, and for leading thousands of souls astray by his serpent-like seductions, attacking the Archbishop's concubinate marriage, and in general denouncing a career which Pole saw as rooted in deception, self-indulgence and ambition.

One of the three principle charges at the trial had been that Cranmer had perjured himself in swearing solemn obedience to the Pope at his conse-cration, so Pole also accused Cranmer of perjury. This was in fact a hard charge for Cranmer to rebut: to be of use to Henry in granting the divorce, Cranmer's standing as Archbishop of Canterbury had to be impeccable. To ensure this, he had to swear the usual oaths of allegiance to the Pope. Given his belief that the Pope was Antichrist, this was a tall order. However, under pressure from Henry, Cranmer satisfied a very uneasy conscience by making a solemn protestation in private before lawyers, that the oaths of obedience he would take to the Pope during the consecration ceremony would not prevent his proceeding with the Reformation of the English Church in obedience to the King. As Thomas Martin, the chief prosecutor, put it at his trial, 'He made a protestation one day to keep never a whit of that which he would swear the next day'. However one may seek to excuse it, this was undoubtedly an unedi-fying episode, and it appeared all the more squalid to Pole, since More, Fisher and the Carthusians had gone to their deaths precisely because they would *not* swear an oath they did not believe. For Pole, therefore, this charge of perjury lay at the root of all the evils of Cranmer's archiepiscopate: it showed him to be not the shepherd who enters by the door, but the wolf who breaks into the sheepfold to kill and destroy. 'The Church in England has never suffered more, the Church of Christ has never had a more grievous enemy than you.'[25]

Within days of its dispatch, Pole regretted sending this letter, since the Spanish theologians he had sent to work on Cranmer were getting nowehere, and told him they 'despaired of the salvation of that miserable man's soul'. Pole wondered whether it was right to waste medicine on hopeless cases.[26] He had told Cranmer himself that it might be more fitting for him to call down the fire of God's vengeance on Cranmer and the 'house' or schismatic church he had created when he had abandoned the Church of God, than to reason and plead with him. However, he declared, he took encouragement from the fact that it was never too late to repent, and Cranmer was now asking for a private conference with him.

In fact, Pole never did speak in person to Cranmer, but just two weeks later he wrote another almost equally long letter to him, this time in English, in which he brought the charge of perjury into sharper focus. At his trial, Cranmer had refused to recognize the jurisdiction of the presiding papal delegate, James Brookes, Bishop of Gloucester, on the grounds that he was the representative of a usurped foreign power, and whose allegiance to the Pope was incompatible with his obedience to the Queen. Dangerously, given the uncomfortable charge of perjury against himself, Cranmer wrote to the Queen calling the Pope Antichrist and denouncing Brooke as a perjurer. For good measure, he wrote separately to the Queen, in effect accusing her too of perjury for betraying her coronation oath by obedience to the Pope.[27]

The Queen passed these letters to Pole to deal with. He decided to use the occasion for a last urgent effort to persuade Cranmer to repudiate his heresies. The resulting reply has often been condemned for its harshness to a defeated old man at bay, and it certainly pulls no punches: but its tone sprang partly from Pole's outrage that Cranmer of all people should accuse others, including the Queen herself, of perjury, and partly from his genuine anguish at Cranmer's apparent determination to die an unrepentant heretic. Under the ferocity, there was a genuine pastoral concern. Equally, however, there is no disguising his revulsion at what seemed to him Cranmer's demonic errors, both about the papacy and about the sacrament of the altar. And at the centre of Pole's revulsion lay Cranmer's entry into the Primacy of all England on the basis of that perjured oath.

> you, geveng your othe to the truthe, yow mocked with the same, as the Jewes mocked with Christ, when thei saluted him saing Ave Rex Judaeorum and afterwards did crucifie hym. For so did yow to the Vicar of Christ, Knowledgeng the Pope of Rome by the words of your othe, to be so, and in mynde intending to crucifie the same authoritie. Whereof came the plague of deape ignoraunce and blyndnes unto yow.

Even if Cranmer had intended 'a thousande reformations in your mynde', no good could flow from so bad a beginning, 'yow now entryng to the mownteyne of God, which was to that high Archbushoprick, and to the Primacie of the Realm ... by fraud and dissimulation'.[28]

Pole's letter concluded with an urgent appeal to Cranmer to throw himself on God's mercy and recant. In fact, Cranmer's recantation, when it came, was not the result of Pole's fierce pleading, but of natural timidity, spiritual and mental isolation, and the relentless persuasions of his Oxford minders. As we know, however, that repentance did not last.[29] The truly horrific decision to burn Cranmer anyway, despite his recantations, must surely have been the Queen's, but Pole must at least have acquiesced in it. Moreover, the messenger carrying this decision, and justifying it from the pulpit at Cranmer's execution, was Henry Cole, Provost of Eton and a former member of Pole's Italian household. Notoriously, Cole's sermon at Cranmer's burning justified his death on three grounds. Here are Cole's words as Foxe summarized them:

> First that being a traytor, he had dissolued the lawfull matrimonie betweene the Kinge her father and mother: besides the driuing oute of the Popes authoritye, while he was Metropolitane.
>
> Secondly, that he had ben an heretike, from whom as from an author and onely fountaine, all heretical doctrine & schismaticall opinions that so many

yeres haue preuailed in Englande, did first rise and spring: of which hee had
not bene a secrete fauorer only, but also a most earnest defender euen to the
ende of his life, sowing them abroad by wrytings and argumēts, priuately
and openly, not without great ruine and decay of the catholicke church.

And further, it seemed meete, according to the lawe of equalitie, that
as the death of the Duke of Northumb. of late, made euen wyth Thomas
More Chauncellour that dyed for the Churche, so there shoulde be one
that shoulde make euen wt Fisher of Rochester: and because that Ridley,
Hooper, Ferrar, were not able to make euēn wyth that man, it seemed
meete, that Cranmer shoulde be ioyned to them to fill vp this part of
equalitie.'[30]

Each of the three core elements of Cole's sermon, it has to be admitted, can
be found in Pole's relations with Cranmer – the insistence on his special
culpability in the divorce, the schism, and the spread of heresy were central
issues in Pole's two letters to Cranmer in prison, and the emphasis on the
centrality of the martyrdoms of More and Fisher is something specially
characteristic of Pole and his circle. Until March 1556, the regime, apart
from the Cardinal himself, had been strangely silent about More, Fisher
and the other Henrician martyrs.[31] Their centrality in Cole's funeral sermon
for Cranmer suggest some direct input from Pole: if he did not instigate
Cranmer's execution, he certainly accepted it and had some part in Cole's
attempt to justify it.

Whoever was responsible, the decision to burn Cranmer famously backfired.
It provoked the weary old man to a desperate last stand, and a magnificently
defiant death. We need not exaggerate this setback to the regime: the magnificence of Cranmer's death would only emerge in Elizabeth's reign, in John
Foxe's narrative. In 1556 only those present at the burning in Oxford itself
were aware of Cranmer's volte-face, and though his six recantations were
hastily published without acknowledgement of his final change of heart, later
that year Catholic apologists would make much of the radical doctrinal instability which his repudiation of his many recantations revealed.[32] But there can
be little doubt that a penitent Cranmer alive and under house-arrest would
have been a greater asset to Mary's regime than the martyr responsible for the

magnificent and heroic gesture of holding his hand in the fire. Nothing about that death seemed magnificent, however, to Pole and his associates, who saw in Cranmer's actions only desperation, and a tragic return to damnable error. And Cranmer's relapse, of course, confirmed the Queen in her conviction that he had been shamming repentance all along to save his life, and that burning him had therefore been the right decision.[33]

Pole, perhaps, was not so sure: later the same year he took immense personal pains over the conversion of another iconic leader of the Edwardine Reformation. Sir John Cheke, Edward VI's quondam tutor, had fled to the continent and there had become a key figure in the Protestant diaspora. Mary's Council now had Cheke kidnapped, and brought to England for trial. Pole not only despatched one of the regime's most effective persuaders, the golden-tongued Abbot John Feckenham, to consult with the captive, but he granted Cheke the personal interviews he had denied Cranmer. The lengthy recantation Pole eventually composed for Cheke reiterated many of the issues, even the very phrases, that had cropped up in his correspondence with Cranmer, such as the final paragraph, warning against a pretended conformity to Catholicism for fear's sake: this was, he wrote, in a phrase lifted directly from his second letter to Cranmer, 'a mere mocking of Christ, and more dishonouring, than when the Jews saluted him saying *Ave Rex Judaeorum* with their mouth, the same time they brought him to be crucified as a malefactor'.[34] Cheke's recantation gave the Marian church the propaganda triumph which the death of Cranmer had denied them.

But for the remaining two years of Pole's life, Cranmer would continue to haunt the cardinal's thoughts, and to surface again and again in his writing and preaching. Within a month of his consecration as Archbishop of Canterbury, Pole set about purging the diocese of Canterbury from the effects of Cranmer's archiepiscopate. He issued instructions for a general visitation, and a diocesan special heresy commission was established.[35] The new Archbishop composed an extensive instruction to guide the work of these commissioners, specifying in depth how the laity of the diocese who had fallen into error were to be dealt with. This instruction, and his subsequent sermons for the diocese, reveal how deeply Pole had brooded on Cranmer and his work.[36]

For Pole, the truths of the faith were never arrived at by reason, or individual judgement, but received from the testimony of the Church, transmitted through its bishops. In discussing this tradition, Pole constantly recurred to a verse in Deuteronomy, 'Ask your father, and he will show you, and your elders, and they will tell you'. Here was the key to a secure grasp of the gospel: the bishop was your spiritual father, ask him, and he will show you.

But in his instructions to the Canterbury heresy commission, Pole asked how would this have worked 'three years ago, when the Busshope of Canterburye was an heretique himselfe'? Pole was clear that those who had accepted Cranmer's eucharistic teaching because he was their bishop were to be treated as innocent, however erroneous their beliefs: for 'ytt is nott the opinion alone that maketh a man an heretique, be it never so much against the faythe'. Provided they were not stubborn, and willing to be corrected now by Pole, then those who innocently absorbed such errors deserved instruction, not punishment.[37]

But a theoretical difficulty remained. Cranmer's case seemed to cast doubt on the security of tradition and the force of the maxim 'ask thy father'. What did Cranmer's fall suggest about the continuity of tradition in the See of Canterbury? Pole's answer to this question was that one's spiritual father must be able to show *his* spiritual father, just as in a physical pedigree one must be able to appeal to an unbroken line of descent: the pedigree of Catholic truth must be as concrete and complete as a family tree. Cranmer and the other reformers appealed indeed to the Fathers of the primitive church, but this was a paper theory, that unchurched what Pole called 'their nexte fathers'. On the evangelical account, for centuries their benighted Catholic ancestors had lived and died in ignorance of true Christianity. For Pole, this was to repudiate the Deuteronomic command, 'ask thy father'. Pole by contrast appealed specifi-cally to his own Episcopal pedigree, the long line of his predecessors in the See of Canterbury: 'the ladder of the fathers spirituall by the succession of busshopes which all have agreed in oone, the last following that same self fayth'. It was a line that ran from Christ and St Peter, down through the popes to St Augustine of Canterbury and his successors in the see, including Lanfranc, who had defended the Catholic doctrine of the Mass, down to modern times, 'untyll busshope warrames tyme, which professed the same'. But after Warham had come Cranmer, 'whiche nother had his father carnall nor spirituall afore him of his opinion'. By the novelty of his teaching he had revealed himself to be a spiritual monster, a son without a father, self begotten, a heretic. And since Cranmer was 'not hable to showe his nexte father of whom he received his opinion, this sheweth he was not the father God sendeth the church unto to learne the trewith'.

As Pole declared in another Canterbury sermon, developing the same train of thought, in the long ladder of truth Cranmer was

> a broken steppe, which is now taken awaye, and a new one of that same matter that your fathers steppes were made of putt in his place, there being but one broken steppe amongst so meny sounde and good, and suche an one that you being upon itt, not only yow founde no resting place ... but wythall travayle there yow took a sorrier fawlle than iff you had faullen from heaven to earth and from thence to hell, as ye dyd.[38]

We take it for granted that the Marian regime's decision to burn Cranmer was a spectacular own goal, the creation of a martyr out of a defeated and broken apostate, and in an obvious sense it was. But Pole's broodings in the wake of Cranmer's death alert us to the fact that had the cardinal not died on the same day as his cousin the Queen in November 1558, English perceptions of the shape and meaning of Cranmer's life might have been very different. Pole's instructions to the Canterbury heresy commission, and the sermons for the diocese of Canterbury in which he reflected further on Cranmer's apostasy, and which he intended for publication, constituted a powerful theological apologetic for Catholic tradition, vividly and concretely identified with the succession of orthodox sacramental teaching by the Archbishops of Canterbury from Augustine and Lanfranc to Warham and Pole himself, a succession in which Cranmer was the one broken step. Death was to prevent the publication of Pole's sermons: but even so, his reflections on Cranmer would help shape Catholic thinking about the martyred heresiarch for centuries.

Pole's distinctive emphasis on the succession of teaching by the archbishops of Canterbury was perhaps too specific and too idiosyncratic to be easily generalized. But the other themes of his letters to, and preaching about, Cranmer were taken up at once and developed in Catholic Reformation historiography. Pole's right-hand man, Nicholas Harpsfield, compiled a devastating Latin account of Cranmer's execution in 1556, drawing heavily on Pole's ideas and emphasizing, like him, the perjury with which Cranmer's archiepiscopal ministry began, his uncanonical marriage, and the spiritual instability which had marked his end. The fact that this account was composed in Latin suggests that it was intended for a European as well as an English audience.[39] Harpsfield went on to provide a savagely comic account of Cranmer in English in his *History of the Pretended Divorce*. This was the work in which the notorious box in which the Archbishop was alleged to carry Mrs Cranmer about made its first appearance.[40] These books remained in manuscript, but their key ideas passed almost unaltered into Nicholas Sanders' hugely influential Latin work on *The Origin and Growth of the Anglican Schism*, published posthumously in 1585.[41] Sanders' book, denounced by Protestants as the 'pestilent and seditious book of Dr Slanders' rapidly established itself as the most widely read Catholic account of the English Reformation for the next three hundred years: in the generation after its first publication it went through an astonishing six Latin editions and was translated into French, German, Spanish, Portuguese, Italian and Spanish. John Foxe's account of Cranmer's death would create for English Protestants the figure of a noble archiepiscopal martyr. Pole and his followers presented Catholic Europe with a very different Cranmer, a concubinate priest, feebly subservient to brute tyranny, untruthful from the start, and unstable to the end. That unflattering portrait would shape Catholic perceptions of Cranmer and his Reformation down to modern times. And in that sense at least, Pole had the last word on Cranmer.

9

Rome and Catholicity in mid Tudor England

On 10 or 11 March 1554 a group of state officials and prominent churchmen met for supper in the lodgings of Sir John Brydges, Lieutenant of the Tower of London. They included Thomas Brydges, Sir John's brother, Sir John Bourne, principal Secretary of State to Queen Mary, and Sir Roger Cholmeley, Lord Chief Justice under Edward VI, though now in eclipse for his ill-advised support for Queen Jane in 1553. The churchmen included Dr John Feckenham, formerly a monk of Evesham, lately chaplain to Edmund Bonner and prebendary of St Paul's: in Edward's reign, Feckenham had himself spent two years as a prisoner in the Tower, suspected of complicity in the Prayer-Book rebellions of 1549. Unsurprisingly, his star was now in the ascendant, and less than twenty-four hours earlier he had been elected Dean of St Paul's.

This notable company had gathered to have supper with an equally illustrious prisoner, Nicholas Ridley. As Bishop of London under Edward VI and a key figure in the radicalizing of English eucharistic doctrine and practice, Ridley was now a marked man, and was due to be taken to Oxford in company with Thomas Cranmer and Hugh Latimer for a show heresy trial within the next few days: indeed the imminence of his departure was almost certainly the reason for the supper. It was, of course, an edgy meal: inevitably, the talk turned to heresy and how one could recognize it. Unsurprisingly, Ridley was on his guard: despite universal protestations of good will, no-one seemed willing to give him an explicit assurance that whatever he might say would not be used in evidence against him, though in the event none of it was.

The main focus of the conversation was eucharistic doctrine, and in attempting to persuade Ridley of the truth of Catholic sacramental teaching, Feckenham appealed to an argument from living tradition: as Ridley reported,

> 'Forty yeares agoe' quoth M. Fecknam, 'all were of one opinion' about the Mass.

Ridley dismissed the apologetic value of such universal acceptance, since

> 'Forty yeares ago' (quoth I) 'all held that the Bishop of Rome was supreme head of the vniuersall Church.'
>
> 'What then?' was master Fecknam beginning to say. &c. but M. Secretary tooke the tale, and sayde, that was 'but a positiue law.'

Ridley, however, was having none of this minimalism:

> 'A positiue law?' quoth I, 'No Syr, he [the pope] would not haue it so: for it is in his decrees, that he challenged it by Christes owne word. For his decree sayth … .The Church of Rome was aduaunced aboue all other Churches in the world, not by any Sinodicall constitutions, nor yet any counsell, but by the liuely voyce of the Lord, according as the Lord sayd to Peter: Thou art Peter. &c. And in an other place he entreateth … Thou art Cephas, that is to say, the head'.
>
> 'Tush', (quoth M. Secretary) 'it was not counted an article of our fayth. '[1]

In this story, which of course comes from Ridley via Foxe, notice that the two clergy, Catholic monk and Protestant bishop alike, were agreed that before the break with Rome everyone in England had accepted the supremacy of the Pope over the church as an article of faith. When the layman, Sir John Bourne, pooh-poohed the very idea, Ridley rounded on him, quoting not only Canon law but Pope Boniface VIII's claim to universal papal supremacy in the Bull *Unam Sanctam*. Ridley of course had an axe to grind: for him the universal acceptance of papal supremacy in early Tudor England represented the *reductio ad absurdam* of the whole argument from tradition. For Feckenham, by contrast, the acceptance of papal authority by everyone in early Tudor England was a strong indication of Catholic truth – *quod semper, quod ubique, quod ab omnes*.[2] It's a revealing exchange, and one that brings us to the nub of my concerns in this chapter. Were Ridley and Feckenham right? *Did* early Tudor Catholics accept papal primacy? If they did, what are we to say about the almost universal repudiation of papal obedience under Henry, and what account are we to give of the return to papal obedience under Mary?

In his essay 'Is the Pope a Catholic?' Peter Marshall elegantly traced the efforts made during the 1530s and early 40s, both by the Henrician regime itself and by the very large number of conservative conformists uneasy about their acquiescence in the Royal Supremacy, to devise an account of catholicity which excluded communion with or obedience to the Pope.[3] Marshall's essay is a valuable contribution to the history of Tudor casuistry, and a salutary reminder of the shifts to which decent men and women might be driven in attempting to reconcile self-respect with self-preservation. But it should not blind us to the fact that most of those involved in this enterprise were almost certainly acting, to a greater or lesser degree, in bad faith. It is, of course, perfectly true that at the beginning of the sixteenth century there was a wide area of legitimate disagreement about the precise nature and scope of papal primacy. Conciliarist theories fostered by uncertainties over papal authority during the early fifteenth century were entertained by early Tudor humanists as they were everywhere else in Europe, and were shared even by some of those who would eventually give their lives for papal authority: everyone knows William Roper's famous anecdote about Thomas More's objections to the unguarded exaltation of papal primacy in Henry VIII's *Assertio Septem Sacramentorum*, and More's advice to Henry that papal authority should be 'more slenderly touched' there.[4]

But nuances of interpretation of the meaning or exact extent of papal primacy are worlds away from the wholesale rejection of all papal authority. In 1509 nobody in England except the Lollards doubted that communion with and obedience to the Bishop of Rome were in some sense fundamental to Catholic unity and Catholic identity. In the fifteenth and early sixteenth century the overwhelming majority of English people accepted as axiomatic that the See of Rome was 'the well of grace', the necessary source of dispensations, absolutions, and licences that could facilitate, absolve or dispense individuals and institutions in a vast range of situations: those able to afford to do so routinely had recourse to papal power, for the Pope and the Pope alone could allow illegitimate men to be ordained to the priesthood, permit first cousins to marry, dissolve invalid unions, or permit bishops to hold more than one diocese. Henry's own first marriage was made possible only by the invocation of this universally acknowledged papal dispensing power.[5] Outright rejection of papal authority as the work of Antichrist, and the corresponding denial of all but a personal moral leadership of the apostles in Peter, was indeed to be advanced by some of the ideological architects of Henrician apologetic for the break with Rome, and even a deeply conservative courtier like Henry Parker, Lord Morley, might consider it prudent to establish his loyalty by denouncing 'the desteable ydolatrye of this wicked monster of Rome'.[6]

But there is abundant evidence of continuing loyalty to the Pope and belief in his primacy in England even in the dangerous 1530s,[7] and in 1509, everyone would have thought that to denounce the Pope as an idolatrous monster excluded those doing so from Catholic communion. It's notable that the most cogent Henrician defence of the Royal Supremacy, Gardiner's *De Vere Obedientia*, wriggles hard to avoid such abusive demonization of the papacy, and Gardiner hedges his bets about the existence of a papal primacy of some kind.[8] For despite his prominence as a defender of the Henrician schism, Gardiner himself was certainly a reluctant schismatic: his secret negotiations with Cardinal Contarini at Regensburg in 1541 make it absolutely clear that unlike his royal master he thought a return to papal obedience both possible and desirable. It's hard to believe that conservative-minded colleagues like Cuthbert Tunstall and John Stokesley were not equally uncomfortable in the schism that their ferocious royal master had forced upon them. The Henrician conservative Bishop George Day of Chichester was certainly speaking for many when he admitted to John Bradford in 1555 that in Henry's reign 'I went with the world, but, I tell you, it was always against my conscience'.[9]

I am sceptical, therefore, of the notion that the twenty years from 1534 to 1554 saw the emergence of a distinctive English Catholic theology: Catholicism without the Pope. The conservative writings in those years by Gardiner, Tunstal, Smyth and others in defence of the sacraments and the authority of the institutional church seem to me not stages in the evolution of a coherent Anglo-Catholic system, but a series of increasingly beleaguered stands in defence of chosen doctrinal bunkers as the Reformation engulfed them, skirmishes in a theological war whose battle-plan was fatally undermined by the absence of a coherent ecclesiology.

These considerations have a direct bearing on how we are to understand the restoration of papal communion in Marian England. Who was more typical in their attitude towards the papacy, Sir John Bourne – 'Tush, it was not considered an article of our faith' – or Dr Feckenham, with his nostalgia for a pre-schismatic England in which there had been widespread acceptance of papal primacy as an article of faith? Some recent accounts of Mary's reign have opted firmly for what I cannot resist calling the 'Bourne Supremacy'. The most clear-cut of these is Lucy Wooding's *Rethinking Catholicism in Reformation England*, which argues that for most Marian churchmen, the return to papal obedience was an unwelcome irrelevance, the papacy itself at best an embarrassing administrative necessity, part of a package deal for the restoration of traditional religion, but a part to which they attributed no positive value in its own right. So for Dr Wooding, the Marian Church was in seamless continuity with the Henrician past in finding no real religious *use* for the papacy. Marian apologists, she thinks, wrote and spoke of papal authority rarely, if at all, and then 'purely in terms of an administrative purpose', since for them 'the Pope had no particular function to fulfil as a spiritual head'. Over the preceding twenty years the rhetoric of the Royal Supremacy, she argued, 'had been thoroughly assimilated within Catholic thought', and 'the papacy had become irrelevant to the Catholic faith in England'. That situation would only change after Queen Mary's death, and then as a result of external pressures – the irreversible consolidation of the Elizabethan Settlement, the assimilation of the English Catholic clerical diaspora into the post-Tridentine Church in Europe, and perhaps especially the utter dependence of that diaspora on the financial and institutional support of the Counter-Reformation papacy. Only when English Catholic apologists found themselves 'clinging to the papacy for safety's sake' would the Marian reluctance to talk about papal authority begin to be eroded.[10]

That analysis of Marian attitudes to the papacy seems to me to involve a fundamental misreading of the evidence, but the germ of Dr Wooding's argument was perhaps implicit in the sharp distinction which John Bossy drew many years ago between the Marian Church as a coda to the history of the medieval *Ecclesia Anglicana*, and Elizabethan recusancy as a new beginning and an assimilation to English circumstances of the novel energies of the Counter-Reformation.[11] And the continuities which Dr Wooding thought she perceived between Henrician and Marian attitudes to the papacy are also assumed in other accounts of Marian Catholicism. Ellen Macek's study of traditionalist Catholic apologetic between 1535 and 1558, *The Loyal Opposition*, similarly asserts the persistence of Henrician anti-papalism into the Marian Restoration. Macek's book barely mentions the papacy, and has no index entry for pope, papacy or papal – and like Dr Wooding, Dr Macek dismisses the significance of the papacy for traditionalist understanding of Catholic belief. Macek sees the reformist programme of Cardinal Pole for the reconstruction of Marian Catholicism as having been undermined specifically by traditionalist mistrust of Pole's papalism, while for the cardinal's conservative colleagues and subordinates, she argues, Paul IV's mistreatment of the cardinal was a grim confirmation of their 'earlier warnings about papal interference in English affairs'.[12]

Even the briefest survey of the official teaching of the Marian Church on the papacy will show how very wide of the mark these assessments are.[13] Indeed Mary's regime almost literally attached bells and whistles to the whole notion of papal authority, in the form of a major annual celebration of its religious importance. From 1556 Pole's Legatine Synod ordered a nationwide annual commemoration of the reconciliation with Rome, to be kept as a gala day.[14] This was to be marked in every parish in the land with a solemn procession, a mass with special prayers of thanksgiving for the return of the realm to Catholic unity under the Pope, and a compulsory sermon expounding both the doctrine of papal primacy and the practical benefits of the restoration of Catholic unity. For priests who could not preach themselves, the regime obligingly produced a printed model sermon on the subject by John Harpsfield.[15] In London this celebration was held at St Paul's, the clergy and wardens of every parish in attendance, priests in copes, the wardens bearing the parish banners. This high-profile commemoration was a new invention, the first of what was to prove a series of Tudor and Stuart annual religious commemorations of national deliverance. Its success is best measured by the fact that Mary's Protestant successors were to adapt the device for their own purposes – Elizabeth's accession day, Gunpowder treason, and the rest of what David Cressy has labelled Bonfires and Bells.[16]

But of course, in the case of the Marian regime, the bonfire half of Bonfire and Bells involved a gruesomely literal endorsement of papal primacy. Not to put too fine a point on it, Mary's regime burned anyone who denied papal primacy. Denial of the authority of the Catholic Church and specifically the authority of the Pope was one of the two charges most often laid against the victims of the Marian burnings. The issue of papal authority was thereby placed as a test of Catholicity on a par with the other key issue, the presence of Christ in the sacrament of the altar. Certainly, the precise terms in which the issue was put to suspected heretics varied, and in some cases it was phrased in as conciliatory a way as possible, to encourage the wavering to conformity. But in other instances it might be uncompromisingly explicit. The ex-Dominican Bishop John Hopton of Norwich was one of the most active of the Marian bishops against heresy: unsurprisingly, the first of the articles used in his diocese accused suspects 'that they beleeued not the Pope of Rome to bee supreme head immediately vnder Christ in earth of the vniuersall Catholike Church'.[17] By contrast, Bishop Bonner's articles for the London diocese were more emollient, less provocative, emphasizing the universality of the church rather than the authority of its visible head, and smuggling in the obligatory reference to the Church of Rome by listing Rome as one Catholic church among many, albeit the first. So, it was alleged against suspects

> that thou hast not beleued … the faith and religion, which both the Church of Rome, Italy, Spayne, England, France, Ireland, Scotland, and all other churches in Europe, beyng true members and partes of the sayd Catholike and vniuersall Church do beleeue & teach, … : but contrarywise, thou hast beleeued, and doest beleeue, that that fayth and religion, which the sayd church of Rome, & all the other Churches aforesayd, haue heretofore beleued, and do beleue is false, erroneous, and naught.[18]

The Henrician King's Book had insisted that the Church of Rome was just one Catholic church alongside 'the churches of France, Spain England or

Portugal'. So it's tempting to see in the formulation of Bonner's London articles in Mary's reign some lingering reluctance on his part to reduce the question of the unity and authority of the Catholic church to the single question of papal supremacy. This may well be so: but it shouldn't be construed, nevertheless, as a rejection of or resistance to papal primacy itself. The fundamental Marian compendium of Catholic orthodoxy, the *Profitable and Necessary Doctrine*, together with the two homilies on the primacy, were issued in 1555 on Bonner's own authority, and they were unequivocal in their assertion that the Catholic church by Christ's ordinance, had 'one principall head or chiefe governor here upon earth ... the chief vicar and substitute of Christ.', an office ordained 'for the preservation of the unity thereof'.[19]

And if the language of Bonner's articles was more restrained than that of some other bishops, there is no evidence whatever of a generalized official Marian reluctance to use the language of papal primacy and even supremacy. Even Stephen Gardiner himself made no bones about his unequivocal repudiation of Henricianism. When Rowland Taylor piously blessed the memory of Henry and rebuked Gardiner for reneging on the Oath of Supremacy he had sworn to the dead king, Gardiner brushed him aside: 'Tush, tush, that was herodes oath ... I have done well in breaking it and I thank God I am come home agayne to our Mother, to the catholike Church of Rome'.[20]

This was remarkable enough from the leading Henrician clerical apologist: unsurprisingly, the activists round Cardinal Pole were even more downright. Nicholas Harpsfield, Archdeacon of Canterbury, one of the most effective Marian hammers of heretics, and right-hand-man to Pole in the diocese of Canterbury, sometime after 1557 mounted a wholesale literary attack on Henry and Henricianism in his *Treatise of the pretended Divorce*: in it, Harpsfield insisted that the authority of the Holy See was such that the Pope had power 'to dispense even with those things which the Apostles themselves have in the Church ordained'. The Pope could overturn even the decisions of a general Council, because 'the Pope hath his authoritie not of the Councils but of God himself'.[21]

The rhetorical distance between what could be seen as a carefully nuanced placing of Rome as *primus inter pares* in Bonner's articles and Harpsfield's gung-ho high papalism, setting Pope above Councils, alerts us to a plurality of voices, if not of doctrines, within Marian Catholicism and, in Harpsfield's case, to the centrality of Cardinal Pole in establishing the understanding of the place of the papacy which became the official Marian line.

I've discussed Pole's distinctive teaching on the papacy at some length elsewhere,[22] so I don't want to linger too long on it here, but we need to recall its main outlines.[23] As we have seen in chapter eight, Pole first articulated his thinking about the papacy in the long Latin open letter he sent to Henry in May 1536 and which was later published, apparently without his permission, under the title *Pro ecclesiasticae unitatis defensione*. Book I of this treatise had contained the usual exegesis of the usual New Testament papal proof-texts – "thou art Peter and upon this Rock I will build my Church", "Simon Peter I have prayed for you", "Feed my Lambs, feed my sheep", and so on. Book II however was more original. For a start, it included a sustained and ferocious attack on Henry himself as a tyrant led astray by lust. But it also set out a *providentialist* rather than a juridical argument for papal authority, claiming the special care of Christ for England, manifested specifically through the papacy. England had been the first nation to accept Christianity, when in the second century Pope Eleutherius had sent missionaries at the request of the mythical King Lucius. Ever since, English destinies had been inextricably linked to the papacy: the popes had repeatedly conferred unique benefits on England, most notably Gregory the Great's mission of Augustine to re-evangelize the country after the Saxon invasions. England had flourished so long as it remained in filial obedience to the popes, and had been afflicted with every kind of ill whenever it had deviated from that obedience, of which the ills of Henry's reign, tyranny begetting rebellion, were the latest and worst examples. This providentialist argument, that obedience to the papacy brought temporal blessings to a nation, just as separation from it brought corresponding calamity, was of course by no means unique to Pole. As early as 1520 the Sienese Dominican Ambrosius Politi Catharionus had argued in his *Apologia pro veritate Catholicae fidei* that the subjection of the Orthodox churches to Turkish rule was a direct consequence of their lapse from the papal obedience they had accepted at the Council of Florence, and he warned that evangelical Germany was rushing headlong to similar disaster.[24] A decade on, Thomas More claimed in his *Dialogue concerning Heresies* of 1529 that those dire warnings had been fulfilled, in his evocation of the chaos that had overtaken Germany.[25] Pole, who certainly knew More's book, gave the argument a further distinctive twist by integrating it into a broader account of the special relationship of England to the papacy stretching back to Pope Eleutherius, and even more by his daring interpretation of the deaths of Thomas More himself, and of John Fisher and the London Carthusians, as a divine endorsement of the truth of papal primacy, and a further manifestation of God's special care for the English.[26] Pole insisted that More and his fellow martyrs were the first modern martyrs to die for the unity of the church under the Pope, as opposed to some more general Christian truth. Their deaths were therefore a direct message from God, written in blood, a proof greater even than scriptural or patristic testimony, establishing definitively that papal primacy was not a mere human administrative arrangement, but an essential article of faith. And when in November 1554 he came as papal legate to absolve England from schism, Pole updated this argument in the long program-matic speech he made to both Houses of Parliament, highlighting once more the role of More and Fisher, and stressing the twenty years of calamity – war, rebellion, famine, disease, economic collapse, religious division and the spread of heresy and sacrilege – which had flowed from Henry's repudiation of papal obedience.[27]

From 1555 onwards, therefore, it was Pole's very distinctive brand of papalism which was to prove decisive for the official teaching of the Marian church. The book of Homilies published by Bishop Bonner as a companion piece to his *Profitable and Necessary Doctrine* in 1556, and subsequently prescribed by Pole for use throughout England, contained *two* sermons on the primacy (out of a total of thirteen) by John Harpsfield, brother of Nicholas and Archdeacon of London. Harpsfield's homilies rehearsed the usual arguments for Petrine primacy and its transmission to the bishops of Rome, but the sermons culmi-nated with an application of the general doctrine to England, drawing directly on Pole's ideas. Harpsfield insisted on the special providential relationship between England and Rome, 'for from that see came the fayth into this land … in the days of King Lucius', and reminded his hearers 'what miseries have be falne emongest us, synce our disobedience against the see of Rome, and synce that tyme that temporall princes dyd take upon them, that office which is spiritualle, and not belonging to the regall power, but greatly distant and different from the same'. He urged his hearers therefore to 'esteme the primacy and supremitie of the see of Rome, as an aucthoritie instituted by Chryst, for the quietness of the Crysten people, and for the preservation of christendome in the catholyke, true fayth, and for the defence of it against all heresie'.[28]

The official Marian line on England and the papacy therefore, was that until the time of Henry, Catholic England had understood its filial dependence on the mother Church of Rome and its bishop, and it had flourished so long as it understood and lived up to that dependence. Conversely, from the moment when, under the influence of a wicked king, it had abandoned papal obedience, it had thereby ceased to be a Catholic nation, and became instead the target of divine chastisement. But what of the Bourne Supremacy, 'Tush, it was not counted an article of our faith'? And how could the story of Thomas More, warning his ardently papist king against getting carried away, and urging him to touch on papal authority 'more slenderly', be accomodated within this framework?

This apparent lack of interest in the papacy on More's part was rather a pressing issue for Pole and those around him. In the first year of the Marian Restoration, there had been a deafening silence about More and the other Henrician martyrs by the restored Catholic authorities. This was not surprising. In response to Pole's *De Unitate* in 1536 Tunstall, Bonner and Gardiner had all denounced More and Fisher as traitors. Gardiner in particular was the author of the official justification of Fisher's execution, the tract *Si Sedes illa Romana*.[29] However sincere their return to Papal Obedience, these Henrician conservatives cannot have been anxious to have men they had vehemently denounced as traitors exalted now as martyrs. For Pole, however, the fate of Fisher and especially of More was central to understanding the true nature of papal primacy: as we have seen, their martyrdom for Catholic unity was for him the clinching proof that papal primacy was indeed of the *esse* not the *bene esse* of the Church. So, for Pole, the idea that More might somehow have been unsound on this very topic was intolerable.

Yet Pole certainly knew the story of More's warning to Henry against excessive devotion to the Pope. That anecdote originated with More's son-in-law, William Roper, but in 1556 it was incorporated by Nicholas Harpsfield into his full-scale biography, celebrating More's 'peerless prerogative' as 'the first of any layman in England that died a martyr for the unity of the Catholic church'.[30] Harpsfield's life of More was a programmatic tract, designed to embody Pole's understanding of the recent religious history of England in biographical form. The book was certainly compiled with Pole's blessing, and very possibly at his request. It was completed in time for New Year 1557, and Pole certainly read it that year. And he evidently brooded on the story of More's youthful disregard of papal authority. At the end of November 1557, Pole took steps to correct any impression of More's unsoundness on the papal office implied in Roper's anecdote. The cardinal gave a high profile public airing to a story of his own about More, simultaneously corroborating Roper's claim that More had once thought the papal primacy a matter of political convenience, while proving that this was a temporary lapse on the part of the greatest of Tudor martyrs, and that More had come explicitly and vehemently to disown such a view, embracing instead full-blooded Catholic belief in the centrality of papal authority.

St Andrews Day 1557 was marked with special solemnity in London. There was the usual procession, mass and sermon at St Paul's, which the Mayor, Aldermen and all the City clergy attended. The Mayor and Aldermen however then went from St Paul's to join the court at Whitehall, together with all the bishops and all the judges, to witness the solemn installation of Sir Thomas Tresham as Prior of the restored order of St John of Jerusalem. After another procession and mass sung by Abbot Feckenham, the Cardinal then preached a second St Andrew's Day sermon, on the fruits of the national reconciliation with Rome.[31] The sermon was aimed especially at the Mayor and Alderman, chastising them directly for their apparent unwillingness to eradicate or silence the vociferous evangelical minority in the City, and especially among the City's apprentices. To sweeten this frontal attack on what he saw as the City's lax enforcement of the Catholic Restoration, Pole devoted a long section of the sermon to praise of Sir Thomas More, precisely as an exemplary ' cytysen of yours … borne amonge you'. When all the rest of the realm was falling away from the unity of the church, Pole claimed, More had 'overcome all, shewinge suche constancye of fayth as he myghte be a marvelouse example to staye all other'.[32] Pole borrowed this emphasis on More as a Londoner directly from Harpsfield's life, where it is a prominent theme, but he went beyond Harpsfield in relating a City anecdote which is not to be found in Harpsfield's life of More. Pole's first-hand source for this story was the London-based Luchese silk merchant, Antonio Buonvisi, 'whom I thinke you all knowe, dwellynge from his youthe amonge you'. Buonvisi had been one of More's closest friends, and had bought More's City house when the More household relocated to Chelsea.

In Edward's reign, Buonvisi's own household in Leuven had become a refuge for Catholic exiles, including both the entire Roper family, and the young Nicholas Harpsfield.

Pole now related a conversation between Buonvisi and More in the early 1530s, in which More had aired his prophetic fears that the appearance of sacramental heresy in England might be a prelude to the ruin of the church and 'the chaunge of relygyon in this realme'. This premonition, Pole insisted, was the result of a supernatural instinct planted in More by God, since as yet there was no hint of the break with Rome, and the king had seemed ultra-Catholic, 'very styffe concernynge the use of the sacramente after the olde form and honoure'. Buonvisi therefore had asked More what his opinion was concerning papal primacy itself, 'to the whiche question he sodenlye making answer, sayd as his natural reason gave: and that was howe he tooke not that for a matter of so great moment and importance, but rather as inventyd of men for a political order, and for the more quyetnes of the ecclesiastical bodye, than the verye ordinaunce of Chryste'.

Here was the Bourne Supremacy with a vengeance, the martyr showing himself radically unsound on the issue of papal supremacy. But having given this 'sudden and first answere', Pole went on, More was stricken with compunction, 'as though hys conscience had been stroken for so sayinge'. More therefore urged Buonvisi not to take this first answer as his considered judgement, since he had never studied the question properly. They arranged to talk again on the matter in ten or twelve days. In the interim, More duly set about reading and thinking, and when he and Buonvisi next met, according to Pole, 'Mr Moore brake out into a great reproach of his owne selfe, for that he was so hastye to answer yn so greate a matter touchynge the Prymacye of the pope, sayenge Alas, Mr Bonvyse, whither was I fawlinge, when I made you that answere of the prymacye of the chyrche? I assure you, that opinion alone was ynough to make me fawle from the rest, *for that holdyth up all*'.[33]

More functions powerfully in Pole's St Andrew's day sermon, therefore, as a supernaturally inspired witness to the centrality of papal primacy in catholic orthodoxy: on this account, More came to see papal primacy as the doctrine 'that holdyth up all'. The Cardinal went on to demonstrate this interconnectedness between the lynch-pin doctrine of papal primacy and Catholic orthodoxy more generally, by reminding his audience that despite Henry's avowed orthodoxy on everything except papal authority, 'the unytie was not so soone disolvede, but that the faythe of the sacraments began to quayle yn so many hartes'. Inexorably therefore, under Edward 'at laste openlye yn the Parliament the sacrament of sacraments was caste out', 'gevynge you space … to prove and taste the bytternes of the fruyte received by the swarvynge from the unytie of the churche'.[34]

We have no way of assessing the impact on the Marian laity of this incessant insistence by Pole and his lieutenants on the necessity of papal obedience to the maintenance of Catholic unity and truth. What we can say with certainty is that it made a deep impact on the higher clergy. At Elizabeth's accession, both houses of Convocation signed a protestatation affirming both the Catholic doctrine of the mass and the papal supremacy, and the majority of cathedral dignitaries, of the university professoriate, and the heads of colleges at Oxford and Cambridge were to refuse the revived Oath of Supremacy, and most were duly deprived of their posts.[35] In the House of Lords, Abbot Feckenham, Cuthbert Scott, Bishop of Chester, and perhaps most significantly Nicholas Heath, Archbishop of York and Lord Chancellor, all made eloquent defences of papal primacy. Heath in particular was greatly liked by Queen Elizabeth, as a former Henrician conservative who had accepted the first Edwardine prayer-book. The Queen had hoped he might endorse the new settlement. Instead, he, like the others, made a determined and eloquent stand for the necessity of papal primacy. There was no question here of a papacy seen as an administrative convenience. All three speeches demonstrate acceptance of a full-blooded doctrine of papal authority, and all bear the unmistakable marks of Pole's distinctive intellectual synthesis. St Peter and the popes after him, Scott insisted, had been appointed 'to be the foundation, grounde and staye of Christe's churche': without the papacy 'what certainty can we have of our faith, or howe shall we staye ourselves, waveringe in the same in this our time?'[36] The failings of individual popes made no difference: not even Paul IV's overt hostility to the Queen and Pole could revive old reservations about papal interference. Archbishop Heath tackled this issue head on. Paul IV, he declared, had indeed been a 'very austere stern father unto us', but that ill-treatment was irrelevant: it was the Pope's office, not his person, which mattered. Christ had not left the church that he had dearly bought 'by the effusyon of his most precious blood without a head' without Peter's authority, the church's unity was broken, and by leaping out of Peter's ship, England 'must nedes be overwhelmed by the waters of schism, sects and divisions'.[37] These remarkable utterances represent the internalization by the episcopate and higher clergy during Mary's reign of a very high doctrine of papal primacy, which saw in the papacy the divinely chosen instrument of unity, and the providential beacon and safeguard of Catholic truth. These brief speeches are as full-blooded in their insistence on the religious necessity of papal primacy as anything in the more copious writings of Robert Bellarmine a generation later.

The Elizabethan Settlement would temporarily silence the Marian theological establishment. Most of the bishops and key activists were imprisoned, and though many university teachers would scatter to the Low Countries, France, and Italy, many clung on in the hope that the Catholic cause might somehow prevail within their own institutions. By the early 1560s, however, that outcome looked less and less likely, the exiles were regrouping, and by 1564, at Leuven in particular, a theological counter-offensive had been launched.[38] Inevitably, the question of papal authority was prominent among the themes tackled by these Catholic writers in exile. And what characterizes this Louvainist writing about the papacy is not, as Dr Wooding argues, its slow and reluctant absorption of alien ideas about papal authority, borrowed from the European Counter-Reformation, but its seamless continuity with the lines laid down in Marian England by Pole and his colleagues. Nicholas Harpsfield, a man at the heart of the Marian project, would play a seminal role in the formation of Elizabethan Catholic polemic.[39] And a younger generation too of Marian activists would shape the Elizabethan mission. Nicholas Sander and William Allen, whom we think of as Elizabethan activists, were in fact products of Marian Oxford and its Dominican theological schools. One other example will have to stand for many more. Thomas Dorman was a protégé of Thomas Harding at Winchester and New College, and a Fellow of All Souls at a time when the Spanish theologians introduced into Oxford by Pole were promoting a strong belief in papal primacy. In 1564 Dorman pitched into the developing controversy between Bishop Jewel of Salisbury and Dorman's mentor Thomas Harding, by publishing a treatise on the papacy and the mass. Dorman considered the proposition that 'The Bishop of Rome is the head of Christ's Universall Church here on earth', and he deployed a range of patristic sources to establish this. But the heart of his argument was precisely that embodied in Pole's anecdote about More, and replicated in most other Marian writings about the papacy: abandon the unity of papal communion, and you open the floodgates of heresy. So, like the Marian apologists, Dorman recited the afflictions of Christianity in England – heretics in the place of Catholic bishops, orthodox Catholic scholars exiled from the universities, the sacraments banished, the pulpits given over to tinkers and tradesmen, feast-days uncelebrated, Catholic ceremonies denounced and forbidden as pagan superstition. And the single root of all this was the repudiation of the papacy.

> now as we felt none of alle these miseries besides a thousande more, so long
> as we kepte ourselves within the unitie of one heade, so is every man able
> to beare wytnesse, that as soone as the divell, the author of all heresies, had
> once obtained and broughte about the banishment in our country of that
> one bishop … .all these rushed in upon us, as the dore that should have
> kept them out being set wide open.[40]

The early Tudor clergy and laity alike had turned their back on papal primacy, and had followed their king into schism. But many of those, like Gardiner and Heath, who had acquiesced in the Henrician and even the early Edawrdine religious changes in the name of obedience to royal authority, had been appalled by the radicalization of reform after 1547. They had seen the mass abolished, the sacrament dishonoured, the altars torn down. Reflection on that bitter experience made them receptive to the claim that the Royal Supremacy itself was the root of England's ills. Reginald Pole had never waivered in his affirmation of papal authority, and he had found in the deaths of More and Fisher what he took to be a direct divine testimony to the indispensability of communion with Rome as a condition of Catholicity. Under Mary, that understanding of the nature of the church's unity was to prevail, and the majority of the Marian higher clergy would accept ejection, imprisonment or exile rather than repudiate it. This revolution was not the product of the 1560s and 1570s, nor the outcome of external European pressures. In this, as in so much else, the brief Marian interlude was to prove decisive for the shape of Elizabethan Catholicism.

IV

Catholic voices

10

The conservative voice in the English Reformation

On 25 November 1558 the parishioners of Much Wenlock, Shropshire, were gathered in their parish church of Holy Trinity for Mass, it being St Catherine's Day. As the vicar, Sir Thomas Butler,[1] made his way to the altar, he was intercepted by the sheriff, Master Richard Newport, newly arrived from London with the news that Queen Mary had died a week before. At Newport's command, the vicar came down into the body of the church at the offertory where, as he later noted down in the parish register, he declared in a loud voice, 'Friends ye shall pray for the prosperous estate of our most noble Queen Elizabeth, by the Grace of God Queen of England, France and Ireland, defender of the faith, and for this I desire you every man and woman to say the Pater Noster with the Ave Maria', and then 'we in the choir sange the canticle *Te deum Laudamus, pater noster, ave maria, cum collecta pro statu Regni prout stat in processionale in adventu Regis vel Regine mutatio aliquibus verbis ad Reginam*. And then went I to the altar and said out the Mass of St Catherine'. On the following Sunday the vicar put on the parish's best cope, called St Milburge's cope, which had somehow survived the depredations of Edward's reign and, accompanied by the leading men of.the town, processed once more into the nave to proclaim the new queen: once more the congregation recited the Our Father and the Hail Mary for the queen's prosperity, the choir sang the Latin litanies and collects for a Catholic ruler, Mass began with the festive processional *Salve festa dies,* and after Mass there was a bonfire at the church gate with a dole of bread, cheese and beer for the poor folks.[2]

This Catholic celebration of the accession of a Protestant queen, complete with careful citation of the Sarum rubrics, was of course replicated all over England in the winter of 1558. Sir Thomas Butler, to whose notes we owe our knowledge of the incident, was certainly a religious conservative. This much is made clear by his warm and admiring obituary accounts of the personalities and careers of former monks and musicians of the local priory of St Milburge, by his pious prayers for the repose of the souls of deceased parishioners and clergy, and by his evident pleasure in the resumption of the celebration of the Sarum rite in Mary' s reign. He began to say Mass 'more antiquo et secundum usu Sarum' again on the first Sunday of September 1553, the same date given for its general resumption in Yorkshire by another and more famous conservative parish priest, Robert Parkyn.[3] But if we can be fairly certain of Butler's religious sympathies, it is certainty by indirection – we deduce them from his tone of voice and choice of words, not because he declares himself explicitly for or against the religious changes which swept and swept again through the town of Much Wenlock in the middle years of the century. As he stood that November by his church gate to watch the bonfire lit in honour of the accession of a queen whom he must have realized was likely to sweep away the very rituals with which the parish had marked the proclamation, he may well have recalled another November bonfire on the same spot in 1547, when the bones of St Milburge were burned on a pyre made up of local pilgrimage images. He had recorded that holocaust in the clipped Latin he generally chose for his notes of momentous religious changes, but allowed himself no comment except that 'hoc fuit ex percepto et injunctione visitator sive Commissioner in visitacione Regia'.[4]

Butler's is certainly a conservative voice, but a voice self-consciously on guard against its hearers, aware that what he says is being taken down, even if it is by his own hand, and may be used in evidence. Nor is his reserve in expressing his innermost feelings about religious revolution and counter-revolution very surprising, given that his notes were inserted into what was, after all, a public record kept by Royal Injunction: the registers of births, deaths and marriages imposed on parishes in the 1530s by Thomas Cromwell.

Historians of the Reformation, newly sensitive to the broad groundswell of conservative religious feeling in Tudor England, have perhaps worked too hard the few genuinely unguardedly Catholic voices that dared to articulate explicit anti-reforming opinions in the middle of the century. Robert Parkyn, curate of Adwick le Street in the deanery of Doncaster, is the best known of these and his vivid and highly coloured narrative of the Reformation, first published by A. G. Dickens in the *English Historical Review* in 1947, features prominently in every recent treatment of the period.[5] In fact, however, it is a most unusual document. Composed sometime during Mary' s reign, it offers a rare Catholic overview of the process of Reformation. Its point of view is announced in its epigraph from Proverbs, *Regnantibus impiis: ruina hominum* (when the wicked are in charge, humankind goes to wrack and ruin), and in its opening paragraph, which traces from 1532 the emergence and progress of the Reformation movement 'to the grett discomforth of all suche as was trew Christians'. Throughout Parkyn's account we are never left for a second in doubt about his feelings, as in his description of the suppression of the religious houses in 1539 when:

> all was suppressed furiusly under footte (even as tholly temple of Hierusalem was handled when the Chaldees had dominion therof) and many abbottes & other vertus religius persons was shamfully put to deathe in diversse places of this realme. And all this ungratiusnes cam thrughe cowncell of one wretche and hereticke Thomas Crumwell, and such other of his affinitie, wich Crumwell was headyde for highe treasson in the yeare after.

Parkyn's glee in recounting the Marian restoration is equally unbridled, especially in the passages on the discomforture of those of his colleagues among the clergy – not least the Archbishop of York – who had dared to marry:

> Hoo it was ioye to here and see howe thes carnall preestes (whiche had ledde ther lyffes in fornication with ther whores & harlotts) dyd lowre and looke downe, when they were cammandyde to leave & forsake the concubyns and harlotts and do oppen penance accordynge to the Canon Law, which then toyke effectt.[6]

The pedigree of Parkyn's rhetoric in such passages is easy enough to identify. It owes a good deal to the vivid invective of Thomas More's controversial writings against Luther, the married friar, and against Tyndale and the early English reformers. But just as great, perhaps, is its debt to the petitions and articles of the rebels in the Pilgrimage of Grace, and of the Western rebels of 1549, with their denunciations of low-born heretical bishops and councillors like Cromwell, and the 'abhominable actes by them comytted and done', and their demands for the return of 'all … auncient olde Ceremonyes used heretofore, by our mother the holy Church'.[7]

But such a pedigree, of course, is sufficient indication of the problems that conservatives had in articulating their view of the Reformation process as it unfolded. Criticism of Crown religious policy from the prophecies of the Nun of Kent onwards had been rapidly identified with treason in Henry's reign: under Cromwell it was indeed true that careless talk cost lives.[8] Up to 1533 More was able to comment on the Reformation as it happened. The voice of the *Dialogue concerning Heresies* or the *Confutation of Tyndale's Answer* is bang up to date.[9] It is a stream of reportage and comment as well as theological reasoning, by turns indignant, sorrowful, scurrilous and amused, offering a lay commentary on current events as well as a storehouse of arguments against the new religion. But the arrest and execution of More for treason meant the eclipse of his writings, and with them the silencing of the most massive, coherent and distinctive vernacular response to the threat of religious radicalism. Subsequent defenders of Catholic opinions among the Henrician and Edwardine conservative clergy might borrow the substance of More's arguments, but his voice – in particular his bruising satire and his hostile commentary on the actions of contemporary reformers – would not be heard again until Mary's reign, when the London tradesman Myles Huggarde would redeploy something of More's supple and wide-ranging invective against heresy to considerable effect.[10]

There is an important connection between public rhetoric and private dissent, a connection which has been insufficently remarked by historians seeking to account for the comparative quiescence of the Tudor populace in the face of reform. So, without any recognized or established anti-reforming rhetoric to legitimate or serve as an example for more humble comment, conservative chroniclers in their narratives, or churchwardens in their parochial accounts, might note successive stages of the religious reforms of Henry's and Edward's reigns, but they rarely expressed an opinion or commented on them in any way which might disclose dissent or invite official retaliation. Commenting on this phase of the Reformation in the parishes, the Elizabethan protestant cleric Michael Sherbrook shrewdly remarked that the authorities 'by the colour of those words Superstition and Idolatry' made 'the ignorant churchwardens and such other like of the Parishioners … afraid to speak any word against their doings, contrary to the Law (least they should have been taken up for hawks meat as all Papists were).'[11]

In the later years of Henry's reign some theological resistance was indeed mounted by conservatives like Stephen Gardiner, powerful enough to secure a hearing and resist suppression,[12] and lesser figures like Richard Smyth, particularly on the issue of the sacrament of the altar, where the conservatives could count on Henry's sympathy.[13] But there was never enough security to permit the emergence of a consistent conservative public rhetoric, or the formation of a recognizable conservative voice, and the fragility of the whole conservative rearguard action was spectacularly revealed in Edward's reign by the unprincipled recantation of Richard Smyth,[14] and the progressive marginalization of steadier conservatives like Gardiner and Tunstall. Those who might have helped form such a voice were simply not allowed to speak. Roger Edgeworth, for example, prebendary of Bristol and Wells, mounted a series of sermons on 1 Peter into which he wove trenchant denunciation of Protestant advance, but the series was cut short by the removal of his preaching licence and his imprisonment at the very beginning of Edward's reign, and was not resumed till Mary's accession.[15] There were of course polemical retorts to Protestantism produced abroad, some of them in English: but at home, silence was imposed on the conservative cause.[16]

The very radicalism of Edward' s reign might have been expected to force this silent conservatism into public speech, and this, in the West Country at least, was of course what happened in the rebellions of the summer of 1549. Nor is there any shortage of evidence for more widespread hostility towards the Edwardine religious regime. In 1550 John Ponet complained that judges in their circuits, magistrates on their benches, bishops and their officers in the church courts, schoolmasters in grammar schools, stewards in manorial courts, and priests in confession, were all urging the people to conservative resistance – 'believe as your forefathers have done before you, follow ancient customs'.[17] This rallying to ancient custom and the beliefs of their forefathers is to some extent reflected in the local records: for example, the bitter comments of one of the churchwardens of Long Melford in Suffolk on the sales of church goods forced by the Edwardine commissioners, when the church's treasures were: 'scateryd abrode and delyvered to certen lyght persons wyche payd lytle or nothyng for them, [and] many of them spoyld & manglyd'.[18] Sir Christopher Trychay's summary of the impact of the Edwardine years in his parish is well-known:

> Anno Domini 1548 was hye warden of this churche Lucy Scely and by her tyme the church goodis was sold away with out commission ut patet postea and no gefth gevyn to the church but all fro the churche and thus hyt continyd fro Lucys time un to Richard Cruce and from Cruce un to Richard Hucly and fro Hucly un to Richard Robyns and fro Robyns un to Robyn at more and by al these mens tyme the wyche was by tyme of Kyng Edward the vi the church ever dekeyd and then deyde the Kyng and Quyne Maris grace dyd succed and how the church was restoryd a gayn by her tyme here after ye schall have knolyge of hyt.[19]

What is notable about these examples, however, heartfelt as they are and, I believe, representative of the feelings of the majority of English men and women in the reign of Edward VI, is that they are all retrospective, with all of them written not in Edward's reign but in Mary's, as Parkyn's narrative was. However much such men might hate the reforms of Edward's reign, at the time they kept their council when they came to set pen to paper. The lack of an adequate mid-Tudor Catholic literary response to the radical phase of the English Reformation in the middle of the century has been widely commented on.[20] Any explanation of that failure must, I think, begin with the Henrician regime's astonishing success in crushing conservative resistance, and above all in the execution of Thomas More and the consequent eclipse of his controversial and religious writings, which had a sterilizing effect on the development of an adequate Catholic public rhetoric in the middle of the century – equivalent to what might have happened more generally in English writing had Tyndale been strangled before he produced his New Testament, or had Shakespeare never written his plays.

At any rate, one even more striking but insufficiently remarked consequence of the lack of a public literature of criticism of, and dissent from, Crown religious policy was the lack of just such an accessible conservative rhetoric, and hence an astonishing conformity of expression even in private or local sources – the lack of any public forum for criticism meant that it became harder even to think the unthinkable. The Morebath accounts, indeed, give us a telling glimpse of the force of such verbal and mental conformity even in a resolutely conservative community. Edward's reign forced Morebath to adopt emergency measures to cope with the collapse of parochial institutions and parochial funding: the normal management of the parish by the churchwardens gave way to a managerial committee made up of the leading members of the parish elite – the 'Fyve men'. In 1552 and 1553 these men had to handle a good deal of Crown business, including the recovery of the parish bells, confiscated like every bell in Devon after the Prayer-Book Rebellion, from the Crown commissioners. This contact with the authorities changed the conventions of parish record-keeping, and in 1552 and 1553 the Five Men prepared accounts notably different in style from anything which preceeded them – no doubt in part because these accounts were written out not by the parish priest, who had acted as parish scrivener and accountant since the 1520s, but by a lay parishioner, John Scely. Each of these accounts begins with a formal dating:

> The cownte of the v men the xiii day yn may (id est the Sonday a fore Whytt Sonday) yn the ere of our Lorde 1553 and yn the ere of our Soverante lorde Edwarde the vi of Englande France and Yrelonde kyng defender of the fayth and yn yerthe of ye churche of Inglonde & also of yerlonde ye supreme hedd.

This formula would be perpetuated by the warden in 1554, Lewis Trychay, the priest's brother, thereby giving Mary the title of Supreme Head which she deplored. Thereafter it was of course discontinued. The priest, copying these accounts into the parish book in Mary's reign, adds a significant but characteristically restrained marginalium: 'Note the style of the kyng'.[21]

The advent of Mary changed all this, because there now emerged a public rhetoric of criticism of the Reformation, legitimating and giving form to conservative popular opinion. I have tried to emphasize elsewhere, and it is worth insisting on here since it is often denied, that from the beginning the Marian regime was extremely sensitive to the role of such official utterance in forming public opinion and a shared public 'voice'.[22] Edmund Bonner's preface to one of the key publications of the Marian years, *The Profitable and Necessary Doctrine* with its attached *Homilies*, puts its finger on precisely this point, in a remarkable account of the role of propaganda in shaping public support for the Reformation. Bonner wrote that:

'Where as in the tyme of the late outragious and pestiferous scisme, beyng here in thys churche and realme of England, al godlynes & godnes was dyspysed, and in maner banyshed, and the Catholique trade and doctryne of the churche (wyth a newe envyouse and odious terme) called and named papistrye, like also as devoute religion and honest behavioure of men was accounted and taken for superstitioune and hypocrisye. And thereupon (by sondry ways and wiles) pernicious and evil doctryne was sowen, planted and set forth, sometyme by the procedyng prechers sermons, sometymes by theyr prynted treatises, sugred all over with a lose lybertye (a thynge in dede most delectabel and pleasaunt unto the fleshe and unto al unruly persons) sometymes by readyng, playynge, singinge and other like meanes, and new devises, by reason whereof great insolency disorder, contention and much unconvenience, dayly more and more dyd ensue … to the notable reproach, rebuke and sclaunder of the hole realme. The people wherof, by sondry wicked persons, were borne in hande that they had gotten God by the fote, and that they were brought out of tirranie, darknesse and ignoraunce ynto lybertie, lyght, and perfytte knowledge, wher in very dede they were broughte from the gode to the bad, and from Godes blessing (as the proverbe is) into a warme sonne, infected with all errour and naughtyness, drowned in sensualitie and malice, and armed with unshamfast boldness, presumption and arrogancie.[23]

It is not long before we begin to catch the echoes of this official rhetoric of the Marian authorities taken up in the local sources – the fierce comments of the churchwardens of Stanford in Berkshire, for example, on the Edwardine period, which they characterize as 'the wicked time of schism ... when all godly ceremonies and good usys were taken out of the church'.[24] For the first time, conservative Catholicism could invoke the language of peaceable obedience and good citizenship in defence of inherited religion. Catholics, not Protestants, now appear as the upholders of law, so that Protestants who spoke out against Catholic doctrine were liable to be denounced not merely as heretics, but as traitors and rebels, impugners of the Queen's proceedings.[25] The difference is startlingly symbolized in the transformation of the tone of a conformist source, the London chronicle of the Windsor herald Charles Wriothesley. Wriothesley of course was an establishment man, and so hardly qualifies as a pure conservative. His sympathies were certainly with the initial phases of reform, a fact attested in his note on the first public use of Cranmer's English Litany in 1544, as 'the Godlyest hearing that ever was in this realme', or his description of the iconoclastic demonstrations and preaching of Bishop Barlow at St Paul's in November 1547 as 'to the extolling of Godes glorie and the great compfort of the awdience'. But he was no radical, describing full-blown Protestants as men of 'the new sect', welcoming the Act of Six Articles, and frequently revealing his regret at the fate of conservative opponents of the regime. He was certainly ill at ease with the more extreme aspects of the Edwardine reforms, and it is therefore no great surprise to see him rally to the new rhetoric of restoration and conservatism. With the weight of the Crown behind the Counter-Reformation, even a supporter of reform swings behind the old church.[26]

Unsurprisingly, therefore, from the accession of Mary, Wriothesley's chronicle records not popish disobedience, but the unruliness of the Protestant rabble. Wriothesley records with horrified disapproval the behaviour of 'certeine lewd and ill disposed persons' and the 'commotion' of the rude people, culminating in a knife thrown at the preacher, when Canon Gilbert Bourne preached a Catholic sermon at St Paul's on Sunday 13 August. Thereafter, Wriothesley's tone in recording the re-establishment of the old religion holds a new respect, as when he notes the resumption of the mass in

London in late August, 'not by commaundement but of the peoples devotion', or when he records the restoration of reservation of the Blessed Sacrament in St Paul's 'after the olde custom of the churche'. So he describes as a 'villanouse act' the famous incident in April 1554 when a dead cat, tonsured and dressed in Mass vestments and with a mock eucharistic host between its front paws, was found on the gallows in Cheapeside. Even Bonner's draconian 1554 Visitation of the London diocese is described in approving terms, and the bishops interrogatories are noted as 'divers goodlye articles in printe for the true religion'.[27]

I have dwelt on the shifts in Wriothesley's tone and rhetoric to underline the entirely new situation brought about by Mary's accession: the passing of the initiative – and the weight of rhetorical advantage – to the conservative cause. Defenders of Catholicism now had available to them a range of rhetorical devices or, if you like, of voices – which had been largely unusable in public and in print under hostile government – not least that most important of all conservative rhetorical devices, the appropriation of the proximate as well as the remote past as a criterion of right faith. This, as Cardinal Pole told the citizens of London, was the acid test of truth in religion:

> So ys also every trewe faythfull man knowne, not by the faythe he hath founde of himselfe, or taken of the fathers so fur off ... but by the faythe of his next father, contynuing the same until he come to his first father ... And thys fayth was yt for the which those great defenders of the catholyke faythe, the Bishop of Rochester and Master Moore dyede ... and thys was verye constancy, to dye for the fayth that they were borne in, and that they receyved of their fathers ... And of them when they dyede ... yt maye be sayde, the which was saide of the patriarches and all the faithful after them, *Appositi sunt ad patres:* whiche is the greatest comfort that any faythfull man at his death can have, and that the heretykes have not; that cannot showe their fathers faythe, but swerve from the same.[28]

Pole's invocation of the memory of More in the context of that appeal to continuity with the past was by no means arbitrary. More himself had made potent use of the argument for faithfulness to the religion of our parents. Indeed, his defence of Purgatory in the *Supplication of Souls* capitalizes heavily on filial loyalty and the sense of continuity and obligation in human relationships. In its opening lines, the souls in purgatory call out to the living:

> In most pytuouse wyse continually calleth and cryeth uppon your devoute charite and moste tender pyte for helpe comfort and relyefe your late aquayntance kindred spouses companions playfelowes and frendes and now your humble and unaquaynted and half-forgoten supplyauntes pore prysoners of gode the sely sowlys in purgatory.[29]

In More's treatise, as elsewhere in his writings, Protestantism is presented as a solvent of human community, divorcing the present from the past, husband from wife, child from parent, and abolishing the bonds of memory, responsibilty and trust. More's rhetoric in that passage itself draws on a distinctive Tudor vernacular genre, the English bede-roll – the call for prayers for benefactors familiar to every early Tudor man and woman from the bidding of the bedes at Mass.[30]

This was a difficult ploy to circumvent. Protestants did, of course, believe that one could do nothing for dead parents, children and spouses, and that the bonds of prayer were of no assistance to the dead. Equally, they believed that the faith of our fathers was not the good old way, but a farrago of error and idolatry: woe to the soul who was indeed gathered to their fathers, since the likelyhood was that, seduced by popish error, the fathers were roasting on the hobs of hell. But it was difficult to say so without forfeiting the sympathy of the great Tudor public. The Marian authorities capitalized on this by including among the articles objecting to suspected Protestants that:

> thy father and mother, all thine ancestors, all thy kindred, acquaintance and friends, did so believe and think in all the same as the … church did therein believe … (and hence that) thyself hast had no just cause or lawful ground to depart or swerve from the same faith … except thou wilt follow and believe the erroneous opinion or belief that hath been … brought in by certain disordered persons of late, at the uttermost within these thirty or forty years last past.

This forced the suspects to the damning admission that 'though my father and mother … did believe as you say, yet they were deceived in so believing'.[31]

This was a ploy designed to discredit the speaker with a conservative audience, but there were Protestant controversialists who did not shrink from stating this conviction in cold print. Thomas Becon, in his *Displaying of the Popish Mass,* daringly parodies More's source, the bede-roll. The passage is a full-frontal assault on Tudor *pietas:*

> And here in your mind and thought ye pray for Philip and Cheny, more than a good meany, for the souls of your great grand sir and of your old beldame hurre, for the souls of father Princhard and of mother Puddingwright, for the souls of goodman Rinsepitcher and goodwife Pintpot, for the souls of Sir John Husslegoose and Sir Simon Sweetlips, and for the souls of all your benefactors, founders, patrons, friends and well-willers. Do ye allege charity, and say it is a charitable deed to pray for them that are departed? I answer; Ye are antichrists, and turn the roots of trees upwards. Will ye have charity before faith? It is not charity that moveth you to pray for the departed, but blind affection, corrupt zeal, cankered custom, and hope of gain.[32]

Becon's parody of one of the most distinctive and potent forms of conservative utterance is as brilliant as it is brave, but it may well have been counter-productive – what he here dismisses as blind affection and cankered custom were powerful forces in sixteenth-century sensibility.

Proper assessment of the weight and effectiveness of the conservative case in Mary's reign would certainly have to get to grips with the centrality of More's writings and reputation for the Marian authorities and the Marian public, which extends to most aspects of the mid- and late-Tudor Catholicism. The collected edition of More's works published in 1557[33] has a fair claim to being the key book for an understanding of Marian Catholicism, though its format, an expensive folio, also indicates something about the limitations as well as the ideals of that regime.[34] But, what I want to emphasize here is the emergence in the mid-1550s of a confident and flexible conservative voice, nourished by a vigorous preaching campaign (including a carefully orchestrated series of sermons at Paul's Cross), as much as by printing.[35] It was a voice capable of performing in a range of registers, by no means narrowly clericalist or elitist, even if it is only in the work of Myles Hogarde that the demotic tang of the best of More's controversies is properly heard again. Hogarde, indeed, self-consciously deploys not only More's arguments, but More's tone of voice, and his savage attack on the Protestant martyrs of Mary's reign is indebted not just to More's theological analysis of the nature of martyrdom, but to More's blackly comic style of ridicule of the persons of the martyrs, and their supporters. In a parodic passage of this sort, which might almost have come from Foxe, Hogarde mocks those who

> crie by the waie as they passe to deathe: 'be constant dere brethren, be constant in the faithe, sticke to it, it is not the temporall paine which you ought to regarde, your brekfast is sharpe, your supper shalbe merye. Therefore the lord strengthen you'. With these and suche like vayne woordes, they brynge the poore men in such fooles paradise, that thei with such vaine arrogance, and small charities, sticke not to adventure themselves into the fiery flambes.[36]

It has been customary to see in Hogarde a 'might-have-been' – the one isolated example of a vigorously conservative lay voice which the Marian regime otherwise notably failed to encourage. Indeed, his acknowledged skill as a controversialist is used as a stick to beat the Marian regime, for failing to make better use of his talents or to produce other writers in his mould. Hogarde was indeed *sui generis*, but I have argued elsewhere that his writing is, in fact, representative of a wider recovery of conservative confidence in the later 1550s. His was not an isolated voice, but the best example of a more general development. We can test this claim by considering Hogarde's handling of a crucial polemical theme in his best book, the *Displaying of the Protestants*, a work which first appeared in June 1556, and immediately ran to a revised second edition a month later. One of the principal concerns of that work was to justify the burnings of heretics which were then taking place (and in which Hogarde himself played a part), and to discredit the claims of those being burned to the status of martyrs.[37]

As part of this endeavour, Hogarde adopted a favourite Marian polemical theme: the variation and inconstancy of Protestantism, even on the most fundamental issues. And since most of the Marian martyrs were condemned principally for their eucharistic beliefs, he chose to focus on Protestant inconsistency in eucharistic belief and practice. With a sure instinct for popular taste, Hogarde preferred the concrete and the anecdotal to the abstract in his controversial writings, and so he directed his attack not at the minutiae of reformed doctrine, but at the rapid succession of ritual changes brought about by the Communion Order of 1548 and the two prayer books of 1549 and 1552. He was here touching a nerve. It was, of course, the ritual innovations of 1549 which had precipitated the Prayer Book Rebellion in the West Country, and the eventual replacement of stone altars by trestle tables placed in the central aisle of the parish church had produced profound disturbance, and in some cases mortal confrontations. In particular, the reformers had been concerned to prevent non-communicating attendance at celebrations of Communion, and there is a perceptible toughening of attitude about this between the two prayer books, with the non-communicants being turned out before the Communion service proper commenced. This concern to prevent adoration of the host led to a series of experiments with the placing of the table, and with screens and curtains to prevent non-communicants catching a glimpse of the communion bread. The key case, widely commented on by the chroniclers, was the re-ordering of St Paul's by Bishop Ridley at Easter 1551 when, as Charles Wriothesley noted, he

> altered the Lordes table that stood where the high aulter was, and he removed the table beneath the stepps into the middes of the upper quire in Poules, and sett the ends east and west, the priest standing in the middest at … the communion on the south side of the bord, and after the creed song he caused the vaile to be drawen, that no person shoulde see but those that receaved, and he closed the iron grates of the quire on the north and sowth side with bricke and plaister, that non might remain in at the quire.[38]

In Hogarde's hands, all this becomes proof of the wavering inconstancy of the effeminate (that is married) bishops, 'which were ever learning and never able to come to the truth'. First, he wrote

> they placed their table alofte where the hygh altare stode. Then must it be set from the wall that one might goe between, the ministers being in contention on whethere parte to turne their faces, either towardes the weste, the Northe, or southe … Thus turning every waye, they myste the

right waye, but yet they coulde not hytte it. Then downe it must come from Sursum to Deorsum. In some places beneath the steppes, in the quier, covering it round about with curtaines for feare of bugges. Within a whyle after it skipped out of the quire into the body of the church. And in some places, neyther in the quyer, not yet in the body of the church, but betwene both ... They hailed it about in the maner of a Cocke pytt, where all the people myght see them, and their communion.

He went on to a similar burlesque description of the variation of practice in administration – first: thick unleavened bread without the embossed name of Jesus, then leavened bread:

lyke to other common bread ... from the which though many crombes did fall they forced not, so lightly they esteemed the matter. For suche Sacramente, such minister, such carpenters, such toles ... the Holy Ghost hath wrought in the Catholike churche the perfit faith and right use of the sacrament of the altar ... in the holy masse, till these bunglers toke in hand the same, meaning as thei thought to amend it. But as their presumption was vaine so in thende it proved. For God seing their inconstant vanities in misusing his sacramentes, brought all their attempts to a vaine effect.[39]

This is robust stuff, and Hogarde is certainly playing a strong card in ridiculing successive transformations of Protestant eucharistic practice, an area where old attitudes died hard and where he could be confident of appealing to conservative lay feeling. But the point I want to insist on is that in this appeal he is by no means alone, a lonely pioneer of neo-Morean scurrility. He is in fact deploying a hard-worked trope in the conservative polemic of Mary's reign. Robert Parkyn homes in on the same variation in practice between the two prayer books:

for the table (whereatt theolly Communion was ministered in the qweare) was hadde down in to the bodie of the churche in many places & sett in the mydde allee emonge the people ... uppon wich table a loaf of whytte bread such as men use in their howses with meate and a cuppe of wyne was sette without any corporax ... the priest or minister ... straightly forbidding that any adoration should be done there unto, for that were idolatrie, said the

boke, and to be abhorride of al faithfull Christians ... Oh how abhominable
heresie and unsemynge ordre was this, let every man pondre in his owne
conscience.[40]

And preaching in Bristol, Roger Edgeworth homed in on the same subject.
This, he told his hearers, 'is the verie property of Heresies, thei be ever
unstedfast and not agreinge arnonge theim selves, but some take one way
and some another ... for example, how manie maners and dyverse wayes of
ministeringe the Cammunion have we hadde among us?' He then launches
into a description whose essential features are by now familiar – the common
bread irreverently laid on the tablecloth, the people driven from the chancel
lest they see and worship, 'and anone that way seemed not best, and therefore
was there veils or curtens drawn, yea and in some churches the very Lent cloth
or veil hanged up ... to hide it', the tables in the nave, the ministers turning
'East or West or North or South'. This 'pulling down of altars and setting up of
boards', he tells his hearers, was also the mark of the Arian heretics in the early
church. But now, if we 'convert ourselves to the God of grace, he will solidate,
stay and settle us sure, contrary to all such inconstancy.'[41]

   I have laboured this point enough. But I think the remarkably close convergence in subject matter and approach between the London artisan, West
Country cathedral dignitary, and south Yorkshire parish priest – in polemical
pamphlet, cathedral sermon and historical memoir – does seem to me to
suggest very strongly the existence in Marian England of a shared theological
and controversial platform, and the common discourse which went with it. In
fact, it seems to provide the evidence for the successful creation of just that
public 'voice' which I have argued had been so notably lacking during the
Henrician and Edwardine reformations, and which too many historians of the
Marian church have assumed the Marian regime had also failed to discover.[42]

   That voice was, of course, destined to be employed in opposition, not as the
officially sanctioned voice of the regime. The accession of Elizabeth reimposed
something like the Protestantism of the latter part of Edward's reign, but with
a totally different conservative reaction, symbolized by the refusal of all but
one of the bishops to co-operate with the Crown. There was now a sharper
sense of the religious issues, and of the starkness of choice between the old and

the new religions, memorably expressed forty years on by the teenager, Robert Colton, who declared to Archbishop Whitgift that

> though I am but a poor lad I am not so far to obey you, having a soul to save like any Catholic … I hear say that England hath been a Catholic Christian country a thousand years afore this Queen's reign and her father's. If that were the old high way to heaven then why should I forsake it? I have no goods to leave, I pray you give me leave to save my soul. My soul doth hunger after my maker, God made man, under the form of bread, whom none but the priests can give me; while you do keep both them and me from the old mass, I dare not go to your new communion.[43]

That recusant utterance certainly owed much to the consolidation of Catholic resistance to the regime by the seminary priests – Robert Colton had been brought up in Wisbech and had spoken often with the priests imprisoned there. But from the outset conservative repudiation of the Elizabethan settlement is strikingly vocal, more consistently focused, and more formidable than anything we hear in either Henry's or Edward's reign. That repudiation would, of course, develop in a direction which cannot sensibly be called 'conservative'. The seminary priests might use reworked editions of the Sarum Missal, Breviary and Manual, and they might see themselves as essentially conservators of the old religion. But the character of their Catholicism was as much a product of the Counter-Reformation as was that of the Jesuit or Oratorian orders with whom they had such close contact. The Catholic dissidents of later sixteenth-century England, in many respects, have as much and perhaps more claim to be thought of as radicals as do most of their puritan and even separatist opposite numbers. Proper discussion of that issue would involve an exploration of the contrasting interpretations of Elizabethan Catholicism offered by John Bossy and Christopher Haigh.[44] What I want to point to here is simply the articulacy with which a powerful conservative critique of Elizabethan Protestantism was mounted from the outset of the regime and, at the risk of monotony, to underline the existence of a public voice or rhetoric in which such criticism could be pitched.

The argument for continuity and fidelity to the Christian past articulated by the Boy of Wisbech was a powerful persuasive for sixteenth-century men and women: it was one of the sharpest tools in the armoury of Counter-Reformation polemicists. But the deliberately nostalgic evocation of a Catholic Merry England was a more ambivalent asset. It, too, had a place in Elizabethan and Jacobean Catholic writing, and a long future as one of the dominant notes in conservative rhetoric more generally. As I discuss in chapter eleven, in the early years of the Settlement the voice of aggrieved nostalgia was one which enraged and alarmed the advocates of Protestantism, who responded by mocking as well as attempting to suppress it, sneering at the old women locked into the backward look – 'Alas Gossip, what shall we do at church, since all the saints were taken away, since all the goodly sights we were wont to have are gone'.[45] But in fact, very few of those who lamented these changes made the move into recusancy, and even among those who did, that note of nostalgia was sounded, more often than not self-consciously, as the voice of the defeated. We hear it in some of the classic Catholic narratives of the late Elizabethan period – the *Rites of Durham,* Roger Martin's account of Long Melford, even in Shakespeare's 'bare ruin'd choirs where late the sweet bird sang'.[46] That note could be sounded by determined recusants, like Martin himself who were, at least in theory, potentially subversive refusers of the Elizabethan settlement. But it is notably absent from the harder-nosed Counter-Reformation policy documents like Robert Parson's *Memorial for the Reformation of England,* which was decidedly cool – if not positively dismissive – about England's monastic past.[47] Parson's concerns in the *Memorial* were utilitarian, and he no doubt had a low view of the practical utility of an expensive and unpopular restoration of contemplative monasticism. But his coolness was perhaps also due to the fact that this nostalgic idealization of the Catholic past had became as much the voice of the church papist, and of some backward-looking parish Anglicans, as of conscientiously recusant Catholics. It is, for example, precisely the note heard in the late-Elizabethan history of the dissolution of the monasteries by the Yorkshire conformist cleric Michael Sherbrook – and it is a tone of voice familiar from chroniclers, topographers and antiquaries like Stowe and Weever. In a down- market version, it was also the voice of the conservative man in the pew so often mocked by puritan zealots, George Giffard's Essex countryman declaring that:

I will follow our forefathers: now there is no love: then they lived in friendship, and made merrie together, now there is no neighbourhood, now every man for himelfe, and are ready to pull one another by the throate ... You would have all men divines, I thinke it is not for ploughmen to meddle with the scriptures ... If you say true, then all our forefathers should be condemned, because they did worship images. I doubt not but God was as mercifull unto them as hee is to men now. I thinke they pleased God better than we do now: let us not stand so much in our own light.[48]

For the godly, that voice was the voice of unconverted England, a sign that for all the nation's profession of reformed religion, 'the popish dung doth stIck still between their teeth'. But by the last decade of the Elizabethan era conservatism of this sort was no threat at all to the settlement. Indeed to the godly, it was the unacceptable face of the settlement, a sign of the lack of true Protestant zeal in a conformist nation.

This chapter has been concerned to explore the relation between public polemic and the formation of a distinctive conservative voice in mid-Tudor England. The Marian regime has been consistently criticized for its failure to implement an adequate propaganda offensive against the Reformation and on behalf of the old religion. That propaganda failure has been measured in large part by a quantitative approach to the polemical pamphlet literature of the middle of the century. I have followed another tack: I have suggested that the success or failure of the Marian regime needs to be assessed in other ways. A striking result of the royal patronage of the reform under Henry and Edward was the retarded evolution of a public rhetoric of conservatism, the lack of any real advance on the polemical legacy of More, and the remarkable silence, even in private sources, of explicit articulation of the conservative opinions which historians now agree were widespread in mid-Tudor England. During the Marian period, by contrast, precisely such a shared rhetoric does emerge strongly, and is powerfully in evidence in a number of polemical contexts, and not only, as is sometimes claimed, in the distinctive work of the artisan pamphleteer Miles Hogarde. The premature death of Mary and the accession of her Protestant half-sister ruined the Marian Restoration, but did not mark the eclipse of that voice. However, some of its moods and modes proved more apt than others to the sustenance of a dissident religious community, and one of the most characteristic modes of the conservative voice – the nostalgic and idealized *laudatio tempora acti* – became a feature of conformist as much as of recusant thought and literature, a reminder that there are severe limits to the helpfulness of the phrase 'the old religion' as applied to Elizabethan Catholicism. And that last point is the subject of my next and final chapter.

11

Bare ruin'd choirs: remembering Catholicism in Shakespeare's England

Until fairly recently there was a tendency for scholars of late Tudor England to think of it as essentially a Protestant place, in which Catholicism was a problematic dimension. The Roman Catholic clerical presence in Elizabethan and Jacobean England was a 'mission', and Catholicism was one of the alien elements over against which Early Modern English identity had defined itself. This is true no longer. As I argued in the early chapters of this book, as contemporary English society has increasingly divested itself of its protestant character and folk memories, we have come to look with fresh eyes at the religious complexities – one might be tempted to say pluralism – of even so explicitly confessional a state as early modern England. The continuing and pervasive influence of Catholicism as a political, religious and cultural force in the England of Elizabeth and James – the England of Shakespeare – has accordingly become more visible.[1]

One aspect of this process of reassessment not so far touched on here, has been the recovery of an awareness of the Catholic dimension of early modern English culture, most obvious in music and architecture, represented by William Byrd and Inigo Jones, but more recently and sensationally focused on the reappraisal of Shakespeare's religion – of which not the least significant aspect may be the perception that he might actually have had a religion.[2] What follows is intended to further, in a tentative sort of way, the reappraisal of the religious significance – or at any rate the religious context – of the work of England's national bard. It focuses on a discussion of the language of a single line in sonnet 73.

> That time of yeare thou maist in me behold
> When yellow leaves, or none, or few doe hange
> Upon those boughes which shake against the could,
> *Bare ruin'd quiers, where late the sweet birds sang.*

Few human enterprises are more certainly doomed than the attempt to provide precise historical expositions of Shakespeare's sonnets. These most elusive of poems defeat, and will no doubt continue to defeat, all attempts to decipher the story or stories they tell, or to identify the contemporary allusions they might be held to make, and sonnet 73 is no exception. But its fourth line deploys an image which, whatever its precise reference, could hardly have been written at any time before the late Elizabethan age, and one which represents Shakespeare's appropriation of a highly charged contemporary historical trope, laden with contentious social and religious significance. Shakespeare's one-line evocation of the ruins of England's monastic past, the ruins of England's Catholicism, can hardly have been casual or unself-conscious, for in Elizabethan England these walls had, if not ears, then mouths, and, in the mode in which Shakespeare chose to evoke them, cried out against the cultural revolution which had shaped the Elizabethan religious settlement.

It is well-recognized that the Henrician dissolution of the monasteries was crucial for the emergence in Tudor England of an acute sense of the mutability of even the most apparently permanent institutions: ruins, as Margaret Aston has demonstrated, make historians. The overthrow of monasticism brought not just the destruction and pillage of some of England's greatest buildings, but a massive transfer of land and influence, a drastic shift from clerical to lay patronage within the church, and a fundamental reorientation of English society. Early modern Englishmen and women were intensely conscious of all these elements of tranformation, as Antonio in *The Duchess of Malfi* declared:

all things have their end:
Churches and cities, which have diseases like to men
must have like death that we have.[3]

Protestant conviction complicated these feelings: scholarly reformers like John Bale (himself a former monk) might loathe monasticism, and its 'superstitious mansyons' harbouring 'lasy lubbers and poppysh bellygoddes', and yet lament the destruction of venerable monastic buildings and great monastic libraries, 'those noble and precyouse monumentes' of the past.[4] The first great county chorographer of Elizabethan England was William Lambarde, and his *Perambulation of Kent*, published in 1576, was a seminal influence on the development of Elizabethan antiquarianism and chorography. He was also an ardent Protestant, who reflected thus on the monastic ruins at Canterbury:

And therefore, no marvaile, if wealth withdrawn, and opynion of holynesse remooved, the places tumble headlong to ruine and decay. In which part, as I cannot on the one side, but in respect of the places themselves pitie and lament this generall decay ... So on the other side, considering the maine Seas of sinne and iniquitie, wherein the worlde (at those daies) was almost wholy drenched, I must needes take cause, highly to praise God that hath thus mercifully in our age delivered us, disclosed Satan, unmasked these Idoles, dissolved their Synagogs, and raced to the grounde all monuments of building erected to superstition and ungodlynesse.

And therefore, let every godly man ceasse with me from henceforth to marvaile, why Canterbury, Walsingham, and sundry such like, are now in these our daies becom in maner waste, since God in times past was in them blasphemed moste: and let the souldiers of Satan and superstitious mawmetrie, howle and cry out with the heathen poet ...

The Gods each one, by whose good ayde this empire stoode upright
Are flowne: their entries and their altars eke, abandoned quight.[5]

For Lambarde, bare ruined choirs, therefore, might be poignant reminders of vanished greatness, but they evoked no fond memories of sweet monastic birdsong. The monastic past was an abomination, the monks and their houses 'harborowes of the Devil and the Pope ... which in horrible crimes contended with Sodome, in unbeliefe matched Ierusalem, and in follie of superstition exceeded all Gentilitie'. By the just judgement of God, therefore, Canterbury and places like it 'came suddenly from great welth, multitude of inhabitants and beautiful buildings, to extreme poverty, nakedness and decay'.

Few Elizabethan or Jacobean antiquaries shared Lambarde's doctrinaire hostility to the religious past, whose visible remains increasingly fascinated them and their readers. Notoriously, John Stow's *Survey of London*, one of the highwater marks of Elizabethan antiquarianism, published in 1598 and vastly expanded in 1603, is saturated through and through with nostalgia for the medieval golden age which had shaped the London townscape and its social and religious institutions. At one level, Stow's work is a sustained lament for the decay of sociability and old decency which he believed was one of the major consequences of the Reformation shattering of ancient buildings and the monuments they contained. The destruction of the Catholic past had been motivated by greed, not goodness, typified in the covetousness which had led men to pluck up the very funeral brasses from the 'defaced tombes and prints of plates torn up and carried away', bringing oblivion to the honourable dead and their good works, 'a great injurie to the living and the dead ... but not forborne by many, that eyther of a preposterous zeal or of a greedy minde spare not to satisfy themselves by so wicked a meanes'.[6]

Stow's *Survey*, therefore, did more than lovingly map the bare ruin'd choirs of Shakespeare's London. It offered a benign account of the antique world, 'when service sweate for dutie, not for meede', a world which had been lost in the dismantling of the early Tudor religious system. His famous description of Midsummer religious celebrations like the St John's fires, with its idealized evocation of 'every man's doore being shadowed with green birch, long fennel, St John's wort, Orphin, white lillies and such like', of hospitable houses hung about with lamps in honour of the saints, is notorious for its social romanticism:

In the moneths of June and July, on the Vigiles of festivall days ... in the evening after the sunne setting, there were usually made Bonefiers in the streetes, every man bestowing wood or labour towards them: the wealthier sort also before their doores neare to the saide Bonefiers, would set out tables ... furnished with sweete breade and goode drinke ... whereunto they would invite their neighbours and passengers also to sit, and bee merry with them in great familiaritie, praysing God for his benefites bestowed on them. These were called Bonefiers aswell of good amitie amongst neighbours that, being before at controversie, were there by the labour of others reconciled, and made of bitter enemies, loving friendes, as also for the vertue that a great fire hath to purge infection of the ayre.

Stow's private papers from the 1560s reveal his hostility to successive manifestations of protestant zeal in the city, and his memoranda are openly sympathetic to the Catholic clergy rabbled by the London crowds. Unsurprisingly, he was vehemently, and probably correctly, suspected of being 'a great favourer of papistry', and his house and books were raided and ransacked for incriminating material in 1569.[7] Stow was gradually to come to accept and endorse the Elizabethan Settlement and its leaders like Parker and Whitgift, but the whole drift of his published work was towards a positive reappraisal of the Catholic past, worlds away from the Reformation polemic of Bale or Lambarde.[8] Nostalgia for the visible remains of Catholicism, and a backward and approving look at the religion which had produced them, were therefore hard to separate. The ruins of the monasteries were only the most striking example of the general destruction of the forms of the old religion. From the outset of the Elizabethan Settlement, the fate of religious buildings in general, from monasteries to chantries, from cathedrals to parish churches, were intimately intertwined with the ideological systems they represented. That interconnection had been revealed at the start of Elizabeth's reign in a London event in which Stow took an intense interest, the furore surrounding the burning of St Paul's after the steeple was struck by lightning on Wednesday, 4 June 1561.

St Paul's Cathedral was very much the symbolic focus of Reformation in London: as we saw in the last chapter, in Edward 's and Mary's reigns ritual change there had become for conservative commentators a barometer of the progress of Protestantism more generally, and this remained true as the main features of the Elizabethan Settlement were set in place. The burning of the Cathedral in a freak storm, on the feast of Corpus Christi of all days, therefore, was certain to elicit pointed confessional commentary, and so the Elizabethan regime moved swiftly to forestall such comment. James Pilkington, Bishop of Durham, preached on the fire at Paul's Cross the following Sunday, declaring that the fire was a sign of the wrath of God against the sins of the time, in particular the decay of obedience to properly constituted authority – he called his hearers to 'humble obedience to the lawes and superior powers, whiche vertue is much decayed in our days', and he announced the tightening up of the laws 'agaynst persons disobedyent aswell in causes of religion, as civil – to the great rejoicing of his auditours'. He added that the prophanation of the cathedral by walking, jangling, brawling and bargaining in service time was a particularly heinous offence before God: the nub of his sermon, however, was an answer to the evil-tongued persons who were already spreading it abroad that this 'token of God's deserved ire' was a direct response to the 'alteration or rather reformation' of religion. The sermon therefore concluded with a lengthy review of great church fires of history, designed to show that St Paul's and other famous churches 'both nigh to this realm and far of, where the church of Rome hath most authority', had frequently been the targets of similar acts of God. He concluded that 'every man should judge, examine and amend himself, and embrace, believe, and truly follow the word of God ...' lest worse calamities follow.[9]

Pilkington's sermon was a sign of the seriousness of the early Elizabethan regime's anxiety about the capital which conservative critics of the religious settlement had already made of the fire four days after its outbreak. It was rapidly answered in a pamphlet called *An addicion, with an Apologie to the Causes of the Brinnynge of Paule's church*, attributed to John Morwen, Bishop Bonner's chaplain. This short pamphlet was a highly effective piece of polemic, brief, forceful and telling. It began with a resumé of biblical examples of judgements by burning, from Sodom and Gomorah through the idolators Dathan and Abiram, the prophets of Baal, and the destruction of Jerusalem itself because of the apostasy of Israel. The fire at St Paul's was a judgement not on sin in general, but on London's infidelity and apostasy in particular. St Paul's had been burned because it had first been prophaned by a false religion. Talking, buying and selling in church were bad, but

> there be worse abuses, as blaspheming God in lying sermons, polluting the temple with schismatical service, destroying and pulling down holy altars,

that were set up by good blessed men … yea, where the altar stood of the Holy Ghost, the new bishops have made a place to set their tails upon, and there sit in judgement on such as be Catholic and live in the fear of God.

The new religion was a mushroom growth, 'never heard tell of before Luther's time, which is not forty years old': therefore we must obey Jeremiah the prophet: 'Stand upon the way of the blessed fathers, and consider and ask of the old paths and high-ways, which is the good way, and walk therein, and ye shall find refreshing to your souls'. And Pilkington's portrayal of the Middle Ages as a time of superstition and error was dismissed as a lie – for then, rather

God was served devoutly night and day, the people lived in fear of God, every one in his vocation, without reasoning and contention of matters of religion, but referred all such things to learned men in general councils and universities … then was the commandments of God and virtue expressed in living, now all is talk and nothing in living: then was prayer, now is prating; then was virtue, now is vice; then was the building up of churches, houses of religion and hospitals, where prayer was had night and day, hospitality kept and the poor relieved: now is pulling down and destroying of such houses … by means whereof God's glory is destroyed and the common-wealth impoverished; then was plenty of all things, now is scarceness of all things: therefore *operibus credite*; the fruit will show whether then was superstition and ignorance, or now in these days.[10]

The *Addicion* is a short work – it runs to only six pages of print in the Parker Society edition of Pilkington's works, but it is an accomplished and damaging piece of conservative propaganda, and stung Pilkington into an elaborate *Confutation* more than twenty times as long. Several of its themes had a long future ahead of them as staples of recusant polemic against the Reformation, not least the appeal to walk in the old ways.

In the early years of the Settlement this was a voice which enraged and alarmed the advocates of protestantism, who paid it the compliment of mocking it. In 1562 Pilkington in his commentary on Haggeus, complained bitterly of the widespread murmuring against the cleansing of the churches, such 'lewd sayings' as

"What should I do at the church? I may not have my beads; the church is like a waste barn: there is no images nor saints, to worship and make curtsey to: little God in the box is gone: there is nothing but a little reading or preaching, that I cannot tell what it means: I had as lief keep me at home." This is a woeful saying....

Jewel took up the same woeful sayings for attack in the Second Book of Homilies, in the following year, when he makes two ignorant wives lament 'Alas Gossip, what shall we do at church, since all the saints were taken away, since all the goodly sights we were wont to have are gone, since we cannot hear the like piping, singing, chanting and playing upon the organs that we could before.'[11]

It is in the light of this popular complaint against the official imposition of 'bare ruin'd quiers' not only in the monasteries but in the parishes, that we should understand the early Elizabethan regime's preoccupation with plaster and whitewash, and against which we should read John Shakespeare's involvement in the defacing and whitewashing of images in Stratford. The Elizabethan injunctions of 1559 recognized that the very stones of the parish churches remembered their catholic past, and attempted to bulldoze away that material memory: the clergy were enjoined to

take away, utterly extinct and destroy all shrines, covering of shrines, all tables and candlesticks, trundles or rolls of ware, pictures, paintings and all other monuments of faigned miracles, pilgrimages, idolatry and superstition, *so that there remain no memory of the same* in walls, glasses, windows or elsewhere within their churches or houses. And they shall exhort all their parishioners to do the like within their several houses.[12]

The trouble was, in many communities this purging of the memory just did not happen. Stratford, like other conservative towns, was slow to implement the injunction, and notoriously, John Shakespeare was chamberlain when, three years into the Settlement, the corporation eventually got round to the removal of the rood loft and other images. He was chief alderman in October 1571, and therefore deputy to the protestant bailiff Adrien Queny, when the latter secured the corporation's agreement to sell off the parish's Catholic vestments.[13]

In the late 1920s the editors of the Stratford corporation accounts took these activities as a sign of John Shakespeare's ardent puritanism. Nowadays that seems less obvious, and it is the tardiness of this action which strikes us, together with the fact that the Stratford purges of 1562 and 1571 were almost certainly a response to external prodding rather than spontaneous zeal. Sales of illegally retained Catholic vestments and books were being forced on the localities by the ecclesiastical authorities all over England in the late 1560s and early seventies, as their subversive potential as focuses of vestigial loyalty to the old religion was increasingly felt. This perception had been given frightening particularity in the Northern rebellion on 1569, when concealed altarstones and holy-water vats were resurrected from the dunghills and gardens where they had been buried and became a symbolic focus for resistance to the Elizabethan Settlement.[14]

In 1571, indeed, Stratford had acquired a new bishop, Nicholas Bullingham, recently arrived as Bishop of Worcester. While still Bishop of Lincoln, Bullingham had presided in 1566 over a systematic purge of 'monuments of superstition' from the churches of Lincolnshire, and in the same years had been invoked as visitor against a provost of King's College Cambridge suspected of being popishly inclined: at King's too Bullingham presided over the destruction of a 'great deal of popish stuff' from the chapel. It is no surprise therefore to find the disposal of the remaining relics of popery taking place at Stratford soon after the arrival of this protestant new broom.

The attitudes of the man and woman in the pew towards all this are hard to assess, and must often have been ambivalent. In the late 1560s a Yorkshire yeoman who had been part of the syndicate which had bought up the timber and bells from the steeple of Roche Abbey was asked by his son 'whether he thought well of the religious persons and the religion that was then used'. When he replied that he had indeed thought well of the monks, having had no occasion to think otherwise, his son asked 'then how came it to pass you was so ready to distroy and spoil the thing you thought well of? What could I do, said He: might I not as well as others have some profit of the Spoil of the Abbey? For I did see all would away: and therefore I did as others did'.[15] Consciences continued to stir uneasily about all such spoil. Nicholas Roscarrock told the story of Jane Burlace, a farmer's wife from Rejarra in Cornwall who took up one of the four great stones used as a rest for relics and crosses on the annual rogationtide procession to the parochial chapel of St Neghton, and used it to make a cheese press. When Mistress Burlace died in November 1582, however, her spirit could not rest till this sacrilege had been put right: accordingly, the stone 'was in the night tyme carryed back by one willed so by her after her death or by some thinge assuminge her personage and remaineth, I think, still where it did'. Roscarrock, a recusant antiquary, was hardly a neutral reporter, but he claimed to have had this story 'from report of such as were of her kinsfolkes and friends who had cause to know it', and the ambivalences revealed in the episode must have been common enough.[16]

Shakespeare grew up, therefore, in a world where attitudes towards the material remains of the Catholic past were more often than not a touchstone of loyalty to, or disatisfaction with, the Elizabethan Settlement. Consider, for example, the most universal of all these reminders of the Catholic past, stained glass. The English Reformation was unusual in the extent of its hostility towards pictures in glass, which were virtually never the object of cult. The reader will recall that the Edwardian and Elizabethan injunctions had called for the removal of all Catholic stories and images 'so that there remain no memory of the same in walls, glass windows or elsewhere within their churches'. The Elizabethan injunctions had added the practical qualification that windows were not to be destroyed if this meant the wind and weather would be let in. Zealous protestants bemoaned this pragmatism, which left intact so many 'monuments of superstition', but even William Harrison, the ardent Protestant polemicist whose *Description of England* celebrated and justified the removal of screens, images and all the other furniture of the old religion from the parish churches as 'altogether needless' in a Reformed church, noted phlegmatically

> only the stories in glass windows excepted, which, for want of sufficient store of new stuff and by reason of extreme charge that should grow by the alteration of the same into white glass throughout the realm, are not altogether abolished in most places at once but by little and little suffered to decay, that white glass may be provided and set up in their rooms.[17]

Stained glass remained everywhere, therefore, and was a potential focus of intense ideological feeling. The recusant antiquary and chorographer of Worcestershire, Thomas Habington, in whose house Henry Garnet was arrested after the Gunpowder Plot, left a lavish and detailed account of the great narrative and doctrinal series of windows in Malvern Priory, 'the glasse whereof is a mirror wherein we may see how to beleeve, how to live, how to dye, how to pass through temporality to eternity'.[18]

Consider, by contrast, the attitude of the Cheshire Puritan John Bruen to the glass in his own parish church in the late 1580s where, on succeeding to the lordship of the manor, he found still

> many superstitious images and idolotrous pictures in the painted windowes, and they so thicke and dark that there was ... scarce the breadth of a groat of white glass amongst them: he knowing the truth of God, that though the Papists will have images to bee lay mens bookes, yet they teach no other lessons but of lyes, nor any doctrines but of vanities to them that professe to learne by them: and considering that the dumbe and darke images by their painted coates and colours, did both darken the light of the Church, and obscure the brightness of the Gospell, hee presently tooke order, to pull downe all those painted puppets and popish idols, in a warrantable and peaceful manner, and of his own coste and charge, repaired the breaches, and beautified the windows with white and bright glasse again.[19]

These contested and contending views were not merely current in the 1590s, when Shakespeare's sonnets were being written, but had been built into the heart of recusant complaint literature and apologetic. As government pressure on the recusant community mounted, the material ruins of the monastic and Catholic past became emblematic not only of the condition of the Catholic community, but of the calamities which the Reformation had brought on England itself, in the destruction not only of right doctrine and religious practice, but in the overthrow of charity, social deference, and the roots of community. You may be familiar with the lament for the shrine at Walsingham usually attributed to St Philip Howard:

Bitter, bitter, O to behold
The grass to grow
Where the walls of Walsingham

So stately did show.
Such were the works of Walsingham,
While she did stand;
such are the wracks as now do show
Of that holy land.
Level, level with the ground
The towers do lie,
which with their golden glittering tops
Pierced once to the sky.
Where were gates no gates are now,
The ways unknown
Where the press of peers did pass
While her fame far was blown.
Owls do shriek where the sweetest hymns
Lately were sung;
Toads and serpents hold their dens
Where the palmers did throng.
Weep, weep, O Walsingham,
whose days are nights,
Blessings turned to blasphemies,
Holy deeds to despites.
Sin is where our Lady sat,
Heaven turned is to hell.
Satan sits where our Lord did sway:
Walsingham, O, farewell.[20]

The lament for Walsingham, however, is only one example of a genre current in the 1590s, like this ballad for possession of which Thomas Hale of Walthamstow was indicted before the Essex assizes in 1594:

Weepe, weepe, and still I weepe,
For who can chuse but weepe,
To thyncke how England styll,
In synne and heresy doth sleepe.

The Christian faythe and catholick,
Is everywhere detested,
In holy servyce, and such like,
Of all degrees neglected.

The sacramentes are taken awaye,
The holy order all,
Religious men do begg astraye,
To ground their houses fall.

The Bushopes and our pastors gone,
Our Abbottes all be deade,
Deade (alas) alyve not one,
Nor other in their steede.

The Churches gaye defaced be,
our altars are thrown downe,
The walles left bare, a greefe to see,
That once coste maney a Crowne.

The monumentes and lefe of Sayntes
Are Brent and torne by vyolence,
Some shedd the holy Sacramentes,
O Christe thy wondrous pacyence.[21]

There was far more at stake in all this than the fate of buildings or even a change of doctrine. In this complaint literature, the decay of the externals of Catholicism reflected, and indeed had caused, the collapse of the moral fibre of society: grief for the bare ruin'd choirs was the objective correlative for despair over the collapse of social value. Reformation meant ruin, in more senses than one. William Blundell, Catholic squire of Little Crosby in Lancashire in the early 1590s, expressed the matter thus:

The tyme hath been we had one faith,
And all trode right one antient path,
The tyme is now that each man may,
See newe Religions coynd each day.

Sweet Jesu, with thy mother mylde,
Sweete Virgin mother, with thy childe,
Angells, and Saincts of each degree,
Redresse our countries myserie.

The tyme hath beene the prelate's doare
Was seldome shut against the poore,
The tyme is now, soe wives goe fine,
They care not though the beggar pine....

The tyme hath beene feare made us quake
To sinne, least god should us forsake,
The tyme is now the lewdest knave,
Is sure (hee'l say) God will him save....

The tyme hath been, within this land
One's woord as good was as his band;
The tyme is now, all men may see,
New faithes have kild ould honestie.

Sweet Jesu, with thy mother myld,
Sweete Virgine mother, with thy childe,
Angells and Saincts of each degree,
Redresse our countrees myserie.[22]

These poetic products of the 1580s and 1590s were matched by the emergence,
at about the same time, of a number of prose texts which similarly constructed
an idealized Catholic past, keyed to the contemplation of its physical ruins both
in the parish and the monastery. The best-known and most elaborate of these
texts is the anonymous *Rites of Durham* of 1593, which lovingly reconstructed
not only the layout of every altar, tomb and painted window in the Priory
church, but also the monastic liturgy for which they provided the setting. The
Rites of Durham is written in language deliberately charged with the sweetness
of nostalgia, like the description of the altarpiece of the Jesus altar,

All of the hole Passion of our Lord Jesus Christ most richlye & curiously
sett furth in most lyvelie coulours all like the burninge gold, as he was

tormented and as he honge on the cross which was a most lamentable sight
to beholde.

The monastic liturgy is depicted throughout as beautiful and affecting, 'all
singinge reioycing and praysing God most devoutly' and the humility of
the monks and their charity to the poor is stressed. The villains of the *Rites
of Durham* are those who defaced and threw down the monuments of the
church, 'lewde disposed personns, who despised antiquities and worthiness
of monuments after the suppression of Abbeys', above all the first Elizabethan
dean, the Genevan minister Dean Whittingham and his wife, who took holy
stones to make door steps and salting blocks, and who made a washing house
for laundresses out of the century garth where the priors were buried, 'for
he could not abyde anye auncyent monument, nor nothing that appertayned
to any godlie Religiousness or monasticall liffe'. And in the same mode as
Roscarrock's story of Mistress Burlace's ghost and the cheese press, the *Rites*
includes the story of a mysterious and comely old beggarman who warned a
Durham householder whose courtyard was paved with gravestones from the
cathedral 'that whilest those stones were theire nothinge wolde prosper aboute
the house and after divers of his children and others died so he caused them
to be removed into the Abbey yard wher now they are'.[23]

The *Rites of Durham* was probably compiled by William Claxton, squire
of Wynyard, who died in 1597. Claxton, a dedicated antiquary and a corre-
spondent of Stow's, to whom he loaned many books and manuscripts, was
not, it should be noted, a recusant, though he had close relatives who were. He
may have had the assistance of George Clyff, the last monk of Durham, who
effectively conformed to the new church in 1559, even though he never signed
the Elizabethan articles (despite which he held a series of livings in the diocese
of Durham and even retained his stall in the Cathedral till his death in 1595).
It is worth remininding ourselves that so blatantly papistical a text, and so
positive an assessment of the monastic past, could survive and articulate itself
in literary form down to the 1590s among men who outwardly conformed to
the protestant establishment.[24]

A close parochial equivalent to the *Rites of Durham* is the now famous
and familiar account written by the unquestionably recusant gentleman,

Roger Martyn, of the last days of the old religion in the Suffolk parish of Long Melford. In Martin's oft-quoted account the same saturated sweetness of descriptive language found in the *Rites* is in evidence, for example in the description of the image of our Lady of Pity, 'a fair image of our Blessed Lady, having the afflicted body of her dear son, as he was taken down, off from the Cross, lying along in her lapp, the tears, as it were, running down pittyfully upon her beautiful cheeks, bedewing the said sweet body of her son'. Martin wrote not merely to record the glory which had once filled the bare ruin'd choir of Long Melford, but as a gesture of resistance and of hope for the future: he lovingly details the *disjecta membra* of the pre-Reformation ornaments of the church, some of which were 'in my house much decayed, and the same I hope my heires will repaire, and restore again, one day'. And he offers an implicit criticism of the Protestant present by projecting an idealized account of the ritual life of Henrician Long Melford, in which gorgeous ceremonial and the sacred calendar cemented the bonds of deference and patronage between rich and poor. In a passage on bonefires uncannily reminiscent of Stow's more famous account, on which indeed it may be modelled, Martin presents the same picture of flower-bedecked plenty, shared in neighbourly charity, 'and in all these bonefires, some of the honest and more civil poor neighbours were called in, & sat at the board, with my grandfather'.[25]

This was a recusant document, which inevitably emphasized the superiority of the old religion and its benign effects on society. But as we have seen, such perceptions were not confined to Catholics. Protestant polemicists denounced the conservative folk-culture of conformist parishioners for their backward glances at the flesh-pots of Egypt, revealed in proverbial saws like 'It was merry world when the Mass was, for all things then were cheap'. In 1581, George Giffard's fictional Essex countryman, Atheos, was loud in repudiation of the Pope and all idolatry, but looked back to England's Catholic past as a time of communal harmony and good fellowship.

> I will follow our forefathers: now there is no love: then they lived in friendship, and made merrie together, now there is no neighbourhood, now every man for himelfe, and are ready to pull one another by the throate".

His protestant interlocutor, Zelotes, foamed with indignation at such perverse romanticism:

> Ye follow your owne fond and doting opinion that ye imagine a thing which never was: for the world hath ever bene like it selfe, full of debate and strife, a very few in all ages which have had true love'[26]

Nor was it Catholics alone who applied this romanticism specifically to the monasteries. We have seen that the compiler of the *Rites of Durham*, of all texts, was probably a conformist. He was far from being alone. Michael Sherbrook, Elizabethan Rector of Wickersley in the East Riding of Yorkshire, completed a treatise on the *Fall of Religious Houses* in 1591. It is an extraordinary work from the pen of an Anglican incumbent, for it was a sustained defence of the monasteries as good landlords and benign employers, centres of charity and industry. Sherbrook had no doubt that England had been in steep moral decline since the Reformation,

> for the estate of the realm hath come to more Misery since King Henry 8 his time, than ever it did in all the time before: If it be a Misery to have more thieves, whores, extortioners, usurers and contentious persons striving the one against another in suits of law, and to be short, far more Beggars than ever was before.

The history of Reformation England was one long sequence of 'the going away, or rather driving away of godly devotion, and the bringing in of Carnall liberty, making small Concience, or rather none at all, of most things'. Anyone who compared pre-and post-Reformation England must agree, Sherbrook thought, that the 'Builders and Maintayners' of monasteries 'were far wiser in building of them, than we in destroying them, and the governors of the Common Weale then far better'.[27]

Sherbrooke is an extreme case, though in the light of Ian Doyle's identification of the conformist Anglican authorship of the *Rites of Durham* he looks a little less isolated than he once seemed: at any rate, some of his views were evidently common enough. In 1589 Francis Trigge, a Lincolnshire cleric, published a defence of the Reformation entitled 'An apologie or Defence of our dayes against the vaine murmurings and complaints of many', in which he admitted that 'many do lament the pulling downe of the abbayes, they say it was never merrie world since: they highly commend their liberalitie to the poore, their curtesie to their tenants, their commoditie to the commonwealth'. Trigge flatly rejected all this as so much moonshine: in fact, he thought, the monasteries had been full of

> pryde, idlenesse, fullnesse of breade and unmercifulnesse. In so much that the fatnesse and haughtiness and idleness of monkes, came into a proverbe amongst all men: in so much, that idle persons were called abbey lubbers: fatt men were said to have abbotts faces.[28]

We have travelled a roundabout route, but I hope by now it will be evident where we are going. Sonnet 73 was probably written in the late 1590s. Religion is neither its subject-matter nor the primary source of its poetic energy. Its allusion to the Reformation and the monasteries is certainly oblique and perhaps unconscious. Yet, in the fraught religious atmosphere of the last decade of the old Queen's life, its phrasing decisively aligns Shakespeare against the Reformation: line four's evocation of monastic ruins and the 'sweet birds' who had once sung there must have sent to its first readers a clear and unambiguouslly *un*protestant message. It is not of course a line which need only have been written by a Catholic: I have been documenting that there were conforming Anglicans, like Stow and Sherbrook, whose writings reveal just as positive an attitude to the Catholic past as is implicit in the phrase 'where late the sweet birds sang'.

But we can and should press Shakespeare's words for further nuances of meaning. Consider the significance here, for example, of the word 'late' in

Where *late* the sweet birds sang.

The word 'late' there has in fact been taken by some commentators to rule out the application of the image to the monasteries at all, for in the 1590s the dissolution of the monasteries was two generations back, and so could hardly be described as 'late'.[29] On the contrary, however, I believe the telltale word 'late' once again aligns Shakespeare with a dangerously positive reading of the religious past. Delight in and reverence for the ruins of the old religion made the antiquarian movement as a whole a Trojan horse within the embattled

Protestantism of Tudor and early Stuart England – as we have seen, there were many recusants and fellow-travellers among the ranks of the antiquaries. But open assertions of the virtues of the last stages of monasticism were rare: antiquarian indignation at the depradations of the iconoclasts operated at a fair degree of generality – what such attacks represented was barbarism, the decay of reverence, lack of respect for traditional pieties. But we can see the carefully demarcated confessional limits of this attitude at work in one of the classic antiquarian products of the early Stuart period, *Ancient Funeral Monuments* by Shakespeare's admirer, the Houghton protégé John Weever, published in 1631 but in preparation for two decades before that.

Weever's work, based on his own perambulations of the diocese of Canterbury, Rochester, London and Norwich, and on the collections of Sir Robert Cotton, is a celebration of the value and importance of funeral inscriptions, and as such it shares the general antiquarian hostility to iconoclasm. Weever quotes 'a late nameless versifier' to this effect.

What sacred structures did our elders build
Wherein Religion gorgeousaly sat deckt?
Now all thrown downe, Religion exil'd
Made Brothel-houses, had in base respect,
Or ruin'd so that to the viewers eye
In their own ruins they intombed lie:
The marble vrnes of their so zealous founders
Are digged up, and turn'd to sordid uses;
Their bodies are quite cast out of their bounders
Lie un-interr'd. O greater what abuse is?
Yet in this later age we now live in,
This barbarous act is neither shame nor sinne.[30]

These were the sentiments used by Laud and his associates to justify their campaign to recover the beauty of holiness, and Weever's book, which is dedicated to Charles I, contains many asides which show that he supported the recovery of architectural and ritual dignity within the Church of England's worship. He also displays a regard for the religious customs of his home county of Lancashire which demonstrate an unmistakable animosity to advanced Protestantism and the campaign for a godly England, as in his remark that

> in the country where I was borne, the vulgar sort especially, doe most commonly swear by the cross of their own parish kirke, as they call it: and in ancient times, children used to sweare by the Sepulchres of their parents ... But, with us in these dayes, I see no such reverence that sonnes have to their fathers hands or to their Sepulchres. I heare no swearing by Kirkes, Crosses or Sepulchres. I heare sometimes, I must confesse, forswearing to build Churches; swearing to pull downe crosses, or to deface and quite demolish all Funerall Monuments; swearing and protesting that all these are the remaines of AntiChriste, papisticall and damnable.[31]

Weever, then, is unmistakably friendly to much in the Catholic past, and to the idea of monasticism – he remarked in the dedicatory epistle that 'it may seeme, peradventure, unpleasing to some, for that I do speake so much of, and extoll the ardent pietie of our forefathers in the erecting of Abbeyes, priories, and such like sacred Foundations.' His account of the early Anglo-Saxon monastic movement, based on Bede and Capgrave, is glowing and laudatory: unlike Bale and other Reformation polemical historians, he thinks well of Augustine of Canterbury and appears to credit his miracles. He is also deeply sceptical of the motivation of the Henrician dissolutions, which he sees as driven by greed and sanctimonious hypocrisy.

It is all the more striking, therefore, that Weever adopts an unreconctructedly Protestant account of the *later* history of monasticism, as one long tale of decline and lapse from primitive virtue. He draws heavily on Lambarde in his treatment of the diocese of Canterbury, and retells and adds to many of Lambarde's scandalous anecdotes about popish superstition and gullibility in the later Middle Ages. He also reiterates the usual Reformation catalogue of the vices of the monks – 'pride, covetousnesse, insatiable luxurie, hypocrisie, blinde ignorance, and variable discord amongst the Church-men and all other our English votaries'. Despite the bad faith of the Henrician reformers, therefore, the 'fatal and finall period of the Abbeyes, Priories and such like religious structuires: with the casting out to the wide world of all their religious Votaries' was 'chiefly occasioned by their owne abhominable crying sinnes, more than by any other secondarie meanes'.[32]

Weever's ambivalence about England's monastic past reveals the inconsistencies and unresolved contradicitions within the thinking of the antiquarian movement about the past. For our purposes, however, it is of interest chiefly in highlighting the radically contrasting reading of the monastic past implicit in Shakespeare's phrase 'where *late* the sweet birds sang'. For Weever, monasticism had its glories: it was born in zeal and sanctity, it wrote a golden page in England's history, and its ruins, choice pieces of antiquity, were for that reason noble and to be treasured. But its *final* phase was sordid and disreputable: for Weever at any rate, of *late*, no sweet birds sang in England's quires, but only the carrion fowl of a corrupt system which had bred its own decay. By contrast, Shakespeare's 'where late the sweet bird sang' implies a reading of the last stages of monasticism, and of the roots of the Reformation, far more favourable to Catholicism.

Let me by way of conclusion make it clear what I have *not* been arguing. I do not think Sonnet 73 constitutes evidence that Shakespeare was a Catholic: as we have seen, its rhetoric, and the historical and religious attitudes implicit in that rhetoric, closely resemble the ideologically and theologically charged antiquarian and nostalgic writing about the religious past which seems to have been a special feature of the 1590s. That sort of writing would continue well into the Jacobean and Caroline periods, and it had a future in the mid and late Stuart tradition of writing about sacrilege which we associate with Sir Henry Spelman. Some of these Elizabethan and early Stuart texts were indeed produced by recusants, but others by conformist fellow-travellers like Stow and Sherbrook and Claxton. As far as the evidence of Sonnet 73 takes us, Shakespeare might just as well be placed among the fellow-travellers as among the Catholics. But if we cannot quite be sure that Shakespeare was a Catholic, it becomes clearer and clearer that he must have struck alert contemporaries as a most unsatisfactory Protestant. In the mind and mouth of the most illustrious of all Elizabethans, the Tudor religious revolutions had elicited not even the most equivocal of endorsements.

Notes

Introduction

1 Norman L. Jones, *The English Reformation: Religion and Cultural Adaptation*, Oxford: Blackwell (2002), p. 1.

2 *The Stripping of the Altars: Traditional Religion in England c. 1401–1570*, New Haven and London: Yale University Press (1992).

3 C. Haigh ed., *The English Reformation Revised*, Cambridge: CUP (1987).

4 I discussed the book's origins and intentions in the introduction to the second edition, published in 2005.

5 This is the essential argument of A. G. Dickens, *The English Reformation*, London: Batsford (1989).

6 Christopher Haigh, *Reformation and Resistance in Tudor Lancashire*, Cambridge: CUP (1975); 'Anticlericalism and the English Reformation', *History*, LXVIII, (1983), 391–407, and 'The English Reformation: A Premature Birth, a Difficult Labour and a Sickly Child', *The Historical Journal*, XXXVIII, (1990), 449–59; J. J. Scarisbrick, *The Reformation and the English People*, Oxford: Blackwell (1984).

7 Clive Burgess, 'For the increase of Divine Service: chantries in the parish in late medieval Bristol', *Journal of Ecclesiastical History* XXXVI, (1985), 48–65; idem, 'A fond thing vainly invented' in S. J. Wright ed., *Parish, Church and People: Local Studies in Lay Religion, 1350–1750*, Leicester: Hutchinson (1988), pp. 56–85; Peter Heath, 'Between reform and Reformation: the English Church in the fourteenth and fifteenth centuries', *Journal of Ecclesiastical History*, XLI (1990), 647–78; idem, *The English Parish Clergy on the Eve of the Reformation*, London: Routledge and Kegan Paul (1969); Christopher Harper-Bill, *The Pre-Reformation Church in England, 1400–1530*, Seminar Studies In History, London: Longman (1989).

8 *English Reformations: Religion, Politics and Society under the Tudors*, Oxford: Clarendon Press (1993).

9 For a generalising discussion which tends to conflate several varieties of 'revisionism' as a unitary phenomenon, see the 'Introduction' in N. Tyack ed., *England's Long Reformation 1500–1800*, London: UCL Press (1998).

10 Andrew Graham Dixon, *A History of British Art*, London: BBC Books (1996); Roy Strong, *A Little History of the English Country Church*, London: BBC Books (2007); Stephen Greenblatt, *Hamlet in Purgatory*, Princeton NJ: Princeton University Press (2001).

11 Patrick Collinson, *The Birthpangs of Protestant England*, Basingstoke: Macmillan (1988).

12 *ibid.*, p. ix.

13 A. G. Dickens, *The English Reformation*, London: Batsford (1964); Christopher Haigh, 'A. G. Dickens and the English Reformation', *Historical Research*, vol. 77 no. 195 (February 2004), 24–38.

14 Geoffrey Elton, *Policy and Police: the Enforcement of the Reformation in the Age of Thomas Cromwell*, Cambridge: CUP (1972).

15 Note 7 above.

16 Richard Rex, *Henry VIII and the English Reformation*, Basingstoke: Palgrave Macmillan, 2nd edn (2006); Peter Marshall, *The Catholic Priesthood and the English Reformation*, Oxford: Clarendon Press (1994); *idem* ed., *The Impact of the English Reformation*, London: Arnold (1997).

17 John Bossy, *The English Catholic Community 1570–1850*, London: Darton, Longman and Todd (1975); *idem*, *Christianity in the West*, Oxford: OUP (1985).

18 Peter Burke, *Popular Culture in Early Modern Europe*, Aldershot: Scolar, 2nd edn (1994).

19 R. W. Scribner, *Popular Culture and Popular Movements in Reformation Germany*, London: Hambledon (1987).

20 Victor and Edith Turner, *Image and Pilgrimage in Christian Culture: Anthropological Perspectives*, Oxford: Blackwell (1978).

21 Mary Douglas, *Natural Symbols: Explorations in Cosmology / With a New Introduction*, London: Routledge (1996).

22 Strong, *A Little History*; Simon Jenkins' review appeared in the Sunday Times, September 9th 2007, and is available online at http://entertainment.timesonline.co.uk/tol/arts_and_entertainment/books/non-fiction/article2402095.ece.

23 Chapter 9 below.

24 Chapter 2 below. And see Linda Colley, *Britons: Forging the Nation, 1707–1837*, London: Pimlico (1994); and Colin Haydon, *Anti-Catholicism in Eighteenth-Century England, c. 1714–80: A Political and Social Study*, Manchester: Manchester University Press (1993).

25 Paul Binski, *Westminster Abbey and the Plantagenets, Kingship and the Representation of Power, 1200–1400*, New Haven and London: Yale University Press (1995).

26 Hyder Rollins ed., *Old English Ballads 1553–1625*, Cambridge: CUP (1920), pp. 138–9.

27 H. Clifford, *Life of Jane Dormer, Duchess of Feria*, London: Burns and Oates (1887), pp. 38–9, cited by Christopher Haigh, 'The Continuity of Catholicism in the English Reformation', *Past & Present*, no. 93 (Nov. 1981), 37–69 at p. 37.

28 Arnold Pritchard, *Catholic Loyalism in Elizabethan England*, Chapel Hill NC: University of North Carolina Press (1979); the dilemmas of loyalty for the Catholic elite are explored, amid much else, in Michael Questier's *Catholicism and Community in Early Modern England: Politics, Aristocratic Patronage and Religion c. 1550–1640*, Cambridge: CUP (2006); see also Sandeep Kaushik, 'Resistance, loyalty and recusant politics: Sir Thomas Tresham and the Elizabethan state', *Midland History*, xxi (1996), 37–73; and Peter Marshall, *Faith and Identity in a Warwickshire Family: the Throckmortons and the Reformation*, Dugdale Society Occasional Paper no. 49 (2010).

29 William Cardinal Allen, *An Admonition to the Nobility and People of England and Ireland Concerninge the Present Warres Made for the Execution of His Holines Sentence*, n.p. (1588), RSTC 368.

30 The phrase is A. G. Dickens's, *English Reformation*, London: Batsford, 2nd edn (1989), p. 312.

Chapter 1

1 George Orwell, 'The English People', in Sonia Orwell and Ian Angus (eds), *The Collected Essays, Journalism and Letters of George Orwell*, Penguin: Harmondsworth (1968), vol. III, pp. 15–56.

2 John Rodden, 'Orwell on Religion: The Catholic and Jewish Questions', *College Literature*, vol. 11, no. 1 (1984), 44–58

3 Nicholas Boyle, *Who Are We Now?: Christian Humanism and the Global Market from Hegel to Heaney*, Edinburgh: T&T Clarke (2000).

4 Richard Rex, *Henry VIII and the English Reformation*, Basingstoke: Palgrave Macmillan, 2nd edn (2006), chapter 1.

5 H. Gee and W. J. Hardy, *Documents Illustrative of English Church History*, London: Macmillan (1896), pp. 187ff.

6 R. Sylvester and D. P. Harding (eds), *Two Early Tudor Lives*, New Haven and London: Yale University Press (1990), pp. 248–50.

7 Cited from the online edition at http://internetshakespeare.uvic.ca/Annex/Texts/docs/KyngeJohann/OS/scene/1-tln-93, accessed 6 July 2011.

8 Nicholas Pecock (ed.), *A Treatise on the Prestended Divorce ... by Nicholas Harpsfield*, Camden Society (1878), p. 282.

9 E. Duffy, "The comen knowen multitude of crysten men': *A Dialogue Concerning Heresies* and the defence of Christendom', in George M. Logan ed., *The Cambridge Companion to Thomas More*, Cambridge: CUP (2011), pp. 191–215.

10 *A Dialogue Concerning Heresies* in Thomas M. C. Lawler, Germain Marc'hadour and Richard C. Marius (eds), *The Complete Works of St. Thomas More*, vol. 6, New Haven and London: Yale University Press (1981), pp. 427–8.

11 Best treatment by Diarmaid MacCulloch, *Thomas Cranmer, a Life*, New Haven and London: Yale University Press (1996), pp. 351–513.

12 Miles Hogarde, *The Displaying of the Protestants with a Description of Divers of their Abuses*, London (1556), RSTC 13557, fols 16–17v, 116–17; for an earlier Marian attack on the foreign origins of Protestantism, John Proctor, *The Waie Home to Christ and Truth*, London (1554), RSTC 25754, fols B ii(v)–B iii.

13 Richard Broughton, *The Conviction of Novelty and Defence of Antiquity*, (1632), STC 1126, 14, p. 5.

14 John Proctor, *The Historie of Wyates Rebellion with the Order and Maner of Resisting the Same*, 2nd edn, London (1554), STC 20407, p. 96.

15 K. J. Kesserling, *The Northern Rebellion of 1569: Faith, Politics and Protest in Elizabethan England*, London: Palgrave Macmillan (2010); Arnold Pritchard, *Catholic Loyalism in Elizabethan England*, Chapel Hill NC: North Carolina University Press (1979) and references cited in the Introduction, above, note 28.

16 Philip Hereford ed., *The Ecclesiastical History of the English People*, trans. Thomas Stapleton, London: Burns Oates & Washbourne (1935), pp. xxxiii–xlii.

17 *ibid* p. l.

18 Felicity Heal, 'Appropriating History: Catholic and Protestant Polemics and the National Past', *Huntington Library Quarterly*, vol. 68, No. 1–2 (March 2005), 109–32.

19 Felicity Heal, 'What can King Lucius Do for You? The Reformation and the Early British Church', *English Historical Review*, vol. 120, (2005), 593–614.

20 E. Duffy, *Fires of Faith: Catholic England under Mary Tudor*, New Haven and London: Yale University Press (2009), p. 36.

21 I have used the text of the speech preserved among Pole's manuscripts, now in the Vatican, Vat. Lat. 5968, fols 305–59.

22 Robert M. Kingdon ed., *The Execution of Justice in England, by William Cecil and A True, Sincere and Modest Defence of English Catholics, by William Allen*, Ithaca NY: Cornell University Press (1965), pp. 214–59.

23 On the English College frescoes and the prints derived from them, Anne Dillon, *The Construction of Martyrdom in the English Catholic Community 1535–1603*, Aldershot: Ashgate (2002); L. H. Monsen, 'Rex Gloriose Martyrum: A contribution to Jesuit Iconography', *Art Bulletin*, vol. 63, 130–7; K. Noreen, 'Ecclesiae militantis triumphi: Jesuit iconography and the Counter-Reformation', *Sixteenth Century Journal*, vol. 29, 689–715; C. M. Richardson, 'The English College in the 1580s' in Andrew Headon ed., *The Church of the English College in Rome: Its History & Restoration, Rome*: Gangemi Editore (2009), pp. 34–51; R. L. Williams, "Libels and paintings': Elizabethan Catholics and the International campaign of visual propaganda' in C. Highley and J. King (eds), *John Foxe and his world*, Aldershot: Ashgate (2002).

24 I quote from the version of the text in John Foxe, *Actes and Monuments*, London: John Daye (1583), p. 107.

25 Hastings Robinson ed., *The Zurich Letters*, Cambridge: Parker Society (1842), pp. 157ff.

26 They are printed in William Keating Clay ed., *Liturgies and Occasional Forms of Prayer Set Forth in the Reign of Queen Elizabeth*, Cambridge: Parker Society (1847).

27 *Liturgies* p. 517

28 *Liturgies* p. 578

29 *Liturgies* pp. 644–5, 649.

30 The sometimes tortuous theological shifts behind these changes are analysed in Anthony Milton's *Catholic and Reformed: the Roman and Protestant Churches in English Protestant Thought 1600–1640*, Cambridge: CUP (1995), especially chapter 9.

31 John Hayward ed., *John Donne, Complete Verse and Selected Prose*, London: Nonesuch Press (1978), Holy Sonnet XVIII, p. 287.

32 George Herbert, *The Temple, Sacred poems and private ejaculations. By Mr. George Herbert*, Cambridge: Printed by Thom. Buck and Roger Daniel, printers to the Universitie (1633) RSTC 13183, p. 102.

33 Gillian Evans and J. Robert Wright, *The Anglican Tradition: a handbook of sources*, London: SPCK (1991).

34 For a shrewd analysis of this high-church historiography, Diarmaid MacCulloch, 'The Myth of the English Reformation' *Journal of British Studies*, vol. 30, no. 1 (Jan. 1991), 1–19; for an account of the Church of England in its first century which supports the high-church historiography by presenting the monarchy as a restraint on the full-blooded protestantizing of the Church of England, G. W. Bernard, 'The Church of England c. 1529 – c. 1642', *History*, vol. 75 (1990), 183–206.

Chapter 2

1 The elitist art of the miniaturist Nicholas Hillyard is the exception which proves the rule.

2 Thwackum's remark occurs in *Tom Jones*, Book Three, chapter 3. There are too many editions for a page citation to be useful.

3 above, pp. 26–9.

4 C. Z. Wiener, 'The Beleaguered Isle. A Study of Elizabethan and Early Jacobean Anti-Catholicism', *Past and Present*, no 51, (May 1971), 27–62.

5 An entry into the immense and burgeoning literature on Foxe can be made with J. F. Mozley, *John Foxe and His Book*, London: SPCK (1940); William Haller, *Foxe's Book of Martyrs and the Elect Nation*, London: Jonathan Cape (1963); John N. King, *Foxe's Book of Martyrs and Early Modern Print Culture*, Cambridge: CUP (2006); Elizabeth Evenden and Thomas S. Freeman, *Religion and the Book in Early Modern England: the making of John Foxe's 'Book of Martyrs'*, Cambridge: CUP (2011). The standard

resource for any study of Foxe is now 'The Acts and Monuments Online' (TAMO) website, which makes available annotated editions of all the Elizabethan editions of Foxe's book: http://www.johnfoxe.org/.

6   John Foxe, *Actes and Monuments*, London: John Daye (1583), p 20.

7   Thomas S Freeman, 'Inventing Bloody Mary: Perceptions of Mary Tudor from the restoration to the twentieth century' in Susan Doran and Thomas Freeman (eds), *Mary Tudor, Old and New Perspectives*, London: Palgrave Macmillan (2011), pp. 78–100.

8   J. E. Drabble, 'Gilbert Burnet and the history of the English Reformation', *Journal of Religious History*, 12 (1983), 351–63; Tony Claydon, 'Latitudinarianism and Apocalyptic History in the Worldview of Gilbert Burnet, 1643–1715', *The Historical Journal*, vol. 51, no. 3 (Sep. 2008) 577–97.

9   Cited in Edwin Jones, *The English Nation: the Great Myth*, Stroud: Sutton (2003), pp. 87–8.

10 Jones, *English Nation*, p. 232.

11 For Froude's career, in addition to the ODNB article by A. F. Pollard and William Thomas, Herbert Paul, *The Life of Froude*, London: Pitman (1905); Waldo Hilary Dunn, *James Anthony Froude, a Biography*, 2 vols, Oxford: Clarendon Press (1961–3). For appraisals of his work as a Tudor historian, in ascending order of usefulness, A. L. Rowse, *Froude the Historian, Victorian Man of Letters*, Gloucester: Sutton (1987); G. R. Elton, 'J A Froude and his History of England' in *Studies in Tudor and Stuart Politics and Government: Volume 3, Papers and Reviews 1973–1981*, Cambridge: CUP (2003); J. W. Burrow, *A Liberal Descent: Victorian Historians and the English Past*, Cambridge: CUP (1981), pp. 231–85. Basil Willey, *More Nineteenth Century Studies: a Group of Honest Doubters*, London: Chatto and Windus (1963), pp 106 ff., deals with Froude's religious odyssey. See also, Eamon Duffy, 'Introduction' to *J. A. Froude's Mary Tudor*, London: Continuum (2010).

12 *The History of England from the Fall of Wolsey to the Defeat of the Spanish Armada*, 12 vols, London: Longmans, Green and Co. (1879).

13 *History of England*, vol. 12, p. 378.

14 Keith Thomas, *Religion and the Decline of Magic*, Harmondsworth: Penguin (1973), p. ix.

15 A. G. Dickens, *The English Reformation*, 2nd edn, London: Batsford (1989), p. 13.

16 There is a well-documented modern life of Lingard by Peter Philips, *John Lingard*, Leominster: Gracewing (2008); the delightfully expanisve Edwardian life by Martin Haile and Edward Bonney, *The Life and Letters of John Lingard*, London: Herbert and Daniel (1911) retains its value. Lingard's intellectual milieu and historical work have been studied by Joseph Chinnici, *The English Catholic Enlightenment: John Lingard and the Cisalpine Movement*, Shepherdstown: Patmos Press (1980); by D. F. Shaw, *The English Ranke, John Lingard*, New York: Humanities Press (1969); and most recently by Edwin Jones, *English Nation*, Chapter 6, and his *John Lingard and the Pursuit of Historical Truth*, Brighton: Sussex Academic Press (2004).

17 F. A. Gasquet, *Henry VIII and the English Monasteries: an Attempt to Illustrate the*

History of their Suppression, 2 vols, London: Hodges and Co. (1888–9); F. A. Gasquet, *The Old English Bible and Other Essays*, London: J.C. Nimmo (1897); F. A. Gasquet, *The Eve of the Reformation: Studies in the Religious Life and Thought of the English People*, London: Bell & Sons (1900); F. A. Gasquet, *Parish Life in Mediaeval England*, London: Methuen (1906); E. Bishop and F. A. Gasquet, *Edward VI and the Book of Common Prayer*, London: J. Hodges (1890).

18 The conflict between Gasquet and Coulton was sensitively treated in Dom David Knowles's 1956 Creighton lecture, *Cardinal Gasquet as an Historian*, London: Athlone Press (1957).

19 Philip Hughes, *The Reformation in England*, 3 vols, London: Hollis and Carter (1950–4).

20 Cited in Christopher Haigh, 'A. G. Dickens and the English Reformation', *Historical Research*, vol. 77, no. 195 (February 2004), 33–5.

21 A. G. Dickens, *The East Riding of Yorkshire with Hull and York: a Portrait*, Hull: Brown (1996), pp. 62–3, 66, 111–12.

22 Dickens, *English Reformation*, p. 289.

23 I discuss this shift in the Introduction, above.

24 Haigh, 'A. G. Dickens', p. 37.

25 I have used the Penguin edition, *The Alteration*, Harmondsworth (1988).

26 *The Alteration*, p. 199.

27 *ibid.*, p. 97.

28 Excellent discussion by Christopher Haigh, 'Elizabeth', in Susan Doran and Thomas Freeman (eds), *Tudors and Stuarts on Film, Historical Perspectives*, Basingstoke: Palgrave Macmillan (2008); see also the pertinent remarks in the essay by Tom Betteridge in Susan Doran and Thomas Freeman (eds), *The Myth of Elizabeth*, Basingstoke: Palgrave Macmillan (2003), pp. 254ff.

29 see above, pp. 15–16

30 A. G. Dickens, *East Riding*, pp. 62–3, 66; Andrew Graham-Dixon, *A History of British Art*, London: BBC Books (1996), p. 39.

31 Graham-Dixon, *A History of British Art*, p. 42.

32 *ibid.*, pp. 14–16.

33 Alison Shell, *Shakespeare and Religion*, London: Arden Shakespeare (2010).

Chapter 3

1 A. H. Thompson, quoted in Beat Kumin, *The Shaping of a Community: the Rise and Reformation of the English Parish, c. 1400–1560*, Aldershot: Scolar (1996), p. 186.

2 The standard works on screens are F. B. Bond, *Screens and Galleries in English
   Churches*, London: Oxford University Press (1908); F. B. Bond and Dom Bede Camm,
   Roodscreens and Roodlofts, London: Pitman (1909); Aymer Vallance, *English Church
   Screens*, London: Batsford (1936). There is a good brief account in G. H. Cook, *The
   English Mediaeval Parish Church*, London: Phoenix House (1961), pp. 150–62. On
   the iconography of the screens, Bond and Camm, *Roodscreens*, 2, (for Devon), and
   Bede Camm, 'Some Norfolk rood-screens' in Christopher Hussey ed., *A Supplement to
   Blomefield's Norfolk*, London: Privately printed limited edition (1929), pp. 239–95; W.
   W. Williamson, 'Saints on Norfolk roodscreens and pulpits', *Norfolk Archaeology*, 31
   (1955–7), 299–346; M. R. James, *Suffolk and Norfolk*, London: J. M. Dent (1930), *passim*;
   W. W. Lillie, 'Screenwork in the County of Suffolk', *Proceedings of the Suffolk Institute
   of Archaeology*, 20 (1930), 214–26, 255–64; 21 (1931–3), 179–201; 22 (1934–6), 120–6.
   All these are essentially listings, and unless otherwise stated, identification of saints on
   the rood-screens discussed are taken from these sources. Something more ambitious
   is attempted in W. G. Constable, 'Some East Anglian rood-screen paintings', *The
   Connoisseur*, 84 (1929), 141–7, 211–20, 290–3, 358–63; see also E. Duffy, 'Holy maydens,
   holy wyfes: the cult of women saints in fifteenth and sixteenth-century England' in D.
   Webb ed., *Women in the Church*, *Studies in Church History*, 23, Oxford: Basil Blackwell
   (1990), 175–96, and *The Stripping of the Altars*, London and New Haven: Yale University
   Press (1992), pp. 110–13, 157–60. All the Norfolk screens mentioned in this chapter are
   illustrated and described in Audrey Baker's 1937 Courtauld Institute PhD thesis, *English
   Panel Painting 1400–1558*, edited, updated and extended by Ann Ballantyne and Pauline
   Plummer (London, Archetype Publications, 2011) which unfortunately appeared too
   late to be used in this chapter. There is an invaluable study of the (largely unpainted)
   screens of the Southern Welsh Marches by Richard Wheeler, focused on the structural,
   artistic and architectural historical aspects, rather than on patronage, but containing
   much information pertinent to screens in other parts of the country – *The Medieval
   Church Screens of the Southern Marches*, Little Logaston: Logaston Press (2006).

3 A. Hanham ed., *Churchwardens' Accounts of Ashburton, 1479–1580*, Torquay: Devon
   and Cornwall Record Society (1970), pp. 70ff; J. Erskine Binney ed., *The Accounts
   of the Wardens of the Parish of Morebath, Devon, 1520–1573*, Exeter: Devon and
   Cornwall Record Society (1904), p. 70ff. The devotional activity in Tudor Morebath is
   treated in my *The Voices of Morebath, Reformation and Rebellion in an English Village*,
   New Haven and London: Yale University Press (2001).

4 The fundamental work on dating, based largely on wills from the Norwich Consistory
   Courts, has been done by Simon Cotton, for Norfolk in 'Medieval roodscreens in
   Norfolk – their construction and painting dates', *Norfolk Archaeology*, 40 (1987),
   44–54, (hereafter Cotton, 'Roodscreens') (references for 150 parishes), and for Suffolk
   in an unpublished hand-list, last updated in January 2011 and kindly made available
   to me by Dr Cotton (references for 124 parishes). In the course of other research using
   Norwich Consistory Court Wills I have been able to add just over two dozen further
   parishes, mostly in Suffolk – these are cited individually as they arise. Further material
   on Norfolk bequests in Baker, *English Panel Paintings*, pp. 91–6.

5 A range of examples printed in J. Charles Cox, *Churchwardens Accounts*, London:
   Methuen (1913), pp. 175–80, and Bulier, loc. cit.

6 Surviving examples of musicians' 'squints', both in Wales, illustrated in Vallance,

Screens, plates 32–3; Charles Kerry, *A History of the Municipal Church of St Laurence, Reading*, Reading: privately published by the author (1883), pp. 55–9; David Dymond and Clive Paine (eds), *The Spoil of Melford Church*, Ipswich: Salient Press (1989), p. 3; R. C. Dudding ed., *The First Churchwardens' Book of Louth 1500–1524*, Oxford: OUP (1941), p. 214; Cook, *English Parish Church*, pp. 155–7.

7 The sources for this table, which makes no claims to be statistically representative but simply codifies the information from 280 parishes in which bequests for work on the rood-screen have been found, are cited in note 4 above.

8 Cotton, 'Roodscreens', 52; Paul Cattermole and Simon Cotton, 'Medieval parish church building in Norfolk', *Norfolk Archaeology*, 38 (1981), 255, 271, 257; Norwich Consistory Court Wills (hereafter NCC) Aleyn, 153; NCC Spyltymber, 93; N. Pevsner, *North East Norfolk and Norwich*, Harmondsworth: Penguin (1962), p. 235. Gardener was just one of a number of benefactors paying for furnishings and decoration in the wake of the rebuilding.

9 Rood-stairs survive in literally hundreds of churches: representative examples can be seen in Edingthorpe and Castle Acre in Norfolk, or Hessett in Suffolk. For a turret housing the rood-stairs, see St John's, Needham Market, or the 'Clopton turret' at Long Melford.

10 NCC Spyltymber, 124; Godsalve 20; Alpe, 216; Platfoote, 23; Spyltymber, 85; Briggs, 227.

11 Vallance, *Screens*, p. 65. Hackington indenture printed in *Archaeologia Cantiana*, 44 (1932), 267–8.

12 J. E. Foster ed., *Churchwardens' Accounts of St Mary the Great, Cambridge from 1504 to 1635*, Cambridge: Cambridge Antiquarian Society (1905), pp. 15, 36, 41, 43, 46, 48; Cook, *English Parish Church*, p. 161.

13 Binney, *Morebath*, p. 70.

14 Binney, *Morebath*, pp. 94, 112.

15 Vallance, *Screens*, p. 65.

16 NCC Rix, 243; Popy, 20; Spyltymber, 79.

17 Clive Burgess ed., *The Pre-Reformation Records of All Saints', Bristol: Part I*, Bristol Record Society Publications 46 (1995), p. 16.

18 Cotton, 'Roodscreens', 49. According to his gravestone near the screen, Salmon died in 1486, so in all probability his widow initiated the screen as their joint memorial.

19 F. Blomefield and C. Parkin, *An Essay Towards a Topographical History of the County of Norfolk*, London: Henstede, Humbleyard, Gallow and Brothercross (1805–10) vol. 1, pp. 316–33: Cotton, 'Roodscreens', pp. 48–9; NCC Popy, 27; Johnson, 87.

20 Foxley screen illustrated also in Duffy, *Stripping of the Altars*, plate 124; Cotton, 'Roodscreens', 48; NCC Attmere, 373.

21 *Trunch Miscellany* (cyclostyled pamphlet available at Trunch, n.p., n.d.) pp. 6–7, though I have modified the translation of the inscription given there. The Latin runs 'Orate pro animabus omnium benefactorum istius operis quod factum fuit anno

domini millesimo quingentesimo secundo quorum animabus propitietur Deus. Cui sit gloria, laus, honor, virtus et potestas atque jubilatio, gratiamin actio, amor indeficiens per infinita saeculorum saecula. Amen dicant omnia'; Cotton, 'Roodscreens', 52.

22 NCC Brigges, 152.

23 NCC Platfoote, 115. On this whole subject, Clive Burgess, 'The benefactions of mortality: the lay response in the late medieval urban parish', in D. M. Smith ed., *Studies in Clergy and Ministry in Medieval England*, Borthwick Studies in History 1, York: Borthwick Institute (1991), pp. 65–86.

24 Lillie, 'Screenwork in Suffolk', vol. 21, 189. The Fritton screen is illustrated in Duffy, *Stripping of the Altars*, plate 125. The Ipswich group portraits illustrated in Baker, *English Panel Paintings*, pp. 6, 7.

25 Judith Middleton-Stewart, 'Patronage, personal commemoration and progress: St Andrew's Church, Westhall c. 1140–1548', *Proceedings of the Suffolk Institute of Archaeology* 3, (1986), 312–13; Cotton, 'Roodscreens', 47; Blomefield and Parkin, *Norfolk*, vol. 6, p. 266; NCC Ryxe, 131 – Richard Brown of Cawston, 4 marks 'to the peynting of a pane of the Rode lofte'; for the Attleburgh inscriptions, Camm 'Some Norfolk roodscreens', p. 249. Atereth's 'iiij panys' make up the whole north side of the screen; see also ch. 4 below, p. 96.

26 Blomefield and Parkin, *Norfolk*, vol. 6, p. 278; NCC Spyltymber, 150; Garnon, 16. Mrs. Busby also left money for the gilding of an image of St Saviour, before which she asked to be buried.

27 NCC Robynson, 93; *Archaeologia Cantiana*, 44, 267–8.

28 NCC Garnon, 23; Cox, *Churchwardens Accounts*, pp. 175–6; Cotton, 'Roodscreens', 44; Binney, *Morebath*, p. 70.

29 Ann Eljenholm Nichols, *Seeable Signs: the Iconography of the Seven Sacraments 1350–1544*, Woodbridge: Boydell & Brewer (1994), p. 351.

30 Discussion in P. Lasko and N. Morgan, *Medieval Art in East Anglia 1300–1524*, Norwich: Jarrold and Sons (1973), pp. 39–40, 49, 60; Pauline Plummer, 'The Ranworth roodscreen', *Archaeological Journal*, 137 (1980), 291–5; Baker, *English Panel Paintings*, pp. 12–32.

31 For an exploration of the religious significance of the sequences of Virgin Martyrs which occur on many screens, see Duffy, 'Holy maydens', *passim*.

32 The conventional texts are given in James, *Norfolk and Suffolk*, pp. 218–19; for fifteenth-century representations of apostles and prophets, and related sequences, Emile Male, *Religious Art In France: the Late Middle Ages*, Princeton NJ: Princeton University Press (1986), pp. 211.

33 For illustrations of these screens, Duffy, *Stripping of the Altars*, plates 17, 29, 31–2, 141; Constable 'Some East Anglian rood screen paintings', 146–7; and Baker, *English Panel Paintings, passim*.

34 Blomefield and Parkin, *Norfolk*, vol. 5, p. 440.

35 Ann Eljenholm Nichols, *The Early Art of Norfolk: a subject list of Extant and Lost Art*, Kalamazoo MI: Medieval Institute Publications (2002), pp. 239–43.

36 Norman Tanner, *Heresy Trials in the Diocese of Norwich 1428–31*, Camden Society 4th Series, 20 (1977), p. 148; Nichols, *Seeable Signs*, pp. 72–3. I have discussed devotion to the Latin Doctors more fully in 'The Four Latin Doctors in Late Medieval England', in Julian M. Luxford and M. A. Michael (eds), *Contexts of Medieval Art: Images, Objects and Ideas*, Turnhout: Harvey Miller (2010), pp. 33–41.

37 NCC Attmere, 222.

38 Edward Peacock ed., 'Churchwardens' Accounts of the Parish of Leverton in the County of Lincoln', *Archaeologia*, 41 (1867), p. 349.

39 Ludham screen illustrated also in *Stripping of the Altars*, plates 73, 79, and in Constable 'Some East Anglian rood screen paintings', 214. Walstan is represented at Barnham Broom, Binham, Burlingham St Andrew, Denton, Foulden, Haddiscoe, Litcham, Ludham, Norwich (St James), Outwell and Sparham: the savagely defaced screen at Beeston next Mileham once had an image of Walstan, whose scythe and ermine hem are still visible: Nichols, *Early Art of Norfolk*, p. 235. For the cult of St Walstan, Duffy, *Stripping of the Altars*, pp. 200–5.

40 NCC Multon, 135. All Saints was normally a Trinitarian image, in which the crowned figure of God the Father held the crucifix between his knees, hovered over by the Spirit in the shape of a dove. The 'All Saints' dimension was represented by the souls of the just held by the Father in a napkin at his breast. For a representation, Francis Cheetham, *English Medieval Alabasters*, Oxford: Phaidon, Christies (1984), colour plate 6.

41 Illustrated in Duffy, *Stripping of the Altars*, plate 33, and in Constable 'Some East Anglian Rood Screen Paintings', 292–3.

42 Duffy, 'Holy maydens', 178–80.

43 Ken Farnhill, *Guilds and the Parish Community in Late Medieval East Anglia c.1470–1550*, Woodbridge: Boydell Press (2001), p. 175; Nichols, *Early Art of Norfolk*, p. 23.

44 Blomefield and Parkin, *Norfolk*, vol. 6, pp. 264–7; information about the guilds at Gressenhall, Trimingham and at Cawston from the list of guild dedications in Farnhill, *Guilds*, pp. 172–211.

45 The Annunciation scene from St Michael at Plea is illustrated in Lasko and Morgan, *Medieval Art*, plate 56; the Barton Turf angels are reproduced in Edward G. Tasker, *Encyclopedia of Medieval Church Art*, London: Bratsford (1993), plates 6.3–6.11, and described in detail in Nichols, *Early Art of Norfolk*, pp. 33–4; St Apollonia and St Zita from the same screen are illustrated in *Stripping of the Altars*, plate 60. See also Baker, *English Panel Paintings*, pp. 28, 64–9.

46 Sebastian Sutcliffe, 'The cult of St Sitha in England: an introduction', *Nottingham Medieval Studies*, 37 (1993), 83–9.

47 For which see Jacobus de Voragine, *The Golden Legend*, ed. and trans. W. G. Ryan, Princeton NJ: Princeton University Press (1993), vol. 2, pp. 203–4.

48 *Transactions of the Shropshire Archaeological Society*, 3rd Series, 3 (1903), i–ii.

49 Cotton, 'Roodscreens', 52.

50 For Horsham St Faith, where the images of St Brigid of Sweden and St Catherine of

Siena are borrowed from woodcuts in the Brigittine treatise, *The Dyetary of Ghostly Helthe*, produced by Wynken de Worde in 1520, see *Stripping of the Altars*, plates 61–2 and p.86; for Wyverstone *ibid.*, plate 139; for the Loddon panels, Constable, 'Some East Anglian rood screen paintings', 359. Some sixteenth-century screens, such as those at Wiggenhall St Mary in the Norfolk Marshland, and Belstead in Suffolk, retain single figures in each panel, but move away from the sculptured niche prototype and towards narrative by placing a continuous background, such as a landscape or wall, behind the figures.

51 Constable, 'Some East Anglian rood screen paintings', 294; Baker, *op. cit.* pp. 53–4.

52 Only Gregory and Augustine appear at Gateley, but the other two Doctors may have been on the doors, now gone. 'Puella Redibowne' has not been identified convincingly, but she had a shrine chapel at Cromer, and Alice Man, a widow of the parish of Lound, left money in 1502 both for the gilding of the rood-beam and for the gilding of 'maid redybone', evidently a statue in the church there. NCC Popy, 144; Williamson, 'Saints on Norfolk roodscreens', 308. Two of the saints from Gateley, including Master John Shorne, are reproduced also in Duffy, *Stripping of the Altars*, plate 72.

53 Some of the Southwold donations listed in Cotton, 'Rood screens', 53; D. P. Mortlock, *The Popular Guide to Suffolk Churches*, vol. 3 East Suffolk, Bury St Edmunds (1992), p. 185. The Southwold screen is illustrated in Constable, 'Some East Anglian rood screen paintings', 363–4 and Baker, *op. cit.* pp. 184–9.

54 Illustrated in Constable, 'Some East Anglian rood screen paintings', 142–3 and Duffy, *Stripping of the Altars*, plates 56, 74, 108–9.

55 Ranworth wills and benefactions surveyed in A. W. Morant and J. l'Estrange, 'Notices of the Church at Randworth (sic)', *Norfolk Archaeology*, 7 (1872), 178–211.

56 Duffy, 'Holy maydens', 194–6

57 Plummer, 'Ranworth rood screen', 292–5; D. H. Farmer ed., *The Oxford Dictionary of Saints*, Oxford: OUP (1978), pp. 5–6. See also references in note 30 above.

58 Tasker, *Encyclopedia of Medieval Church Art*, plates 5.230–5.247.

59 NCC Heyward, 74, 76, 78; Hyll, 42. The screen is illustrated in Constable,'Some East Anglian rood screen paintings', 144–5, Baker, *op. cit.* pp. 88–9, and Duffy, *Stripping of the Altars*, plates 56, 59, 79, 131; details of some of the bequests for the screen, and about the inscription, are to be found in Simon Cotton and Roy Tricker, *Saint Andrew, Burlingham*, (cyclostyled pamphlet available at the church, no place or date), pp. 4–5.

60 For the Henrician campaign against St Thomas, Duffy, *Stripping of the Altars*, p. 412.

61 NCC Thyrkyll, 12.

62 For Wenhaston and Ludham, Duffy, *Stripping of the Altars*, plates 55, 137–8. For Binham, Duffy. *Stripping of the Altars*, 2nd Ed. (2005), pp. xxxv–xxxvii.

63 P. Northeast ed., *Boxford Churchwardens' Accounts 1530–1561*, Suffolk Record Society (1982), p. 58; A. G. Legge ed., *Ancient Churchwardens Accounts of the Parish of North Elmham 1539–1577*, Norwich: Goose (1891), pp. 43–4; J. L. Glasscock ed., *The Records of St Michael's Parish Church, Bishop Stortford*, London: Elliot Stock (1882), pp. 47–50; W. H. Overall ed., *The Accounts of the Churchwardens of the Parish of St Michael,*

Cornhill 1456–1608, London: privately printed (1883), p. 65; Cox, *Churchwardens' Accounts*, pp. 180–4.

64 Duffy, *Stripping of the Altars*, pp. 545–8.

65 Binney, *Morebath*, p. 185.

66 The point about plague masses is derived from an examination of the Marian Breviaries, listed in A. W. Pollard and G. R. Redgrave, *A Short-Title Catalogue of Books Printed in England, Scotland, and Ireland and of English Books Printed Abroad 1475–1640*, 2nd edn revised and enlarged, London: Bibliographical Society (1976), nos. 15836–15847.

67 F. Bailey ed., *Prescot Churchwardens' Accounts*, Lancashire and Cheshire Record Society (1953) p. 53. For discussion of the Elizabethan attack on images, Duffy, *Stripping of the Altars*, pp. 568–77.

Chapter 4

1 Much of the surviving documentation on medieval and Tudor Salle is gathered or summarized in W. L. E. Parsons, *Salle: the story of a Norfolk Parish, its Church, Manors and People*, Norwich: Jarrold and Sons (1937), (hereafter cited as *Salle*); brief architectural account by T. A. Heslop in Boris Ford ed., *The Cambridge Guide to the Arts in Britain, Volume 2: The Middle Ages*, Cambridge: CUP (1988), pp. 194–9; R. Fawcett and D. King 'Salle Church', *Archaeological Journal*, vol. 137 (1980), 332–5; F. Blomefield & C. Parkin, *An Essay towards a Topographical History of the County of Norfolk*, London: Henstede, Humbleyard, Gallow and Brothercross (1769), vol. IV, pp. 421–6.

2 Figures from *Salle*, pp. 139–40.

3 The coats of arms are detailed in *Salle*, pp. 32–3.

4 J. Alexander and P. Binski (eds), *The Age of Chivalry: Art in Plantagenet England 1200–1400*, London: Royal Academy of Arts in association with Weidenfeld & Nicolson (1987), pp. 516–17.

5 Listed in *Salle*, pp. 94–5; for Thomas Rose's misdemeanour, *ibid.*, p. 47.

6 Norfolk Record Office (= NRO) Norwich Consistory Court Wills (=NCC), 181/182 Aleyn.

7 NRO, Archdeaconry of Norwich Wills (=ANW), 222 Gloys, Will of Alice Martyn, 1510; cf. NRO, ANW, 173 Cooke, will of Margaret Greeve, 1508 (bequest of 3d. to the plough-light of Kirkgate); parish organizations for women only are discussed, using evidence mainly from the south-west of England, in Katherine L. French, 'Maidens lights and wives stores: women's parish guilds in late medieval England', *Sixteenth Century Journal*, XXIX (1998), 399–425.

8 For plough-lights, R. Hutton, *The Stations of the Sun: a History of the Ritual Year in Britain*, Oxford: OUP (1996), pp. 124–8.

9 NRO, NCC, 444 Ryxe.

10 H. Harrord ed., 'Extracts from Early Norfolk Wills', *Norfolk Archaeology*, 1 (1847), 119.

11 His will is in PCC 44/45 Wylbey.

12 NRO, NCC 202–5 Wolman.

13 My transcription.

14 NRO, NCC 11–12 Brosyard.

15 PCC wills, 20 Wattys.

16 NRO, NCC Spyltimber 291; Pull also left 6d. to each plough-light.

17 *Salle*, p. 83 (John Lutting, chaplain d. 1399), pp. 98–100 (Robert Luce, chaplain d. 1456).

18 They are summarized in H. F. Westlake, *The Parish Guilds of Medieval England*, London: SPCK (1919), p. 209.

19 *Salle*, p. 93.

20 NRO, ANW 222 Gloys (will of Alice Martin 1510).

21 Information on Cawston from F. Blomfield and C. Parkin, *Topographical History of Norfolk*, vol. III, pp. 537–47.

22 NRO, NCC 22 Ryxe (f. 131)

23 NRO, NCC 202–5 Wolman (Thomas Briggs); PCC Wills, I. Godeyn (Geoffrey Boleyn).

24 NRO, NCC 46–7 Platfoote.

25 PCC Wills, 75 Jekyn; *Salle*, p. 76.

26 NRO NCC 11–12 Brosyard (will of Robert Luce, chaplain 1456); NCC120 Gelour (will of Thomas Bucke, chaplain, 1475); NCC 32 Wight (will of William Jekkes, chaplain, 1499); NCC 291 Spyltimber (will of Robert Pull, 1510).

27 NRO NCC 11–12 Brosyard.

28 *Salle*, pp. 73–7, 81–8, 99. Thomas Jekkes asked for burial beside Simon Boleyn.

29 A. E. Nichols, *Seeable Signs, the Iconography of the Seven Sacraments 1350–1544*, Woodbridge: Boydell Press (1994), pp. 345–6.

30 The conventional texts are conveniently listed in M. R. James, *Suffolk and Norfolk*, London: J. M. Dent (1930), pp. 218–19. See also ch 3 above, pp. 69–71.

31 Brown's will, NRO NCC 131 Ryxe and above, ch 3, p. 66.

32 Ch 3 above, pp. 62–9.

33 The discussion of the glass in *Salle*, pp. 61–71, largely based on notes supplied by M. R. James, has now to be supplemented by the account by David King in *Archaeological Journal*, 137, 333–5.

34 For an illustration of the subject and some other examples, Francis Cheetham, *English Medieval Alabasters*, Oxford: Phaidon, Christie's (1984), p. 175.

35 Late medieval belief about the angels is conveniently summarized in *The Golden Legend or Lives of the Saints as Englished by William Caxton*, London: Gollancz (n.d.), vol. 5, pp. 180–99.

36 On the heraldic glass, *Salle*, p. 66–9.

37 T. H. Swales, 'The Redistribution of Monastic Lands in Norfolk at the Dissolution', *Norfolk Archaeology*, vol. 34, (1966–9), 25.

38 Colin Richmond, *John Hopton*, Cambridge: CUP (1981), pp. 244–5.

39 Swales, 'Redistribution', 24–5; E. Duffy, *The Stripping of the Altars*, New Haven and London: Yale University Press (1992), p. 403; and see *Letters and Papers*, vol. 20 Pt 1, 282, no 37 (grant in fee of the sight of the Franciscan priory at Walsingham); A. R. Martin, 'The Greyfriars of Walsingham', *Norfolk Archaeology*, 25 (1935), 227–71, especially 235; representative cross-section of Townsend's activities on behalf of government in Norfolk is provided in G. R. Elton, *Policy and Police: the Enforcement of the Reformation in the Age of Thomas Cromwell*, Cambridge: CUP (1972), pp. 17, 82, 144–5, 342; best discussion of the Walsingham Plot, and the Townsend family's role in suppressing it, C. E. Moreton, 'The Walsingham Conspiracy of 1537', *Historical Research*, 63 (1990), 29–43.

40 C. E. Moreton, *The Townsends and their World: Gentry, Law and Land in Norfolk c. 1451–1551*, Oxford: Clarendon Press (1992), pp. 29–36; F. W. Russell, *Kett's Rebellion in Norfolk*, London: Longmans, Brown, Green, Longmans and Roberts (1859), pp. 8–9.

41 In 1537 'Roger Tonneshonde DCL', rector of North Creake, was described as the King's Chaplain when dispensed for plurality; D. S. Chambers (ed.), *Faculty Office Registers 1534–1549: A Calendar of the First Two Registres of the Archbishop of Canterbury's Faculty Office*, London: Clarendon Press (1966) p. 105. I owe this and several other references to the kindness of Dr David Crankshaw, who commented very helpfully on a draft of this essay.

42 John Le Neve, *Fasti Ecclesiae Anglicanae 1300–1521*, revised and expanded, London: University of London, Institute of Historical Research, Athlone Press (1962), vol. iii, p. 19; Moreton, *The Townsends*, pp. 42–3.

43 In 1534 Townsend signed the formal renunciation of Papal Supremacy which is reproduced as plate xxiv of Denys Hay, *The Italian Renaissance in its Historical Background*, Cambridge: CUP (1976), facing p. 183.

44 The references to his evangelicalism in Susan Brigden, *London and the Reformation*, Oxford: Clarendon Press (1989), pp. 55, 384, appear to be based on the provisions and wording of his will, discussed below.

45 PCC Wills F 21 Dyngeley f. 169v; the extracts transcribed in *Salle*, pp. 130–1 are accurate in substance, but modernize spelling, and have many unacknowledged omissions and paraphrases.

46 See the table of elected officers in E. Duffy, *The Voices of Morebath: Reformation and Rebellion in an English Village*, New Haven and London: Yale University Press (2001), pp. 191–9.

47 *Salle*, p. 147

48 *Salle*, p133.

49 D. MacCulloch, 'Kett's Rebellion in Context', *Past and Present*, 84 (1979), 60; and, less guardedly, A. Fletcher and D. MacCulloch, *Tudor Rebellions*, 4th edn, London: Longmans (1997), p. 79.

50 Russell, *Kett's Rebellion*, pp. 37–8; Moreton, *The Townsends*, pp. 37–8.

51 *Salle*, p. 185. For a different perspective on local collaboration with the Reformation, Ethan Shagan, *Popular Politics and the English Reformation*, Cambridge University Press (2003) esp. chs 5 and 7.

52 His will, made on 12 July 1558, was proved in the Norwich Consistory Court on 7 February following – NRO NCC 322 Jerves.

53 NRO NCC 10 Crawforde (will of John Lockett, Tailor, 1543).

54 See the bitter comments about Townsend's suspicious alliances and his unscrupulous opportunism, made by Sir Nicholas le Strange to Cecil in September 1549, C. Knighton (ed.), *Calendar of State Papers of Edward VI*, HMSO (1992), no 359.

55 NRO NCC 31–7 Lyncolne, and cf. Richmond, *Hopton*, pp. 244–5.

56 *Salle*, pp. 134–6; H. B. Walters ed., 'Inventories of Norfolk Church Goods', *Norfolk Archaeology*, vol. 28 (1945), 17–18 'probably the richest inventory in quality in the county outside Norwich....'; there are still two medieval bells in the tower, one inscribed in honour of the Trinity, and the other simply with the name of its King's Lynn maker.

57 NRO NCC 155 Beeles; Lockett requested burial in the churchyard, so the repaving cannot have been connected with his grave: on the other hand, it is clear that many explicitly Catholic funeral inscriptions survived the Edwardian purges *in situ* at Salle – for a list made *c.* 1602, see C. M. Hood ed., *The Chorography of Norfolk*, Norwich: Jarrold and Sons (1938), pp. 145–7.

58 *Salle*, pp. 135–6.

59 C. H. Cooper, *Annals of Cambridge*, Cambridge: Warwick and Co. (1842), vol. 1, pp. 423–7; C. H. Cooper, *Athenae Cantabrigiensis*, Cambridge: Deighton Bell (1858), vol. 1, pp. 461–2; J. B. Mullinger, *History of Cambridge*, Cambridge: CUP (1873), vol. 2, pp. 73–6; J. Peile (ed.), *Biographical Register of Christ's College 1505–1905*, Cambridge: CUP (1910), vol. 1, p. 26; V. J. K. Brook, *A Life of Archbishop Parker*, Oxford: Clarendon Press (1962), pp. 28–32.

60 Corpus Christi College Cambridge, Parker Library, Ms 97, fols 202, 212, 225. (Norwich Diocesan certificate, compiled for Archbishop Parker *c.* September 1561 – January 1562).

61 Albert Peel ed., *The Second Parte of a Register*, Cambridge: CUP (1915), vol. 2, p. 153; *Salle*, p. 77.

62 *Salle*, pp. 77–9; J. F. Williams, 'An Episcopal Visitation in 1593', *Norfolk Archaeology*, vol. 28 (1945), 82.

63 *Salle*, p. 140.

64 NRO, ANW, 144–8 Lawson.

Chapter 5

1 Chapter 4 above. For a survey of this process of deconstruction to 1558, see E. Duffy, *The Stripping of the Altars*, London and Newhaven: Yale University Press (1992), pp. 379–503. The best survey of the religious dimension of the reign of Edward VI is Diarmaid McCulloch, *Tudor Church Militant*, Harmondsworth: Penguin (1999).

2 R. Hoyle, *The Pilgrimage of Grace and the Politics of the 1530s*, Oxford: OUP (2001).

3 For some notably defensive Suffolk certificates in response to these enquiries in November 1547, *The East Anglian*, New Series vol. 1, (1885), 48–51, 57–70, 83–4, 102–4, 114–16, 128–9, 143, 159–60.

4 Eamon Duffy, *Stripping of the Altars*, pp. 455–7; *Acts of the Privy Council* II, pp. 535–6.

5 *Norfolk Archaeology*, vol. 28 (1942–5), 93, 95, 98.

6 F. C. Eeles & J. E. Brown (eds), *The Edwardian Inventories for Bedfordshire*, Alcuin Club Collections 6 (1905), pp. iii–v; W. Page ed., *The Inventories of Church Goods for the Counties of York, Durham and Northumberland*, Surtees Society 97 (1896), pp. ix–xiii.

7 H. B. Walters ed., *London Churches at the Reformation*, London: SPCK (1939), pp. 17, 23–4; that this procedure was followed widely is evident from the 1547 certificates from East Anglia listed in note 2 above.

8 *Acts of the Privy Council* III, pp. 104, 263.

9 *Acts of the Privy Council* III, p. 228.

10 *Seventh Report of the Deputy Keeper of the Public Records*, HMSO (1846), Appendix 10, pp. 307–8.

11 The surviving Inventories as known in 1846 were listed in the *Seventh Report of the Deputy Keeper of the Public Records*, Appendix 10, pp. 307–36 and more fully as Exchequer (KR) Church Goods, *List and Index Society* vols 69, 76 (1971–2) .

12 The Norfolk inventories were edited by H. B. Walters and others between 1935 and 1957 in *Norfolk Archaeology*, vol XXVI, 245–70, vol. XXVII, 97–144, 263–89, vol. XXVIII, 89–106, 133–80, vol. XXX, 75–87, 160–7, 213–19, 370–8, vol. XXXI, 200–9, 233–98.

13 Clive Burgess ed., *Pre Reformation Records of All Saints Bristol: Part I*, Bristol Record Society (1995), pp. xxiv, xxviii, xli.

14 W. H. St John Hope ed., 'Ancient Inventories of Goods belonging to the Parish Church of St Margaret Pattens in the City of London', *The Archaeological Journal*, vol. 42 (1885), 320–5.

15 Walters, *London Churches*, p. 370.

16 J. Robert Daniel-Tyssen ed., *Inventories of the Goods and Ornaments in the Churches of Surrey in the Reign of King Edward the Sixth*, London: Surrey Archaeological Collections (1869), p. 109.

17 Walters, *London Churches*, pp. 270, 271–2.

18 *ibid.*, p. 134.

19 *ibid.*, p. 223.

20 For the protestant incumbents, Susan Brigden, *London and the Reformation*, Oxford: Clarendon Press (1989), pp. 403, 530.

21 Brigden, *London*, p. 587.

22 Walters, *London Churches*, p. 206; Brigden, *London*, p. 592.

23 Brigden, *London*, pp. 591–2, 627.

24 *ibid.*, pp. 428–9.

25 Walters, *London Churches*, pp. 99, 110–13, 120–4, 246, 452–3; *Surrey Inventories*, p. 14, 88; *Transactions of the Essex Archaeological Society* vol. IV, p. 222; vol. V, pp. 117–20, 278–9.

26 *Surrey Inventories*, pp. 11–12, 14, 23, 24, 25, 26, 27, 29–30.

27 *Transactions of the Essex Archaeological Society*, vol. V, pp. 273–6, 221.

28 *ibid.*, vol. V, pp. 278–9.

29 Brigden, *London*, p. 462.

30 *ibid.*, p. 439.

31 Walters, *London Churches*, pp. 376–7 (removal of the altar in the rood-loft), p. 377 (taking down of the other altars, using the proceeds of *sales* of other items, not the altars, made in 1549), p. 378 (disposal 1551–2 of many Catholic ornaments including altar-cloths).

32 Walters, *London Churches*, p. 187.

33 *ibid.*, p. 259.

34 *ibid.*, p. 553–9.

35 *ibid.*, p. 336.

36 *Surrey Inventories*, pp. 32–3, 34, 36, 37, 98.

37 Walters, *London Churches*, pp. 541, 210, 603. But the distruction of stained glass does suggest a protestant initiative by key parishioners.

38 *Transactions of the Essex Archaeological Society*, NS II, pp. 241–2.

39 Walters, *London Churches*, pp. 88–92.

40 *ibid.*, pp. 382–4, 530–5.

41 *ibid.*, pp. 88, 170, 242, 378, 596; *Surrey Inventories*, p. 66.

42 *Transactions of the Essex Archaeological Society*, vol. V, p. 280.

43 Walters, *London Churches*, pp. 137, 170, 302, 428.

44 *ibid.*, pp. 88, 94, 348.

45 *Surrey Inventories*, pp. 81, 85–8.

46 Walters, *London Churches*, p. 477.

47 *ibid.*, p. 90.

48 *ibid.*, p. 256.

49 *ibid.*, pp. 466–73.

50 *ibid.*, pp. 227–32.

51 *ibid.*, pp. 341; *Transactions of the Essex Archaeological Society*, vol. IV, p. 231; NS II, p. 240.

52 *Stripping of the Altars*, pp. 487–9.

53 J. E. Cussans (ed.), *Inventory of Furniture and Ornaments remaining in all the Parish Churches of Hertfordshire in the last year of the reign of King Edward the Sixth*, Oxford and London: James Parker (1873), pp.15–22.

54 *Surrey Inventories*, p. 132.

55 *Surrey Inventories*, p. 96.

56 Walters, *London Churches*, p. 287; *Surrey Inventories*, pp. 106, 123.

57 Walters, *London Churches*, p. 189.

58 *ibid.*, pp. 193–4, 217, 229.

59 *ibid.*, pp. 158, 189, 282–5, 373–80, 399–401.

60 *ibid.*, p. 86.

61 *ibid.*, pp. 94, 101, 129, 180, 184–7, 408, 462–5, 541; *Surrey Inventories*, pp. 90–1, 98, 106.

62 Walters, *London Churches*, p. 94.

63 Walters, *London Churches*, pp. 87, 189. 205, 213, 237, 295 .

64 *Transactions of the Essex Archaeological Society*, vol. V, pp. 226, 231, 241.

65 *Acts of the Privy Council*, vol. IV, pp. 117, 139, 185.

66 *Archaeologia Cantiana*, vol. XIV, p. 322.

67 *Acts of the Privy Council*, vol. IV, p. 252.

68 *Archaeologia Cantiana*, vol. XIV, p. 322.

69 *Acts of the Privy Council*, vol. IV, pp. 282–3.

70 *Acts of the Privy Council*, vol. V, pp. 348, 354–5.

71 Brigden, *London*, p. 591.

72 *ibid.*, pp. 348, 360.

73 *Acts of the Privy Council*, vol. V, pp. 361, 371, 376.

74 For a particularly well-documented example, *Bedfordshire Inventories*, pp. 17ff.

75 For a Suffolk example, D. Dymond ed., *The Spoil of Long Melford*, pp. 29–30.

76 *Transactions of the Essex Archaeological Society*, vol. V, (1873), p. 223, and *ibid.*, NS vol. I (1877), p. 169.

Chapter 6

1 Maria Dowling, *Fisher of Men: a life of John Fisher 1469–1535*, Basingstoke: Macmillan (1999), pp. 159–69.

2 Henry's dealings with Fisher over the divorce are outlined and discussed in G. W. Bernard, *The King's Reformation*, New Haven and London: Yale University Press (2005), pp. 101–25.

3 Modern biographies add little to the meagre details of Fisher's Yorkshire background contained in the earliest *Life*, edited by F. van Ortroy as *Vie du bienheureux martyr Jean Fisher*, Brussels: Polleunis et Ceuterick (1893), which, however, I have preferred to cite from the more readily available modernized edition by Philip Hughes ed., *Saint John Fisher, The Earliest English Life*, London: Burns Oates and Washbourne (1935), pp. 20–3 (hereafter, *Earliest English Life*); Dowling, *Fisher*, p. 7; the still-valuable Victorian biography by T. E. Bridgett, *Life of Blessed John Fisher*, London: Burns and Oates (1888), pp. 7–11, attempts to expand on Fisher's family.

4 The Spiritual Consolation written for Fisher's step-sister Elizabeth was edited by J. E. B. Mayor, *The English Works of John Fisher*, London: Early English Texts Society (1886), pp. 349–63, and more recently by Cecilia A. Hatt in *English Works of John Fisher,Bishop of Rochester, Sermons and other writings 1520–1535*, Oxford: OUP (2002), pp. 368–75; it is discussed by Edward Surtz, *Works and days of John Fisher*, Cambridge MA: Harvard University Press (1967), pp. 373–7.

5 Fisher's dealings with St John's, including his provision for countrymen and kin, are judiciously discussed by Malcolm Underwood, 'John Fisher and the promotion of Learning' in Brendan Bradshaw and Eamon Duffy (eds), *Humanism, Reform and Reformation:the career of Bishop John Fisher*, Cambridge: CUP (1989), pp. 25–46. See also Richard Rex 'Fisher's College' in P. Linehan, editor, *St John's College, Cambridge: A History*, Woodbridge: Boydell and Brewer (2011), pp. 5–26.

6 Bridgett, *Blessed John Fisher*, pp. 293–4.

7 Fisher included an affectionate eulogy of Melton in his treatise against Oecolampadius in 1527; Dowling, *Fisher of Men*, p. 8; Fisher's intellectual debts to Melton are discussed in Richard Rex, *The Theology of John Fisher*, Cambridge: CUP (1991), pp.

23–6. On Michaelhouse itself, Andreas Loewe, 'Michaelhouse: Hervey de Stanton's Cambridge Foundation', *Church History*, 90.4 (2010) pp. 599–608.

8 Brendan Bradshaw, 'Bishop John Fisher: the man and his work' in Bradshaw and Duffy, *Humanism, Reform and Reformation*, p. 3.

9 Mary Bateson ed., *Grace Book B, Part 1, 1488–1511*, Cambridge: CUP (1903), p. 168.

10 Michael K. Jones and Malcolm Underwood, *The King's Mother: Lady Margaret Beaufort*, Cambridge: CUP (1992).

11 Dowling, *Fisher of Men*, p. 10.

12 Sermon printed in Mayor, *English Works*, pp. 289–310.

13 Dowling, *Fisher of Men*, pp. 12–14.

14 Jones and Underwood, *The King's Mother*, pp. 221ff.

15 Most recent account of the foundation is Rex, 'Fisher's College', above note 5.

16 C. N. L. Brooke, 'The University Chancellor' in Bradshaw and Duffy, *Humanism, Reform and Reformation*, pp. 47–66.

17 The basis for a study of Fisher's relationship with Erasmus is provided by J. Rouscheausse, *Erasmus and Fisher: their Correspondence 1511–1524*, Paris: Librairie philosophique J. Vrin (1968); that relationship was somewhat sourly discussed by Harry Porter, 'Fisher and Erasmus', in Bradshaw and Duffy, *Humanism, Reform and Reformation*, pp. 81–101.

18 On Fisher's Greek and Hebrew, Rex, *Theology of John Fisher*, pp. 55–62.

19 Rex, *Theology of John Fisher*, pp. 63–4.

20 *Earliest English Life*, p. 29.

21 Edited and introduced in Hatt, *English Works*, pp. 209–53.

22 Pole's reminiscence in John Strype, *Ecclesiastical Memorials Relating Chiefly to Religion and its Reformation under the Reigns of King Henry VIII, King Edward VI and Queen Mary*, Oxford: Clarendon Press (1816), vol. III pt 2, pp. 482–510, at p. 495.

23 *Earliest English Life*, pp. 31–8; Stephen Thompson, 'The Bishop in his Diocese' in Bradshaw and Duffy, *Humanism, Reform and Reformation*, pp. 67–80.

24 Dowling, *Fisher of Men*, pp. 142–3.

25 Dowling, *Fisher of Men*, p. 54.

26 Best discussion of the Magdalene controversy, Rex, *Theology of John Fisher*, pp. 65–77.

27 Richard Rex, 'The English Campaign against Luther in the 1520s', *Transactions of the Royal Historical Society*, 5th Series 39 (1989) pp. 85–106; Vincent Nichols, *St John Fisher: Bishop and Theologian in Reformation and Controversy*, Stoke on Trent, Alive Publications, 2011, pp. 117–78.

28 Contemporary account of the book-burning and sermon in Hatt, *English Works*, p. 48, and the sermon itself printed pp. 77–97.

29 Fisher's writings against heresy surveyed in Rex, 'The Polemical Theologian' in Bradshaw and Duffy, *Humanism, Reform and Reformation*, pp. 109–30, and explored individually in the same writer's *Theology of John Fisher*.

30 Rex, *Theology of John Fisher*, pp. 137–46.

31 Bridgett, *Blessed John Fisher*, pp. 88–9.

32 Strype, *Ecclesiastical Memorials*, vol. III pt 2, p. 495.

33 Discussion of the divorce proceedings in Bernard, *King's Reformation*, pp. 1–72. Fisher's resistance discussed *ibid.* pp. 101–25; Dowling, *Fisher of Men*, pp. 132–58.

34 Dowling, *Fisher of Men*, p. 137.

35 Dowling, *Fisher of Men*, pp. 145–6, 148–9.

36 George Cavendish, 'The Life and Death of Cardinal Wolsey', in Richard S. Sylvester and Davis P. Harding (eds), *Two Early Tudor Lives*, New Haven and London: Yale University Press (1962), p. 88.

37 Fisher's offensive comparison was reported by the Imperial Ambassador, Chapuys: for the reaction, Bridgett, *Blessed John Fisher*, p. 170–3.

38 *Earliest English Life*, pp. 105–9; Stanford Lehmberg, *The Reformation Parliament 1529–36*, Cambridge: CUP (1970), pp. 86–9.

39 *Earliest English Life*, p. 112.

40 Richard Rex, 'The Execution of the Holy Maid of Kent', *Historical Research*, vol. 64, Issue 154, (June 1991), 216–20; Bernard, *King's Reformation*, pp. 116–18; for Elizabeth Barton's political significance more widely, Diane Watt, 'Reconstructing the Word: the Political Prophecies of Elizabeth Barton (1506–1534)', *Renaissance Quarterly*, vol. 50, No. 1 (Spring, 1997), 136–63, and her *Secretaries of God: Women Prophets in Late Medieval and Early Modern England*, Woodbridge: D. S. Brewer (2001).

41 *Earliest English Life*, p. 162.

42 J. J. Scarisbrick, 'Fisher, Henry VIII and the Reformation Crisis' in Bradshaw and Duffy, *Humanism, Reform and Reformation*, p. 160–5.

43 *Earliest English Life*, p. 184.

44 Dowling, *Fisher of Men*, p. 107.

Chapter 7

1 C. S. Lewis, *English Literature in the Sixteenth Century, Excluding Drama*, Oxford: OUP (1954), pp. 161–8.

2 See, for example, the writings surveyed in Brendan Bradshaw, 'The Controversial Sir Thomas More', *Journal of Ecclesiastical History*, vol. 36 (1985), 535–69, and the pertinent remarks by J. McConica, 'The Patrimony of Thomas More', in H. Lloyd Jones, Valerie Pearl and Blair Worden (eds), *History and Imagination: Essays in*

Honour of H. R. Trevor Roper, Oxford: Clarendon Press (1981), pp. 56–71, esp. pp. 64ff; J. McConica, 'Northern Humanists before the Reformation', in Cheslyn Jones, Geoffrey Wainwright and Edward Yarnold (eds), *The Study of Spirituality*, London: SPCK (1986), pp. 338–41; Richaed Rex, 'Humanism', in Andrew Pettegree ed., *The Reformation World*, London: Routledge (2000), pp. 51–70. There is an excellent discussion of the relation of Fisher's biblical exegesis to the 'old learning' in J. W. Blench, *Preaching in England in the Late Thfteenth and Early Sixteenth Centuries*, Oxford: Basil Blackwell (1964), pp. 11–20.

3   See his revealing remarks on More's *De IV Novissimis*: 'The colours are too dark. *In the true late medieval manner* More forgets that to paint all black is much the same as not to paint at all. What was intended to be a rebuke of sin degenerates almost into a libel upon life …' (emphasis mine), Lewis, *English Literature*, p. 176.

4   T. E. Bridgett, *Life of Blessed John Fisher*, London: Burns and Oates (1888), p. 15; F. van Ortroy ed., *Vie du bienheureux martyr, Jean Fisher*, Brussels: Polleunis et Ceuterick (1893); *Analecta Bollandiana*, vol. 12 (1893), 208; Philip Hughes ed., *St John Fisher, The Earliest English Life*, London: Burns Oates and Washbourne (1935), p. 184.

5   *Analecta Bollandiana*, vol. 10, 220–1: Hughes, *Earliest English Life*, pp. 34–5. The obvious English Baroque comparison is with John Donne, and the funeral effigy he had made of himself in his shroud. The late Geoffrey Nuttall commented to me that it is perhaps characteristic of the difference between the two men themselves, and of their respective periods, that in choosing a *memento mori* Fisher should prefer an emblem of the universality of death, Donne that *of himself* dead. There are a number of other revealing points of comparison between Donne and Fisher: Donne's *Devotions upon Emergent Occasions* are perhaps the closest parallel in English to Fisher's one literary exercise in the *memento mon* tradition, the *Spiritual Consolation* written for his half sister, Elizabeth White, probably Fisher's least satisfactory work and certainly his least consoling.

6   *Analecta Bollandiana*, vol. 12, pp. 169–70:

7   J. E. B. Mayor ed., *English Works of John Fisher*, London: Early English Text Society (1876), pp. 358, 64. The key writings on this aspect of More are by Geoffrey Elton and Alistair Fox. Elton's principal contributions are 'Sir Thomas More and the Opposition to Henry VIII' (1968), in his *Studies in Tudor and Stuart Politics and Government*, 4 vols, Cambridge: CUP (1974), vol. 1, pp. 155–72; 'Thomas More, Councillor' (1972), Elton, *Studies*, vol. I, pp. 129–54; 'The Real Thomas More' (1980), Elton, *Studies*, vol 3, pp. 344–55. Fox's interpretation is in *Thomas More: History and Providence*, Oxford: Basil Blackwell (1982). See Bradshaw, 'Controversial Sir Thomas More', pp. 535–6, 540–1; Lewis, *English Literature*, p. 163.

8   Lewis, *English Literature*, pp. 163–4; Blench, *Preaching*, p. 236.

9   Sears Jayne, *John Colet and Marsilio Ficino*, Oxford: OUP (1963); Leland Miles, *John Colet and the Platonic Tradition*, London: Allen and Unwin (1962); J. B. Trapp, 'An English Late Medieval Cleric and Italian Thought: The Case of John Colet, Dean of St Paul's', in G. Kratzmauss and J. Simpson (eds), *Medieval English Religious and Ethical Literature*, Cambridge: D S Brewer (1986), pp. 233–50; Harry Porter, 'The Gloomy Dean and the Law; John Colet, 1466–1519', in G. V. Bennett and J. D. Walsh (eds), *Essays in Modern Church History in Memory of Norman Sykes*, London: Black (1966),

pp. 18–43. On pessimism in Renaissance anthropology, see C. Trinkaus, 'Themes for a Renaissance Anthropology', in A. Chastel *et al.*, *The Renaissance*, London: Methuen (1982), pp. 83–125, especially pp. 96–7.

10 Aubrey Townsend ed., *The Writings of John Bradford*, Cambridge: Parker Society (1848), p. 273.

11 *ibid.*, p. 334.

12 Mayor, *English Works*, pp. 127, 109–10.

13 Mayor, *English Works*, pp. 28–9.

14 Mayor, *English Works*, pp. 24–5, 28.

15 Cecillia A. Hatt ed., *English Works of John Fisher, Bishop of Rochester, Sermons and other writings 1520–1535*, Oxford: OUP (2002), p. 248.

16 Mayor, *English Works*, pp. 37–8, 97–8, 100–1.

17 *ibid.*, pp. 283, 29, 25–6.

18 *ibid.*, pp. 43, 113, 167–9.

19 *ibid.*, p. 99; on tears and late-medieval piety, see C. W. Atkinson, *Mystic and Pilgrim*, New York: Cornell Universtiy Press (1983), pp. 58ff. Cf. Blench, *Preaching*, p. 247; and see also John Longland, *Sermones Ioannis Longlandi*, London: Pynson (1518) STC 16797, fol. 68, on the ideal confession – 'sit completa, sit humilis atque *lacrymabilis*' (my emphasis). The texts of the Mass for the gift of tears are in F. H. Dickinson (ed.), *Missale ad Usum Insignis et Praeclarae Ecclesiae SARUM*, Burntisland: E Prelo de Pitsligo (1883, Gregg reprint 1969), p. 8, 19*; for Fisher's tears at mass, *Analecta Bollandiana*, vol. 10, p. 220. But this is a devotional habit by no means confined to the Middle Ages – both Ignatius Loyola and Philip Neri were noted for their weeping at mass.

20 *R.D.D. Ioannis Fischerii, Roffensis in Anglia Episcopi, Opera*, Wurzburg (1597), cols. 1456–7. And for Fisher's doctrine of penance, and the importance of the Magdalene for it, see Richard Rex, 'The polemical theologian', in B Bradshaw and E Duffy (eds), *Humanism, Reform and the Reformation: the Career of Bishop John Fisher*, Cambridge: CUP (1989), pp. 119–20. See also Rex's remarks on the role of private revelations in Fisher's thought, *ibid.*, p. 116.

21 Mayor, *English Works*, pp. 182, 283; cf. G. Ryan *&* H. Ripperger (eds and trans), *The Golden Legend of Jacobus de Voragine*, Salem, (1969), pp. 62, 99–102, 480–1.

22 Wynken de Worde printed seven editions before 1529; see H. S. Bennett, *English Books and Readers, 1475 to 1557*, Cambridge: CUP (1970), p. 250. On the contents of the Primers, Helen C. White, *The Tudor Books of Private Devotion*, Madison WI: University of Wisconsin Press (1951), pp. 52ff.

23 Savonarola's sermon on Psalm 51 is printed in E. Burton ed., *Three Primers*, Oxford: OUP (1834), pp. 130–66. This is a 'reforming' Primer of 1535: White, *Tudor Books*, pp. 91, 96. For Longland's sermons, Blench, *Preaching*, pp. 23ff.

24 A comparison of Longland's sermons with Fisher's is instructive. They share the traditional medieval exegesis – see, for a typical example, their exposition of the

meaning of the four rivers of paradise: Longland, *Sermones*, fols 85b–86a; Mayor, *English Works*, p. 34. Longland's doctrine of purgatory is at least as severe as Fisher's, and Longland supports it with reference both to Thomas Aquinas and St Bonaventura: *Sermones*, fols 6–7b; *English Works*, p. 10. Longland uses the penitential psalms, as Fisher does, as an opportunity to expound the penitential teaching of the Church, with no more sense of anachronism: *Sermones*, fols 55–9. However, he is much less restrained than Fisher in introducing a whole range of Catholic teaching into his exegesis of the texts, as in the excursus on indulgences (fols 61ff), and relics (fols 406ff). And there is nothing in Fisher to match the sheer horror and panic of Longland's treatment of hell – 'O palpabiles tenebras, o tenebras intolerabiles ignis aeterni Cruciabuntur enim die ac nocte in saecula saeculorum' (fols 3a–6).

25 Mayor, *English Works*, pp. 272–5.

26 The funeral sermon, in emphasising Henry's penitence, implicitly underlines his guilt, and Fisher specifically discusses, for example, Henry's resolve to effect a 'true reformacyon of al them that were offycers & mynystres of his lawes', so that *'from hens forward'* (my emphasis) justice might be done, Mayor, *English Works*, p. 271, 221–2. For a rather different sort of discussion of the historical implications of Fisher's account of Henry's repentance, see Geoffrey Elton, 'Henry VII: Rapacity and Remorse', in *Studies*, vol. I, pp. 45–65.

27 Mayor, *English Works*, pp. 298–309.

28 Notably the passage in which he asserts the futility of 'buylding of Colleges' and 'makyng of Sermons' for those who have not made spiritual provision for the hour of death, Mayor, *English Works*, p. 362. But the speaker's repeated insistence on his own total unpreparedness contradicts everything we know about Fisher's daily piety, and seems different in kind from the sense of unworthiness in the presence of a holy God which we would expect from a saint, and which can be seen in the prayer by Fisher printed as an appendix to E. E. Reynolds, *St John Fisher*, Wheathamstead: Anthony Clark Books (1955).

29 A. C. Southern, *Elizabethan Recusant Prose 1559–1582*, London: Sands (1950), pp. 190–3. See above, note 5, for reference to the best-known seventeenth-century example, Donne's *Devotions upon Emergent Occasions*.

30 The classic treatment is R. W. Chambers, *On the Continuity of English Prose from Alfred to More and his School*, Oxford: Early English Text Society, (1932).

31 It is worth comparing Fisher's work with Rolle's *Ego Dormio et Cor Meum*, in G. H. Heseltine (ed.), *Selected Works of Richard Rolle*, London: Longmans, Green and Co (1930), pp. 89–100, which concludes with a similar series of petitions in the form of a 'song' to the Holy Name. For Fisher's devotion to the Holy Name of Jesus, see *Life*, vol. X, 221; for the passage cited in the text, see Mayor, *English Works*, p. 376. English devotion to the Holy Name had a distinctive Yorkshire pedigree, starting with Rolle, and was promoted at Cambridge Trinity by Thomas Rotteram and John Alcock.

32 R. Woolf, *The English Religious Lyric in the Middle Ages*, Oxford: Clarendon Press (1968), pp. 210–11.

33 Hope Emily Allen ed. *English Writings of Richard Rolle*, Oxford: Clarendon Press (1931), p. 36.

34 Mayor, *English Works*, pp.400–1.

35 J. A. W. Bennett, *The Poetry of the Passion*, Oxford: Clarendon Press (1982), pp. 32–61. Fisher explicitly invokes Bernard and the *planctus* tradition, Mayor, *English Works*, p. 401. See also Douglas Gray, *Themes and Images in the Medieval English Religious Lyric*, London: Routledge and Kegan Paul (1972), pp. 18–30, 122–45.

36 R. T. Davies, *Medieval English Lyrics: A Critical Anthology*, London: Faber (1966), nos. 106, 152.

37 Mayor, *English Works*, p. 411. Bennett discusses the origin of the passage, *Poetry of the Passion*, pp. 46–7.

38 P. H. Barnum ed., *Dives and Pauper*, Oxford: Early English Text Society (1976), vol. 1(1), 84–5; Longland also uses this passage, *Sermones*, fol. 19a.

39 Mayor, *English Works*, pp. 416–17.

40 *ibid.*, pp. 391–2.

41 J. C. Olin ed. and trans, *Christian Humanism and the Reformation: Desiderius Erasmus, Selected Writings*, New York: Fordham University Press (1965), pp. 96–7.

42 Mayor, *English Works*, p. 390.

43 Erasmus, *Enchiridion Militis Christiani. An English Version (the 1534 English translation)*, ed. A. M. O'Donnell, Oxford: Early English Text Society, (1981), p. 178.

44 Mayor, *English Works*, p. 159.

45 *Analecta Bollandiana*, vol. 12, pp. 192–3.

46 Mayor, *English Works*, pp. 90–1. Fisher used the same image of the soul suspended over a pit, but without the vividness or menace, in *De Necessitate Orandi, Opera*, col. 1708; Mayor, *English Works*, p. 207.

47 I have worked from the text in *Opera*, and have referred to the English translation produced at Paris in 1640, *A Treatise of Prayer and of the Fruits and Manner of Prayer. By the Most Reverend Father in God JOHN FISHER … translated into English by R.A.B.* The translation of 1560 was not available to me.

48 Edward Surtz, *The Works and Days of John Fisher*, Cambridge MA: Harvard University Press (1967), p. 295; *Opera*, col. 1712. Fisher's teaching in this treatise should be compared with that of Walter Hilton, *The Scale of Perfection*, ed. E. Underhill, London: John M Watkins (1923), pp. 55–82.

49 Wolfgang Riehie, *The Middle English Mystics*, London: Routledge (1981), p. 39, and chs. 3 and 5 *passim*.

50 David Knowles, *The English Mystical Tradition*, London: Burns and Oates (1964), pp. 96, 107–9.

51 *Opera*, col. 1728, my emphasis.

52 D. Jones (ed.), *Minor Works of Walter Hilton*, New York: Benziger (1929), pp. 82–90.

53 Simon Tugwell OP, *Ways of Imperfection*, London: Darton, Longman and Todd (1984), pp. 107–10, 152–69.

54 *Opera*, col. 262.

55 Bridgett, *Fisher*, p. 170.

56 *ibid.*, p. 174; above, chapter 6, pp. 146–7.

57 *Analecta Bollandiana*, vol. 12, 198–9, 226–32

58 *Letters and Papers*, VII, no. 557 (27 April 1534), 221–2; Bridgett, *Fisher*, pp. 63, 176.

59 Francis Cheetham, *English Medieval Alabasters*, Oxford: Phaidon, Christies (1984), pp. 28f.

60 W. H. St J. Hope, 'On the Sculptured Alabaster Tablets Called St John's Heads', *Archaelogia*, 52 (1890), 669–708. Susan Foister, 'Paintings and Other Works of Art in 16th Century English Inventories', *The Burlington Magazine*, 113 (1981), 275.

61 See, for example, Blench's comments on its fine writing, *Preaching*, p. 135.

62 Hatt, *English Works of John Fisher*, p. 227: the passage is quoted *in extenso* in Blench, *Preaching*, p. 135.

63 Hatt, *English Works*, pp.228–9: Blench, *Preaching*, p. 136.

64 Hatt, *English Works*, p. 230.

65 *ibid.*, pp.230–1.

66 The play of the Death of Herod is printed, with helpful comments, in Peter Happe (ed.), *English Mystery Plays*, Penguin: Harmondsworth (1975), pp. 332–42.

67 Hatt, *English works* p. 231.

68 E. Duffy, *Fires of Faith:Catholic England under Mary Tudor*, New Haven and London: Yale University Press (2009), p. ??

69 Dr Hatt thinks not – Hatt, *English Works*, p. 216 note 25 – but does not sufficiently address the peculiarity of the sermon's publication in 1532.

70 J. J. Scarisbrick, 'Fisher, Henry VIII and the Reformation crisis', in Bradshaw and Duffy, *Humanism*, pp. 155–68.

71 The case for the reformers' devotional medievalism was made by Gregory Dix, *The Shape of the Liturgy*, London: Dacre Press (1945), pp. 605ff. An even more entertaining, if somewhat less secure, case against Cranmer's 'emotionalised' piety, was made by Harry Williams, 'Unchristian Liturgy', *Theology*, 61 (1958), 401–4.

72 McConica, 'The Patrimony of Thomas More', *passim*.

73 On Syon see D. Knowles, *The Religious Orders in England, Volume III, The Tudor Age*, Cambridge: CUP (1961), pp. 212–21. On the devotional ethos of the Syon and Carthusian circles at this time, see Roger Lovatt, 'The *Imitation of Christ* in Late Medieval England', *Transactions of the Royal Historical Society*, n.s., 18 (1968), pp. 97–121, and M. G. Sargent, 'The Transmission by the English Carthusians of Some Late Medieval Spiritual Writings', *Journal of Ecclesiastical History*, 27 (1976), 225–40;

on Syon, M. B. Tait, 'The Bridgettine Monastery of Syon (Middlesex)', Oxford D.Phil. thesis 1975: Roger Ellis, *Viderunt eam filie Syon: the Spirituality of the English House of a Medieval Contemplative Order*, Analecta Carthusiana 68 (1984); *idem*, 'Further thoughts on the Spirituality of Syon Abbey' in W. F. Pollard and R. Boenig (eds), *Mysticism and Spirituality in Medieval England*, Cambridge: D. S. Brewer (1997); Vincent Gillespie, 'Syon and the English Market for Continental printed books', *Religion and Literature*, vol. 37 (2005), 27–49.The list in the text is derived from an examination of M. Bateson, *Catalogue of the Library of Syon Monastery, Isleworth*, Cambridge: CUP (1898), and Tait, 'Syon', chapters 7 and 8.

74 On Whytford see White, *Tudor Books*, pp. 153–61; and Tait, 'Syon', pp. 275–96: E. A. Jones and Alexandra Walsham (eds) *Sym Abbey and its Books: Reading, Writing and Religion c1400–1700*, Woodbridge, Boydoll and Brewer 2010.

75 The point is generally made in accounts of Whytford, but for a specific example see the treatment of the commandment to keep the Sabbath holy, anticipating many later 'protestant' and 'puritan' concerns, in *Werke for Housholders*, London (1537) STC 25413, sigs. D–D ii v. See also Tait, 'Syon', p. 292.

76 STC 3277, 14553, and 25421 respectively. Their work is discussed by Tait, 'Syon', chapter 7.

77 On the 'golden chalices, wooden priests' theme, see E. Ruth Harvey, 'The Image of Love', in *The Complete Works of St Thomas More*, VI (2), ed. T. M. C. Lawler, Germain Marc'hadour, and Richard C. Marius, New Haven and London: Yale University Press (1981), pp. 729–59. Its source in Gratian is in *Decretum*, III, ed. E. A. Friedberg, Leipzig, (1879–81), I, 1305–6. For Savonarola's use of the same material, P. Villari, *Life and Times of Girolamo Savonarola*, London: T F Unwin (1889), vol. I, 184. (I owe the Villari reference to Richard Rex.) For Fisher's interest in Savonarola, *Opera*, cols. 109, 637–8.

78 *Opera*, cols. 17 15–16; the passage in question is quoted by Bridgett, *Fisher*, p. 435. Once again, there are striking similarities with Savonarola: cf. Villari, *Savonarola*, vol. II, 58–9.

79 See for example, the confusing usage of Daniel Kinney in referring to More's 'Erasmian' writings in his otherwise excellent introduction to the collection of More's earlier writings that comprise volume 15 of the Yale *Complete Works* (New Haven and London, 1986). Kinney is concerned to differentiate between More's humanism and that of Erasmus, yet nevertheless persists in calling More's humanist letters 'Erasmian'. On the range and variety of opinion and devotional temper in early Henrician England, and on the elements of continuity and tradition in English humanism, see Jan Rhodes, 'Private Devotion in England on the Eve of the Reformation', (Unpublished Durham PhD thesis 1974), pp. 9, 199, and *passim*.

Chapter 8

1 Diarmaid MacCulloch, *Thomas Cranmer, a Life*, New Haven and London: Yale University Press (1997).

2 The most recent biography, especially focused on the European career, is by Thomas F. Mayer, *Reginald Pole, Prince and Prophet*, Cambridge: CUP (2000); two older biographies retain their value, the older, by Martin Haile, *The Life of Reginald Pole*, London: Pitman and sons (1910), for its copious extracts from Pole's correspondence, and that by W. Schenk, *Reginald Pole, Cardinal of England*, London: Longmans, Green (1950), for its concise narrative. Mayer's article on Pole for ODNB is an indispensable supplement to his full-scale biography.

3 Dermot Fenlon, *Heresy and Obedience in Tridentine Italy: Cardinal Pole and the Counter Reformation*, Cambridge: CUP (1972).

4 J. G. Dwyer trans. and ed., *Pole's Defence of the Unity of the Church*, Westminster MD: NewMan (1965), p. 191–2.

5 J. S. Brewer *et al*, *Letters and Papers, Foreign and Domestic of the Reign of Henry VIII*, 21 vols, London: HMSO (1862–1932), vol. 4, part 3, no. 6252.

6 Pole to Henry, 7 July 1530, printed in N. Pocock, *Records of the Reformation, the Divorce 1527–1533*, Oxford: Clarendon Press (1870), pp. 563–4; calendared T. F. Mayer ed., *Correspondence of Reginald Pole* ongoing, four volumes to date, Aldershot: Ashgate (2002–), vol. 1, no. 57, pp. 66–7.

7 Pole's biographer, Tom Mayer, dismisses Pole's claims to innocence in Mayer, *Cardinal Pole in European Context*, Aldershot: Ashgate (2000), ch. XI 'A Fate Worse than Death: Reginald Pole and the Parisian Theologians'.

8 The situation in 1530–1 is well analysed in John Guy, *The Public Career of Sir Thomas More*, Brighton: Harvester Press (1980), pp. 113–74.

9 Pole's account in Haile, *Life*, p. 79.

10 J. E. Cox (ed.), *Miscellaneous Writings and Letters of Thomas Cranmer*, Cambridge: Parker Society (1846), pp. 229–30: interestingly, Diarmaid MacCulloch categorizes Pole's memorandum to Henry as 'opposition literature' – *Thomas Cranmer*, pp. 53–4.

11 According to the ODNB memoir by Tom Mayer, Starkey lived for some after his return in the London house of Pole's brother, Henry Lord Montague.

12 *Correspondence of Reginald Pole*, vol. 1, nos 73, 74; Haile, *Life*, p. 137–8.

13 *Correspondence of Reginald Pole*, vol. 1, nos 76, 78.

14 Brewer, *Letters and Papers*, vol. IX, no. 917.

15 Reginald Pole, *Reginaldi Poli Cardinalis Britanni, ad Henricum Octauum Britanniae Regem, pro Ecclesiasticae Unitatis Defensione*, [Rome, no date, but 1539]; The best modern edition of the *De Unitate*, with a helpful introduction, is the translation into French by Noelle-Marie Egretier, *Reginald Pole, Défense de l'Unité de l'Eglise*, Paris: J Vrin (1967); there is a not altogether reliable English translation by J. G. Dwyer, note 4 above.

16 Mayer, *Pole in European Context*, chapter VII, 'A Diet for Henry VIII: the failure of Reginald Pole's 1537 Legation'; Mayer, *Reginald Pole*, pp. 62–102; Haile, *Life*, pp. 185–271.

17 The narrative in M. H. and R. Dodds, *The Pilgrimage of Grace and the Exeter Conspiracy*, Cambridge: CUP (1915), vol. 2, pp. 277–328, remains valuable.

18 Cranmer, *Writings and Letters*, pp. 325–8; MacCulloch, *Cranmer*, pp. 149–50.

19 Cranmer, *Writings and letters*, pp. 126–7.

20 MacCulloch, *Thomas Cranmer*, p. 151.

21 *Correspondence of Reginald Pole*, vol. 1, no 92, and 118: MacCulloch, *Cranmer*, p. 47.

22 MacCulloch, *Thomas Cranmer*, pp. 554–605.

23 *Correspondence of Reginald Pole*, vol. 3, no. 1414.

24 For the publication history, Thomas H. Mayer, 'A Reluctant Author: Cardinal Pole and his Manuscripts', *Transactions of the American Philosophical Society*, (1999), no. 7, pp. 55–60; the Latin text was printed in the 1854 edition of John Strype, *Memorials of Archbishop Cranmer*, Oxford: Clarendon Press (1854), vol. 3, pp. 614–44; there is a French translation in Angelo Maria Querini, (ed.), *Epistolarum Reginaldi Poli*, Brescia: J. M. Rizzardi (1744–57), vol. V, pp. 238–74.

25 Querini, *Epistolarum*, vol. V p. 244.

26 *Correspondence of Reginald Pole*, vol. 3, no. 1415.

27 Both letters printed in Cranmer, *Writings and letters*, pp. 447–54.

28 *Correspondence of Reginald Pole*, vol. 3, no. 1421; Strype, *Memorials of Cranmer*, vol. II, pp. 972–88.

29 MacCulloch, *Thomas Cranmer*, pp. 584–605.

30 John Foxe, *Actes and Monuments*, 1583 edition, p. 1885, from the Acts and Monuments Online site, http://www.johnfoxe.org/ accessed 26 August 2011.

31 E. Duffy, *Fires of Faith:Catholic England under Mary Tudor*, New Haven and London: Yale University Press (2009), pp. 177–8.

32 Reactions to the execution discussed in Duffy, *Fires of Faith*, pp. 155–8; for an example of Marian propagandist use of the waverings of 'that execrable man Cranmer' in 1556, James Cancellar, *The Pathe of Obedience*, London: John Wailande (1556), RSTC 4564, sig. E ii(v) E iii.

33 Haile, *Life*, p. 486.

34 The recantation, unmistakeably the work of Pole, is printed in John Strype, *The Life of Sir John Cheke*, Oxford: Clarendon Press (1821), pp. 117–27.

35 *Correspondence of Reginald Pole*, vol. 3, no. 1549b.

36 Duffy, *Fires of Faith*, pp. 149–52; the instruction, misleadingly headed 'A frament (sic) concerning the sacrament of the altare', is in Vatican Archives, Vat Lat 5868, fols 227ff, (Bodleian Library Microfilm).

37 Vatican Archives, Vat Lat 5868, fol. 227v., (Bodleian Library Microfilm).

38 Vatican Archives, Vat Lat 5868, fols 227–8, 232, 467, (Bodleian Library Microfilm).

39 [Nicholas Harpsfield,] *Bishop CRANMER'S RECANTACYONS*, ed. Lord Houghton with introduction by J. Gairdner, *Philobiblion Society Miscellanies*, 15 (1877–84).

40 Nicholas Pocock (ed.), *A treatise* on the *pretended divorce between Henry VIII. and Catharine of Aragon, by Nicholas Harpsfield, archdeacon of Canterbury*, London: Camden Society (1878).

41 T. M. Veech, *Dr Nicholas Sanders and the English Reformation, 1530–1581*, Louvain: Bureaux du Recueil, Bibliothèque de l'Université (1935); ODNB; A. F. Allison and D M Rogers, *The Contemporary Printed Literature of the English Counter-Reformation between 1558 and 1640*, 2 vols, Aldershot: Scolar (1989–94), vol. 1, pp. 135–40, vol. 2 pp. 138–9; Peter Milward, *Religious Controversies of the Elizabethan Age*, London: Scolar (1978), pp. 13–15; Christopher Highley, "'A Pestilent and Seditious Book": Nicholas Sanders *Schismatis Anglicani* and Catholic Histories of the Reformation', *Huntington Library Quarterly*, vol. 68 (2005), 151–71.

Chapter 9

1 John Foxe, *Actes and Monuments*, London: John Daye (1583), pp. 1426–8, quotations on p. 1428.

2 This is of course the so-called Vincentian Canon, the criterion of Catholic doctrine: quod ubique, quod semper, quod ab omnibus creditum est ('what has been believed everywhere, always, and by all'). Vincent's *Commonitorium*, was a favourite book with Marian Catholic apologists, and an English translation had appeared in 1554 as *A Boke Written by One Vincentius Leriniensis*, London (1554), RSTC 24747.

3 Peter Marshall, *Religious Identities in Henry VIII's England*, Aldershot: Ashgate (2006), pp. 169–98.

4 Richard S. Sylvester and Davis P. Harding (eds), *Two Early Tudor Lives*, New Haven and London: Yale University Press (1962), p. 235.

5 J. A. F. Thompson, 'The Well of Grace: Englishmen and Rome in the Fifteenth Century' in Barrie Dobson ed., *The Church, Politics and Patronage in the Fifteenth Century*, Gloucester: Sutton (1984), pp. 99–114.

6 For Henry Parker, Lord Morley, see Richard Rex, 'Morley and the Papacy: Rome, Regime and Religion', in Marie Axton and James Carley (eds), *Triumphs of English: Henry Parker, Lord Morley, Translator to the Tudor Court*, London: The British Library (2000), pp. 87–105, especially pp. 87–9.

7 Anthony Shaw, 'Papal Loyalism in 1530s England', *Downside Review*, 117 (1999), 17–40; Ethan Shagan, *Popular Politics and the English Reformation*, Cambridge: CUP (2003), pp. 29–60

8 Pierre Janelle ed., *Obedience in church and state: three political tracts by Stephen Gardiner*, Cambridge: CUP (1930), pp. 67–171. For two very different approaches to the Henrician debates over Papal and Royal Supremacy more generally, Richard Rex, 'The Crisis of Obedience: God's Word and Henry's Reformation', *Historical Journal*, vol. 39 (1996), 863–94; Jean-Pierre Moreau, *Rome ou l'Angleterre? Les Réactions Politiques des Catholiques Anglais au Moment du Schisme 1525–1553,* Paris: Presses Universitaires de France (1984).

9 Foxe, *Actes and Monuments,* (1583) p. 1616.

10 Lucy Wooding, *Rethinking Catholicism in Reformation England,* Oxford: OUP (2000), pp. 128, 191, 198–200.

11 John Bossy, *The English Catholic Community 1570–1850,* London: Darton Longman Todd (1975), pp. 11–34.

12 Ellen A. Macek, *The Loyal Opposition: Tudor Traditionalist Polemics, 1535–1588,* NewYork: Peter Lang (1996), p. 177.

13 Dr Wooding's characterization of the Marian Church's theological indifference to the papacy was challenged by the late Dr William Wizeman, *The Theology and Spirituality of Mary Tudor's Church,* Aldershot: Ashgate (2006), pp. 127–36.

14 Decree no. 1 of Pole's Legatine Synod, in Gerald Bray ed., *The Anglican Canons 1529–1947,* Church of England Record Society vol. 6, Woodbridge: Boydell and Brewer (1998), pp. 74–7.

15 John Harpsfield, *A notable and learned sermon or homilie, made vpon saint Andrewes daye last past 1556 in the Cathedral churche of S. Paule in London, by Mayster Ihon Harpesfeild doctour of diuinitie and canon residenciary of the sayd churche, set furthe by the bishop of London.* London (1556). RSTC 12795.

16 David Cressy, *Bonfires and Bells: National Memory and the Calendar in Elizabethan and Stuart England,* Berkeley and Los Angeles: Weidenfeld and Nicolson (1989).

17 Foxe, *Actes and Monuments,* p. 1912.

18 Foxe, *Actes and Monuments,* p. 1602.

19 Edmund Bonner, *A profitable and necessarye doctrine with certayne homelies adioyned thervnto / set forth by the reuere[n]d father in God, Edmunde Bishop of London …,* 2nd edn, London (1555), RSTC 3283.7, fol. 33v.

20 Foxe, *Actes and Monuments,* p. 1520.

21 Nicholas Harpsfield, *A Treatise on the pretended Divorce between Henry VIII and Catherine of Aragon,* London: Camden Society (1878), p. 41.

22 Eamon Duffy, *Fires of Faith: Catholic England Under Mary Tudor,* New Haven and London: Yale University Press (2009), pp. 29–56, esp. pp 34–6, and above, ch 1 pp. 22–3.

23 Duffy, *Fires of Faith,* pp. 35–46.

24 David N. Bagchi, *Luther's Earliest Opponents,* Minneapolis MN: Fortress Press (1991), p. 63.

25 Thomas More, *A Dialogue Concerning Heresies,* eds Thomas M. C. Lawlor, Germain Marc'hadour and Richard C Marius, New Haven and London: Yale University Press (1981) in volume 6 of the *Complete Works,* pp. 247–8.

26 Duffy, *Fires of Faith,* p. 36 and above, pp. 183–5.

27 *ibid.*, pp. 43–5.

28 Edmund Bonner, *Homelies sette for the by the right reverende father in God, Edmund Byshop of London*, 2nd edn, London (1555), RSTC 3285.7 (issued with the *Profitable and Necessary Doctrine*) fols 48v-54.

29 Janelle ed., *Obedience in Church and State*, pp. 21–65.

30 E. V. Hitchcok ed., *The Life and death of Sir Thomas Moore … by Nicholas Harpsfield*, Oxford: Early English Text Society, OS no. 186, (1932), pp. 158–60.

31 For the sermon and the circumstances surrounding its preaching, Eamon Duffy, 'Cardinal Pole Preaching', in E. Duffy and D. Loades (eds), *The Church of Mary Tudor*, Aldershot: Ashgate (2006), pp. 187–200.

32 The sermon does not survive in Pole's manuscripts, but an incomplete version was printed from Foxe's papers by John Strype, *Ecclesiastical memorials Relating Chiefly to Religion and its Reformation under the Reigns of King Henry VIII, King Edward and Queen Mary*, Oxford: Clarendon Press (1816), vol. III, pt 2, pp. 482–510, quotations at p. 490–3.

33 *ibid.*, p. 493

34 *ibid.*, p. 494.

35 Duffy, *Fires of Faith*, pp. 196ff.

36 John Strype, *Annals of the Reformation and Establishment of Religion … during … Queen Elizabeth's happy Reign*, Oxford: Clarendon Press (1824), vol. 1 pt 2, pp. 412–13.

37 *ibid.*, pp. 399–407.

38 On the Louvain exiles, Christopher Highley, *Catholics Writing the Nation in Early Modern Britain and Ireland*, Oxford: OUP (2008), pp. 25–47, and the introduction to Christopher Coppens, *Reading in Exile*, Cambridge: LP Publications (1993).

39 The fullest discussion of Harpsfield's polemical importance under Elizabeth is Jonathan Dean, *Catholicae Ecclesiae Unitatem: Nicholas Harpsfield and English Reformation Catholicism*, Unpublished Cambridge PhD thesis, (2004).

40 Thomas Dorman, *A Proufe of Certeyne Articles in Religion, denied by M. Iuell, sett furth in defence of the catholyke beleef therein…*, (1564), RSTC 7062, fol. 3.

Chapter 10

1 Catholic priests in the sixteenth century were addressed as 'Sir', (Latin 'Dominus') rather than the now conventional 'Father'.

2 Butler's register was destroyed in a fire in 1859, but extracts from it made by an antiquarian clergyman were printed in the *Cambrian Journal* for 1861, and again in J. C. Cox, *The Parish Registers of England*, London: Methuen (1910), pp. 25–35. I have worked mainly from Cox's edition (quotations at pp. 32–5), but have included one expansion from an edition of the register prepared by Dr Will Coster of Simon de

Montfort University (below, note 4). I am very grateful to Dr Coster for access to this edition.

3   Cox, *Parish Registers*, p.30.

4   *ibid.*, p. *29* and Coster transcript. This was done on the instructions and injunctions of the Commissioner or visitor in the Royal Visitation.

5   Reprinted in A. G. Dickens, *Reformation Studies*, London: Hambledon Press (1982), pp. 287–3 12. For Parkyn's career, see Dickens's essay 'The Last Medieval Englishman' in the same collection, pp. 245–83 .

6   Dickens, *Reformation Studies*, p. 311.

7   A. Fletcher ed., *Tudor Rebellions*, London: Longmands (1979), pp. 120–1, 128–30, 135–6.

8   G. R. Elton, *Policy and Police: The Enforcement of the Reformation in the Age of Thomas Cromwell*, Cambridge: CUP (1972).

9   For More's literary and polemical objectives in those works, Eamon Duffy, '"The comen knowen multitude of crysten men": *A Dialogue Concerning Heresies and the defence of Christendom*', in George M. Logan ed., *The Cambridge Companion to Thomas More*, Cambridge: CUP (2011), pp. 191–215; *idem*, 'Thomas More's Confutation, a literary failure?', forthcoming in T. Grass (ed.), *The Church and Literature, Studies in Church History*, vol. 48 (2012). The best general survey remains Louis A. Schuster, 'Thomas More's Polemical Career, 1525–1533', in *The Complete Works of St Thomas More*, vol. 8, pt 3, New Haven and London: Yale University Press (1973), pp. 1137–1363.

10 On this Marian polemic, see now my *Fires of Faith, Catholic England under Mary Tudor*, New Haven and London: Yale University Press (2009), pp. 57–78.

11 Michael Sherbrook, 'The Fall of Religious Houses', in A. G. Dickens ed., *Tudor Treatises*, Yorkshire Archaeological Society, Record Series, 125 (1959), pp. 138–9.

12 J. A. Muller, *Stephen Gardiner and the Tudor Reaction*, London: SPCK (1926); G. Redworth, *In defence of the church catholic: the life of Stephen Gardiner*, Oxford: Basil Blackwell (1990); see also the important memoir of Gardiner by Colin Armstrong in the Oxford Dictionary of National Biography.

13 This conservative resistance is surveyed in Ellen A. Macek, *The Loyal Opposition: Tudor Traditionalist Polemics 1535–1558*, New York: Peter Lang (1996); Jean-Pierre Moreau, *Rome ou l'Angleterre? Les Réactions Politiques des Catholiques Anglais au Moment du Schisme 1525–1553*, Paris: Presses Universitaires de France (1984); Lucy Wooding, *Rethinking Catholicism in Reformation England*, Oxford: OUP (2000), on which see chapter nine above.

14 Andreas Loewe, *Richard Smyth and the Language of Orthodoxy: Re-imagining Tudor Catholic Polemicism*, Studies in Medieval and Reformation Thought *XCVI*, Leiden (2003).

15 Janet Wilson ed., *Sermons very Fruitful!, Godly and Learned by Roger Edgeworth*, Cambridge: D. S. Brewer (1993), p. 30.

16 The best account of the imposition of the Edwardine reforms is Diarmaid

MacCulloch, *Tudor Church Militant: Edward VI and the Protestant Reformation*, London: Allen Lane (1999).

17 Cited in A. Gasquet and E. Bishop, *Edward VI and the Book of Common Prayer*, London: J. Hodges (1891), pp. 257–8.

18 D. Dymond and C. Paine (eds), *The Spoil of Melford Church*, Ipswich: Salient Press (1989), pp. 29–30. On these confiscations more generally, see chapter 6, supra.

19 J. Erskine Binney ed., *The Accounts of the Wardens of the Parish of Morebath, Devon, 1520–1573*, Exeter: Devon and Cornwall Record Society (1904), p. 200. For Trychay's 'voice', and the voices to be found in churchwardens' accounts more generally, see my *The Voices of Morebath: Reformation and Rebellion in an English Village*, New Haven and London: Yale University Press (2001), pp. 17–46.

20 For example, J. W. Martin, 'The Marian Regime's failure to understand the importance of printing', *Huntington Library Quarterly*, 154, 1980–1, 231–47.

21 Binney, *Accounts*, p. 172; Duffy, *Voices of Morebath*, pp. 142–51.

22 Duffy, *Fires of Faith*, pp. 17–21.

23 *A Profitable and Necessary Doctryne with certeyne Homelies adioyned thereunto Set Forth by the Reverende Father in God Edmonde Byshop of London*, London (1555), STC 3238, preface (no pagination).

24 W. Haines ed., 'Stanford Churchwardens Accounts 1552–1602', *The Antiquary*, 17 (1888), 70.

25 Duffy, *Fires of Faith*, pp. 101, 105.

26 W. D. Hamilton ed., *A Chronicle of England during the Reigns of the Tudors from AD 1485–1559 by Charles Wriothesley, Windsor Herald*, London: Camden Society (1875–7), vol. l, p. 148; vol.2, p. 1.

27 *ibid.*, vol. 2, pp. 97–8, 101, 104, 114, 122.

28 J. Strype, *Ecclesiastical Memorials Relating Chiefly to Religion and its Reformation under the Reigns of King Henry VIII, King Edward VI and Queen Mary*, Oxford: Clarendon Press (1816), vol. 3, pt. 2, pp. 500–1.

29 *The Workes of Sir Thomas More Knyght sometyme Lorde Chancellour of England*, London (1557), p. 288, and in *The Complete Works of St Thomas More*, ed. Frank Manley *et al.*, New Haven and London: Yale University Press (1990), vol. 7, p. 111.

30 On the bede-roll, E. Duffy, *The Stripping of the Altars*, New Haven and London: Yale University Press (1992), pp. 327–37.

31 Duffy, *Fires of Faith*, pp. 102–6.

32 Thomas Becon, *Prayers and other Pieces*, ed J. Ayre, Cambridge: The Parker Society (1844), p. 276; J. W. Martin, *Religious Radicals in Tudor England*, London: Hambledon (1989), and D. Loades, *Politics, Censorship and the English Reformation*, London: Pinter (1991).

33 *The Workes of Thomas More Knyght*, London (1557).

34 On More and the Marian regime, Duffy, *Fires of Faith*, pp. 179–87.

35 Duffy, *Fires of Faith*, pp. 17–21.

36 Miles Hogarde, *The Displaying of the Protestants, with a Description of Divers their Abuses*, London, (1556), RSTC 13557, ff. 42v–43.

37 Duffy, *Fires of Faith*, pp. 174–7.

38 Hamilton ed., *A Chronicle*, vol. 2, p. 47.

39 Hogarde, *Displaying*, fols 80v–83v.

40 Dickens, 'Robert Parkyn's Narrative of the Reformation' in *Reformation Studies*, p. 304.

41 Wilson ed., *Sermons very Fruitful*, p. 365.

42 I have handled these points more fully in *Fires of Faith*, pp. 71–8.

43 Cited in P. Caraman ed., *The Other Face*, London: Longmans, Green (1960), p. 197

44 John Bossy, *The English Catholic Community 1570–1850*, London: Darton, Longman and Todd (1975); C. Haigh, 'The Continuity of Catholicism in the English Reformation', in *idem* ed., *The English Reformation Revised*, Cambridge: CUP (1987).

45 Below, pp. 239–40.

46 Chapter 11 below, *passim*.

47 Edward Gee (ed.) *The Jesuits' Memorial for the Intended Reformation of England*, London, Richard Chiswell (1690): For discussion of Parson's book, see Bossy, *English Catholic Community*, pp. 20–4; T. H. Clancy, 'Notes on Person's Memorial for the Reformation of England 1596', *Recusant History*, 5 (1959–60), pp. 17–34; J. J. Scarisbrick, 'Robert Persons' plans for the 'true' reformation of England', in N. McKendrick ed., *Historical Perspectives*, London: Europa Publications (1974), pp. 19–42.

48 George Giffard, *A Briefe Discourse of certeine Points of the Religion which is among the Common Sort of Christians, which may be Termed the Countrey Divinitie* London: Richard Field and Felix Kingston (1612), pp. 6–20 and *passim*

Chapter 11

1 Above, Introduction and chs 1 and 2. Alison Shell, *Catholicism, Culture and the English Literary Imagination 1558–1660*, Cambridge: CUP (2006).

2 Alison Shell, *Shakespeare and Religion*, London: Arden Shakespeare (2010).

3 Cited by Margaret Aston in her essay, 'The Dissolution of the Monasteries and the sense of the past', in *Lollards and Reformers: Images and Literacy in Late Medieval Religion*, London: Hambledon Press, (1984) p. 315.

4 The ambivalences of Bale's attitudes to his own Catholic and monastic past are brilliantly explored in Oliver Patrick Wort, *Reformation Conversion : An Essay on John Bale*, unpublished Cambridge PhD thesis (2010).

5 William Lambarde, *A Perambulation of Kent*, facsimile edn, Trowbridge: Adams and Dart (1970), pp. 267–8.

6 For this and the quotation that follows, John Stow, *A Survey of London*, ed. C. L. Kingsford, Oxford: Clarendon Press (1908), vol. i/229, ii/75; and see Ian Archer, 'The Nostalgia of John Stow' in D. L. Smith, R Strier and D Bevington (eds), *The Theatrical City: Culture, Theatre and Politics in London 1576–1649* Cambridge: CUP (1995), pp. 17–34.

7 Janet Wilson, 'A Catalogue of the "unlawful" books found in John Stow's study', *Recusant History*, 20 (1990), pp. 1–30.

8 Ian Gadd and Alexandra Gillespie (eds), *John Stow (1525–1605) and the making of the English Past*, London: British Library (2004).

9 Official accounts of the burning by the regime in *A true report of the burninyng of the steple and churche of Poules in London* (1561) STC 19930, and in W. Sparrow Simpson ed., *Documents Illustrating the History of St Paul's Cathedral*, London: Camden Society ns 26 (1880), pp. 113–19. See also Alexandra Walsham, *Providence in Early Modern England*, Oxford: OUP (2000), pp. 232–3.

10 Morwen's tract was included with a refutation in *The burnynge of Paules Church in London in the yeare of oure Lord 1561* (1563), reprinted in James Schofield (ed.), *The Works of James Pilkington, BD, Lord Bishop of Durham*, London: Parker Society (1842), pp. 481–6. Morwen had been Edmund Bonner's chaplain and secretary, and a Prebendary of St Paul's. He was to remain an effective Catholic activist and a thorn in the side of the Protestant regime in the North West into the early 1580s; E. Duffy, *Fires of Faith: Catholic England under Mary Tudor*, New Haven and London: Yale University Press (2009), pp. 198–9.

11 Pilkington, *Works*, p. 156; *Sermons or Homelies Appointed to be Read in Churches in the Time of Queen Elizabeth of Famous Memory*, London (1833), p. 381.

12 W. H. Frere ed., *Visitation Articles and Injunctions of the Period of the Reformation, vol III 1559–1575*, Alcuin Club vol. xvi, London: Longmans, Green (1910), p. 16. Injunction 23 my emphasis.

13 R Savage & Edgar Fripp (eds), *Minutes and Accounts of the Corporation of Stratford upon Avon*, Publications of the Dugdale Society, Oxford (1921–30), i pp. 137–41; ii p. 54.

14 See the 'Libel against Erecters of altars and holy water vats' in *Depositions and other Ecclesiastical proceeding from the Courts of Durham*, Surtees Society vol 21, (1845), pp. 129–30, and depositions on pp. 139–40, 163, 164, 167, 170–6. For Bullingham's Lincolnshire iconoclasm, discussed in the next paragraph, Duffy, *Stripping of the Altars*, pp. 572–7.

15 A. G. Dickens ed. *Tudor Treatises*, Yorkshire Archaeological Society (1959), p. 125.

16 Nicholas Orme ed., *Nicholas Roscarrock's Lives of the Saints: Cornwall and Devon*, Exeter: Devon and Cornwall Record Society (1992), pp. 94, 160.

17 William Harrison, *The Description of England*, ed. G. Edelen, Washington: Folger

Library and Dover Press (1994), p. 35–6; Richard Marks, *Stained Glass in England During the Middle Ages*, London: Routledge (1993), pp. 231–2.

18 J. Amphlett ed., *A Survey of Worcestershire by Thomas Habington,*Oxford: Worcester Historical Society (1895), vol. ii, pp. 177–8.

19 William Hinde, *A Faithfull Remonstrance of the Holy Life and Happy Death of John Bruen*, London: Printed by R. B. for Philemon Stephens and Christopher Meredith (1641), p. 78.

20 E. Jones ed., *The New Oxford Book of Sixteenth Century Verse*, Oxford: OUP (1991), pp. 550–1.

21 F. G. Emmison, *Elizabethan Life: Disorder*, Chelmsford: Essex County Council (1970), pp. 59–61.

22 T. E. Gibson ed., *Crosby Records*, Chetham Society, (1887), pp. 28–31.

23 J. T. Fowler, ed., *Rites of Durham: being a description or brief declaration of all the ancient monuments, rites, and customs belonging or being within the monastical church of Durham before the suppression, written 1593*, Surtees Society 103, (1903, reprinted 1964), pp. 33, 61–2.

24 A. I. Doyle, 'William Claxton and the Durham Chronicles' in James P. Carley and Colin G. C. Tite, *Books and Collectors 1200–1700*, London: British Library (1997), pp. 335–55, esp. 347–9.

25 Martin's account is edited in David Dymond and Clive Payne, *The Spoil of Melford Church*, Ipswich: Salient Press (1992), pp. 1–9.

26 George Gifford, *A Briefe Discourse of certaine points of religion, which is among the common sorts of Christians, which may be termed the Countrie Divinitie*, London: Richard Field, and Felix Kingston (1601).

27 Dickens, *Tudor Treatises*, pp. 90–1.

28 Dickens, *Tudor Treatises*, p. 38.

29 For example, S Greenblatt et al (eds), *The Norton Shakespeare,* New York: Norton & Co. (1997), note 1 to sonnet 73, p. 1947.

30 John Weever, *Ancient Funerall Monuments With In the United Monarchie of Greate Britaine and the Islands adiacent, with the dissolved Monasteries therein contained<* London: Printed by Thomas Harper (1631), p. 4.

31 Weever, *Ancient Funerall Monuments*, pp. 37–8.

32 Weever, *Ancient Funerall Monuments*, pp. 73, 115.

Acknowledgements

I am grateful to Peter Marshall, who read the book in typescript and made many invaluable suggestions for improvement. My thanks also to Dr. Lucy Underwood, who compiled the Index. Earlier forms of Chapters 1 and 2 were delivered as the 2009 Firth Lectures at the University of Nottingham in February 2009.

An earlier version of Chapter 3 appeared as 'The Parish, Piety, and Patronage in Late Medieval England: The Evidence of Roodscreens' in B. Kumin and K. L. French (eds), *The Parish in English Life 1400–1700*, Manchester: Manchester University Press (1997), pp. 133–62: it appears here by kind permission of the publishers.

An earlier version of Chapter 4 appeared as 'The Disenchantment of Space: Salle Church and the Reformation' in J. Tracy ed., *Popular Religion and the Early Modern State*, Cambridge: CUP (2005), pp. 324–47, and appears here by kind permission of the Syndics of CUP.

An earlier version of Chapter 5 appeared as 'The End of it All: The Inventories of Church Goods of 1552' in Clive Burgess and Eamon Duffy (eds), *The Late Medieval English Parish*, Donington: Harlaxton Medieval Studies (2006). It appears here by kind permission of the publisher, Sean Tyas.

An earlier version of Chapter 6 was given as the 2007 O'Connell Lecture at St Malachy's College, Belfast.

An earlier version of Chapter 7 appeared as 'The Spirituality of John Fisher' in B. Bradshaw and E. Duffy (eds), *Humanism, Reform and Reformation: the Career of Bishop John Fisher*, Cambridge: CUP (1988), pp. 205–31, and appears here by kind permission of the Syndics of CUP.

An earlier version of Chapter 8 was delivered as the Friends of Lambeth Palace Library Lecture in 2008, and was first published in the *Lambeth Palace Library Annual Review* 2009, pp. 53–68. It appears by kind permission of the Friends of Lambeth Palace.

An earlier version of Chapter 10 appeared as 'The conservative voice in the English Reformation' in Simon Ditchfield ed., *Christianity and Community in the West: Essays for John Bossy*, Aldershot: Asgate (2001), pp. 87–105 and is published here by kind permission of the publishers.

An earlier version of Chapter 11 appeared as 'Bare ruin'd choirs: remembering Catholicism in Shakespeare's England' in R. Dutton, A. Findlay and R. Wilson (eds), *Theatre and Religion, Lancastrian Shakespeare*, Manchester: Manchester University Press (2003), pp. 40–57, and is reprinted here by kind permission of the publishers.

The cover and frontispiece picture is reproduced by kind permission of the Rector of the Venerable English College, Rome, Figures 1 and 4, and colour plates 3, 4 and 6 are used here by kind permission of Mr Mike Dixon, who took the photographs, and colour plate 5 by kind permission of Dr David Griffith. All other photographs are the author's own.

Index

Bullingham, Nicholas (Bishop of
Worcester) 241
Buonvisi, Antonio 206–7
Burgess, Clive 113
Burgess, Thomas 38
Burke, Peter 8
Burlace, Jane 241–2
Burnet, Gilbert 37–8, 48
History of the Reformation (1679) 37–8
Busby, Joan 67
Butler, Thomas 213–14
Byrd, William 33, 233

Calvin, John 19, 31
Calvinism 31
Cambridge, parish church of Great
St Mary's, rood-loft 61
Cambridge, University of 99, 134, 208
colleges of
Christ's College 105, 137
Jesus College 135
King's College 241
Michaelhouse 135
St John's College 134, 137
Campeggio, Cardinal Lorenzo 146, 169
Campion, St Edmund 12, 25
Cano, Melchior 143
Canterbury
heresy commission in diocese of 191–3
parish churches of Holy Cross, Westgate
68
priory of 235
sermons of Thomas Cranmer in 185–6
sermons of Reginald Pole in 191, 193
visitation of (1556) 191–3
Capgrave, John 252
Cardinals, College of 133
Cardmaker, John (protestant martyr) 115
Carthusian Order 168, 174, 188
executed 183–4, 188
houses of 174
members of, 183
Catharionus, Ambrose Politi 203
Apologia pro veritate Catholicae fidei
203

Catherine of Aragon (Queen of England)
144–5, 169, 173, 180, 181
Catherine of Siena, St, *Dialogues* of 174
Catholic League 27, 28
Cawston, Norfolk 86, 87, 106
Cecil, William (1st Lord Burleigh) 24
Chantries 98, 101, 137
dissolution of 101, 102, 110
Chapman, Robert 102
Charles I (King) 251
Charles V, Holy Roman Emperor 12, 141,
148, 171–2, 185
Charterhouse of London 174
members of executed 183–4, 204
Charterhouse of Sheen 174
members of executed 183–4
Chartres, cathedral of 44
Cheke, Sir John 191
Chester, Alice 63, 71
Chesterton, Gilbert Keith 41
Cholmeley, Sir Roger 195
Christendom 12–13, 16–17, 20, 26, 34,
150, 204
Chur, Graubunden 22
Church of England (Anglican Church) 16,
26–31
and 'Anglican particularism' 29–31, 34
and Protestant internationalism 26–9
Circognani, Nicolo 25
Claxton, William 247
The Rites of Durham 230, 246–7, 253
Clemens, Richard 60
Clerk, John (Bishop of Bath and Wells) 147
Clerke, Robert 60
Cloud of Unknowing, The 167, 168
Clyff, George 247
Cochlaeus, Johann 143
Cole, Henry 189–90
Colet, John 152, 154, 174–6
Collinson, Patrick 6–7
The Birthpangs of Protestant England
(1986) 6–7
Colton, Robert 229–30
Commissioners for church goods (1552)
104, 110, 111, 128